OH, CAPT

**The Life Story of the]
Chief of The Lo**

Ronal

SECOND EDITION

Published by:
Paramount Publishing Ltd.
Paramount House
17/21 Shenley Road
Borehamwood
Herts. WD6 1RT.
Tel: 01-207 5599
Telex: 944036 P MOUNT G

ISBN 0 947665 12 9

To
Audrey

without whose support and encouragement
this book would never have been written

The Author

RONALD COX went from Beckenham Grammar School into the 2nd Fife and Forfar Yeomanry and saw action in tanks in Normandy. On demobilisation, he trained as a teacher at Westminster College and then worked for eighteen years in two Croydon Secondary Modern schools. In his spare time he lectured extensively in local history for the WEA, and wrote scripts and interviewed for sound radio. In the late 1960s he read part-time for a Master's degree and then for a PhD, at Leicester University. For his MA thesis he was awarded the University's John Nichols Prize in 1967; an essay based on part of his doctorate research, *'The Old Centre of Croydon: Victorian Decay and Redevelopment'*, was published in PERSPECTIVES IN ENGLISH URBAN HISTORY (edit Alan Everitt), in 1973. Meanwhile, he became a Principal at the Treasury and at the DES and then the first Chief Administrative Officer at Ewell Technical College. From 1971 to 1978 he was the first (and last) Assistant Director of Education (Building and Development) for the London Borough of Croydon. In the latter year he moved across to Croydon College where he is Head of the Educational Studies Section. He is married and has one son and two grandchildren. This is his first book.

SECOND EDITION 1988

First published 1984

Contents

FOREWORD TO THE SECOND EDITION

Eyre Massey Shaw was, without doubt, the greatest single influence on the development of the British Fire Service in that exciting innovative Victorian era when a transitory Britain moved from sail to steam, from semaphore to telegraph and from 4-legged horse power to that of the combustion engine.

He was a remarkable man; years ahead of his time, autocratic yet understanding, a socialite yet a leader respected by all those under his command.

He led by example and, whatever the circumstances, never baulked at the challenge of 'unenlightened authority' when he felt it threatened the progress of his beloved fire brigade.

Ronald Cox's book is the result of years of painstaking research and captures so well those progressive days of a century ago when the seeds of the modern British Fire Service were both sown and nurtured, by a man who was truly a master craftsman in his chosen profession.

By the final page I am sure you will agree that the standards set by Eyre Massey Shaw are still those by which we, approaching the end of the twentieth century, set great store and would wish to be judged.

G. D. CLARKSON, QFSM, BA (HONS)
Chief Fire Officer and Chief Executive
London Fire and Civil Defence Authority

FOREWORD

As the name Horatio Nelson is synonymous with the British Navy, that of Eyre Massey Shaw holds similar pride of place in the annals of British Fire Service history and tradition.

For while it was the ill-fated James Braidwood who was responsible for the creation and development of organised firefighting in London, his exploits and achievements were eclipsed by the flamboyant but immensely competent Eyre Massey Shaw.

Following Braidwood's untimely and tragic death in 1861, Shaw succeeded him as Chief Officer of the London Fire Engine Establishment, re-formed at public expense, and under the control of the Metropolitan Board of Works, as the Metropolitan Fire Brigade in 1866.

Shaw's achievements have been widely chronicled but, until now, in largely fragmented form as part of more widely-based accounts of Fire Service history and development.

It is, therefore, with much pleasure that I welcome this account of Shaw's life and times by Dr. Ronald Cox, who is to be congratulated on the painstaking research he has carried out in connection with this biography.

It is a welcome and valuable addition to the somewhat sparsely-populated bookshelves covering the history of the Fire Service in this country and those largely responsible for its development into the efficient and effective machine that it is recognised as today.

This biography will, I am sure, appeal not only to the Fire Service historian or enthusiast, but to everyone with an interest in London life during the reign of Queen Victoria.

Dr. Cox has uncovered many facts, and some fables, pertaining to Shaw that were hitherto unknown. He has travelled down numerous 'blind alleys' in his insatiable quest for additional or corroborative information, but he has, to use Fire Service jargon, 'got stuck in' and persevered when the going has got tough.

The result is a compelling account of a man who was a personal friend of the Prince of Wales, who moved in the topmost circles of London society and was immortalised by Gilbert and Sullivan in their operetta 'Iolanthe'.

Dr. Cox recounts how, under Shaw's meticulous direction,

the Metropolitan Fire Brigade developed as quickly as the available finances permitted; how he greatly expanded the use of steam fire engines, introduced telegraph systems and rationalised life-saving operations by taking over the Society for the Protection of Life from Fire in 1868 and increased the number of street escape stations; how he would accompany the Prince of Wales to major conflagrations; how, after years of running 'his' Brigade with a considerable degree of autonomy, he resigned in 1891 after two years of a somewhat acrimonious relationship with the newly-formed London County Council and was knighted by the Queen on his last day of service.

It is an absorbing book and I wish it every success.

R. A. Bullers, QFSM, FIFireE, MBIM
Chief Officer, London Fire Brigade

ACKNOWLEDGEMENTS

I have tried, in the course of my research, to note the names of all who have shared with me their time, their knowledge and their enthusiasm. If I have missed out anyone, I hope I shall be forgiven.

It will usually be apparent from the designations which parts of the work specifically benefitted. I have necessarily had to give titles and locations as they applied at the time of my enquiry; these are sometimes not as full as I would wish, for which I apologise.

Whilst insisting that any errors are of my own making, I wish to thank for their help: The Rt. Hon. the Lord Abinger, Bures, Suffolk; R. J. Adam, Department of Medieval History, St. Andrew's, Scotland; J. R. R. Adams, Belfast Library and Society for Promoting Knowledge, Linen Hall Library, Belfast; John Andrews, London Fire Brigade Museum, London SE1; The Archivist, Guildhall Library, London EC2; Neal Ascherson, c/o THE SCOTSMAN, Edinburgh 1; the Rt. Hon. the Lord Avebury, London SW1; R. A. Birchell, Lecturer in American History and Institutions, University of Manchester; Helen Blacker, Shamley Green, Surrey; the Lady Brabourne, Ashford, Kent; David Brown, Producer, Children's Programmes, BBC, Manchester; Syd Brown, Curator, London Fire Brigade Museum, London SE1; Ronald Bullers, Chief of the London Fire Brigade, London SE1; Kieran Burke, Assistant Librarian, Cork County Library; Lt. Col. the Rt. Hon. the Lord Burnham, Beaconsfield, Bucks; J. M. Byrne, Hon. Secretary, Monkstown Golf Club, County Cork; Sir Arthur Chetwynd, Chetwynd Films Ltd., Toronto, Ontario; the Lord Clanmorris, London W8; Gerald Clarkson, Deputy Chief Officer, London Fire Brigade, London SE1; Gloria C. Clifton, Friern Barnet, London N11; H. S. Cobb, Deputy Clerk of the Records, House of Lords Record Office, London SW1; F. Ronald Coe, Kenley, Surrey; H. R. H. Cox, Librarian, Claydon House, Bucks; Messrs. Cox and Cardale, Solicitors, London EC4; E. J. Davis, County Archivist, Buckinghamshire; A. T. Langdon-Down, Clerk to the Worshipful Company of Coachmakers and Coach Harness Makers, London WC2; K. S. Duncan, Director of International Affairs, British Olympic Association, London WC2; the Baron Ebury, Toorak, Victoria, Australia; Brigadier R. Elsdale, Lydney, Glos; William English, Cobh, County Cork; Mrs. M. Foster, Branch Librarian, Sheerness, Kent; John P. Fuller, the Victoria and Albert Museum Library, London SW7; the Duke of Grafton, Thetford, Norfolk; the Hon. Mrs. Eleanor L. Grant, Lagos, Algarve, Portugal; Margaret C. Griffith, Manuscript Assistant, Trinity College Library, University of Dublin; W. M. Grime, Rochdale, Lancs; Messrs. Halsey, Lightly and Hemsley, London SW1; I. G. Hardy, Area Librarian, Exeter; P. Henchy, Director, National Library of Ireland, Dublin 2; Dr. Francis Hennessey, Cobh, County Cork; Lt. Col. Sir Kenneth Weir Hogg, London W1; R. J. E. Horrill, Librarian, Royal Holloway College, Egham, Surrey; H E Hudson, York; Elspeth Huxley, Malmesbury, Wilts; John Ireland, Messrs. Kitson, Dymond and Easterbrook, Torquay; R. H. Kamen, Royal Institute of British Architects' Library, London W1; Erich Kamper, Graz,

Austria; William Kellaway, Secretary and Librarian, University of London Institute of Historical Research, London WC1; Rev. Brian M. Kennedy, The Rectory, Cobh, County Cork; Mr. Kirby, Clerk, Highgate Cemetery, London; J. E. Lamb, Museum Curator, Norwich Union Insurance Group, Norwich; Anthony J. Lambert, Solihull, Warwickshire; A. F. Langraf, Messrs. G. R. Smith and Son, Solicitors, Torquay; Paul Lansdell, Messrs. Glanfield and Lansdell, Solicitors, Torquay; H. G. Lidstone, Torquay, Devon; J. Loyd, Land Agent, Sandringham Estate Office, Norfolk; A. T. Lucas, Director, National Museum of Ireland; Irene M. McCabe, Librarian and Information Officer, the Royal Institution, London W1; Helen McCulloch, Secretary, the Association of London Clubs, London SW1; R. P. McDouall, Secretary, the Carlton Club, London SW1; Katharine Lindsay-MacDougall, Lochgelphead, Argyllshire; Sir John McNee, Winchester, Hants; Jack Minnitt, Manager, Marketing Department, Sun Life Assurance Co. Ltd., London EC2; R. F. Mole, Deputy Secretary, Royal Holloway College, Egham, Surrey; Wendy Morris, Brigade Librarian, London Fire Brigade, London SE1; George Morrison, Chief Fire Officer, Fire Authority for Northern Ireland, Lisburn; the Rt. Hon. the Lord Mowbray, Segrave and Stourton, c/o House of Lords, SW1; H. E. Lockhart-Mummery, Harley Street, London W1; A. R. Neate, Record Keeper for the Director-General, County Hall, London SE1; Sir Alfred Norris, the British Historical Society of Portugal, Lisbon; Patrick and Kitty O'Connor, Castle Kevin, Mallow, County Cork; Pádraig O'Maidin, County Librarian, Cork; Aidan O'Reilly, Cobh, County Cork; David Orr, Librarian, British Association Library, Oporto, Portugal; David Payne, Grand Hotel, Fokestone, Kent; Malcolm Pillar, Torquay, Devon; J. C. Powell, District Librarian, Maidenhead, Berks; the Rev. V. A. J. Ravensdale, St. George's Church, Lisbon, Portugal; the Rt. Hon. the Lord Redesdale, London NW1; R. Refausse, Manuscripts Assistant, Trinity College Library, Dublin 2; Registrar of Shipping, Port of Cork; Mrs. M. M. Rowe, Head of Record Services, Devon Record Office, Exeter; H. Russell, Irish Librarian, Belfast Education and Library Board; Mrs. P. Russell, Information Officer, Lloyd's Register of Shipping, London EC3; Andrew Saint, Historic Buildings Section, Architect's Department, County Hall, London SE1; Dr. Eileen Scarff, Research Assistant, Scottish Record Office, Edinburgh; Professor R. J. Scothorne, Regius Professor of Anatomy, University of Glasgow; the Rt. Hon. the Viscount Selby, Ardfern House, Argyllshire; Major C. J. Shaw of Tordarroch, Conon Bridge, Ross-shire; E. Sibbick, Osborne House, Isle of Wight; G. J. Slater, Public Record Office of Northern Ireland, Belfast; Brian S. Smith, County Archivist, Gloucestershire; Hester Smith, London NW1; William J. Smith, Head Archivist, County Hall, London SE1; D. K. Smurthwaite, Keeper, Books and Archives, National Army Museum, London SW3; J. G. Spence, Caterham, Surrey; D. M. Staples, General Manager, the Rougemont Hotel, Exeter; F. B. Stitt, Archivist, Staffordshire County Record Office, Stafford; Philip L. Sumner, formerly Keeper of Road Vehicles, Science Museum, London SW7; Elizabeth, Countess of Sutherland, Uppat House, Sutherland; W. Swanton, Cobh,

County Cork; Dr. Philip Taylor, Department of American Studies, University of Hull; Michael L. Tebbutt, Curator, Weston Park, Shropshire; Tina P. Thomson, Administrative Assistant, Westminster and County Office, Sun Alliance and London Insurance Group, London W1; Molly Travis, Broadlands, Hants; Carleton J. R. Tufnell, Muirkirk, Ayrshire; Verdi Vanstone, Olde Court, Torquay; Miss M. E. E. E. Ward, Branch Librarian, Broadstairs, Kent; M. R. E. Webb, Sub-Manager, West End Trust Branch, Lloyds Bank Ltd., London SW1; A. Weigall and Nora A. Weigall, Sutton, Surrey; C. W. West, General Manager, Commercial Union Assurance Co. Ltd., London EC3; Mrs. L. A. West, Firefighting Appliances, Science Museum, London SW7; Dr. J. Wilson, Cork; Alan Wright, Head of the Photographic Section, London Fire Brigade, London SE1; Tom Wylie, Museum Assistant, Local History, Ulster Museum, Belfast; Sir Robin Mackworth-Young, Librarian, Windsor Castle, Berks.

I also owe a debt of gratitude to my family, my friends and my colleagues, who enquired frequently about the progress of the research and who re-invigorated me when it was flagging.

At an early stage in the work I had the good fortune to locate Captain Shaw's only surviving descendant, Sir Bernard Shaw. The support, encouragement and hospitality I received thereafter from both him and Lady Shaw made my task infinitely easier and more enjoyable than would otherwise have been the case.

INTRODUCTION

My interest in Captain Shaw, a cousin of George Bernard Shaw, was first aroused by programme notes at a Gilbert and Sullivan Promenade Concert. They referred to the song from IOLANTHE which provides the title for this book.

The entry about Captain Shaw in the DICTIONARY OF NATIONAL BIOGRAPHY whetted my appetite further; at the time I was unaware of its factual inaccuracies. I enquired at my lending library for a book about him. But I was advised that, even though he had at least a mention in almost every book on fire-fighting, there was no full-length biography. If I needed one, I would have to write it myself.

Because of the almost total absence of family papers and as he was a man of action rather than words, I have had to rely almost entirely on original research. That is not a bad thing, for it has brought to light facets of Shaw that had previously gone unnoticed and it has enabled me to correct a surprising number of inaccurate statements that had previously been made about him.

I have chosen to write comparatively little about the mechanical and organisational aspects of the London Fire Service during Shaw's time, for they have already been well-covered — most recently by Sally Holloway in her LONDON'S NOBLE FIRE BRIGADES, 1833-1904. I have, too, been unable to say very much about Shaw as a family man; this is because he was hardly ever off duty. He lived *'over the shop'*; he attended fires at all hours of the day and night; even his holidays abroad inevitably included a round of visits and inspections connected with his work. He was obsessed with fires and fire-fighting; his family took second place. I have been handicapped, also, by the disappearance or destruction of the personal papers of many people who knew Shaw, either socially or because they were amateur or professional fire-fighters. Yet, from the official papers and contemporary journals, there emerges a clear and fascinating picture of a remarkable public servant.

As a young man he rode indifferent horses hard and far across the Irish countryside and sailed small, sometimes home-made, boats round the Old Head of Kinsale. This developed a stamina and a fearlessness that were later to stand him in good stead. His independence and resourcefulness were encouraged by his fleeing from University and from the threat of ordination into the Church, by the trips he made (probably as crew) on timber boats plying between Cork and Quebec, and by a period spent in America. Summoned back from there by his parents, he then gained his first experience of man management. This was as an officer in the North Cork Rifles, a regiment of little note but much notoriety whose only contribution to the contemporary suppression of the Indian Mutiny was indulgence in street battles against the Royal Artillery, sailors on shore leave and the townspeople of Sheerness.

At the moment of the disembodiment of his regiment, by which time he had a wife and four young children to support, he secured the combined posts of superintendent of the police and of the fire service in Belfast.

There were only four (later seven) fire engines and twenty-two men under his control, yet fifteen months later and when still only thirty-three years of age, he was appointed Superintendent of the London Fire Engine Establishment, in succession to Braidwood who had been killed on duty.

So Shaw came to London, where he remained for the rest of his life. He was very soon advising Parliamentary Committees, with an air of authority based on self-confidence rather than experience; and he was quickly taken up by aristocrats like the Earl of Caithness and the Duke of Sutherland and indeed by Bertie, Prince of Wales. Shortly, too, he was elected to White's, the Carlton and the Marlborough Clubs.

But Shaw was no mere dilettante. He was a working fireman in charge of a service that grew as London expanded. He was much involved too in technical matters, composing pioneer instruction manuals and writing books on fire-fighting, giving advice (based on intuition and, later, experience rather than training) nationally and internationally, and adjudicating on a vast number of inventions designed to prevent fires starting, to extinguish them quickly or to facilitate escape.

In the 1880's, when in his fifties and at the peak of his career, he presided over a truly remarkable exercise, personally inspecting and reporting on fire prevention and fire precautions at all of London's forty-one theatres, the whole task being completed in six months. Hardly was that report complete when he was cited in one of the most notorious divorce trials of the period (in company with a duke, a general and the defendant's own doctor). Then, less than a year later, he was sent by the Government to help the Exeter City Coroner investigate the death of 188 people in a terrible fire at a brand new theatre designed by London's leading theatrical architect; and whilst there, was called from his hotel bed to take control of the demoralised local brigade at a house fire, climbing up and down ladders with a sprightliness and enthusiasm more to be expected in a new recruit than in a man only four months short of sixty.

Sixteen months after that, the London County Council came into existence. Shaw at once found himself in conflict with the militant Progressives who wanted their fire brigade to be commanded not, as John Burns put it, by a military man or a society drawing-room darling (a reference back to the divorce case), but by an administrator who would be the servant of the Fire Brigade Committee. After a succession of public squabbles for which blame can be apportioned to both sides, and with growing discontent in all ranks of the brigade, Shaw resigned with great dignity. His impending departure achieved, for four months, more column inches in the national papers than would be conceivable now for any world figure.

Even after retirement, Captain Shaw continued to make news. He suffered at different times the amputation of both legs; he held court in his Bath chair in Hyde Park; when he died, his funeral was almost a State occasion.

So legendary did he become that, as recently as 1975, the LONDON FIREMAN (and a year later the DAILY TELEGRAPH) produced convincing evidence that he had won a yachting Olympic Gold Medal when over seventy and one-legged. My research proves conclusively that the claim was incorrect; yet I am quite surprised that it was. Such was the man.

I hope the reader will gain as much enjoyment from reading this book as I did from researching and writing it. For their first biography, few authors can have chanced upon a subject more interesting yet previously not investigated.

But I hope, too, the reader will remember that although fighting fires may seem to be an exciting occupation, it is also sometimes boring, often unpleasant, frequently dangerous, occasionally fatal and much taken for granted.

CHAPTER ONE
A START IN LIFE

"No lecture attendances are written against his name; instead the word 'off' . . ."

Eyre Massey Shaw, the first and most famous Chief of the London Fire Brigade, was born on 17 January. According to the DICTIONARY OF NATIONAL BIOGRAPHY and WHO'S WHO, the year was 1830; and those who have written about him in the past have used that date uncritically. Yet the Trinity College Dublin registers, the 1871 census and his death certificate all show him to have been two years older; and he was baptised on 22 February 1828.

Not only is information about Shaw hard to come by; it is also particularly unreliable. With his age, he hardly helps himself; on his marriage certificate he is made out to be a year older than he really was.

We do know that the Shaw family were of Scottish descent. They settled in Ireland, in county Kilkenny; and Eyre's great-grandfather, Robert Shaw, went to Dublin where he became a merchant and served as Accountant-General of the Post Office.

Robert's second son, Eyre's grandfather, was christened Bernard, a name that appears at least eleven times subsequently on the family tree. Its most famous holder was George Bernard Shaw, whose great-grandfather and Robert Shaw, the Accountant-General, were brothers.

Bernard Shaw, Eyre's grandfather, became Collector of the Port of Cork. He rented Monkstown Castle, just outside Cobh which is now virtually a suburb of the city of Cork, and lived there until he died, suddenly, in 1808. Eyre's father also was a merchant, with offices on the quayside at Cork, and with a modest house at 4 Shaw's Terrace, now Carlisle Place (the earlier name may or may not be a coincidence). On the death of his elder brother, in 1858, he moved into Monkstown Castle.

Eyre's mother was a Reeves of Castle Kevin, near Fermoy, also in the county of Cork. Her grandmother whose own great-grandfather had settled in Ireland from Hampshire and had married into the Irish peerage, had bought Castle Kevin in the 1740's. It had been built as a fort, was beseiged by Cromwell and was later restored in the Gothick style. It has an imposing gateway and a fine approach past prosperous farmland with cows grazing almost up to the front door. The gaunt Monkstown Castle, by contrast, has been unoccupied for some years. For a short time it was the club-house for Monkstown Golf Club, and was then boarded up and later damaged by fire.

Eyre himself was not born at Shaw's Terrace, at Monkstown Castle, or at Castle Kevin but, probably, at Glenmore Cottage, near the village of Ballymore on the Great Island of Cobh. Originally a small Georgian house, it has since been much altered and enlarged. It stands in a beautiful secluded garden about twenty yards from the water's edge, overlooking Cork Harbour.

After he had retired, Shaw remembered his home as a genial one but of limited means, with the sea an ever-present feature. In Cobh, he said,

Above: GLENMORE COTTAGE, COBH, CO. CORK. Captain Shaw was probably born here. The house is close to the water's edge and overlooks Cork Harbour. (Photo: Mr. W. Swanton).

Left: MONKSTOWN CASTLE, CO. CORK. Captain Shaw's grandfather and father lived here. In recent years the Castle was a golf club-house and was subsequently damaged by fire.

CASTLE KEVIN, MALLOW, CO. CORK. Captain Shaw's maternal great-grandmother bought Castle Kevin in the 1740s and his mother lived there until her marriage in 1822. The house is surrounded by prosperous farm land.

"every man, woman or child, of high or low degree, young or old, could row a boat and sail a boat, and talk of a boat with real practical knowledge. Many, like myself and other members of my family could build a boat and rig a boat, and make the sails, and turn out a craft, not perhaps after the manner exacted at Cowes, but able to encounter the tremendous seas that are found outside Cork Harbour and off the Old Head of Kinsale." The people of Cobh still exercise these skills today.

His more formal education began at a school run by a Dr. Coghlan, the local Protestant curate. Efforts to find out more about this clergyman have failed, beyond the fact that he later went to Torquay, became a Roman Catholic and in due course a Professor at St. Colman's College, Fermoy. Various letters to a priest in Youghal, said by the College to be an authority on its history, received no reply.

In July 1843 when he was 15½, Eyre Shaw registered at Trinity College, Dublin, as a fellow-commoner, that is an undergraduate of superior rank to the ordinary student having the privileges of dining at the Fellows' table and of qualifying for his degree with one fewer examination. The course ended in the Summer of 1847, his Bachelor of Arts (ordinary pass) degree being awarded at Congregation in March of the following year. He obtained a Master's degree, by purchase, six years after that.

His class marks survive. They show that he was not a good student; or, rather, that he fell away as the course proceeded, especially after the first year. His later career suggests that, at this stage, there was a lack of application rather than of ability.

Later in life, he claimed that his period at Trinity College had ended dramatically. *"Being destined for holy orders"*, he wrote, *"I passed through the Divinity School at Trinity and was on the point of being ordained . . . After the ordination sermon had been preached I returned furtively in my College robes, and leaving these and my other small belongings in my College rooms . . . took ship, and after many long weeks found myself at the western side of the Atlantic."*

This story has been repeated many times, but the evidence from Trinity College is different. He registered as a post-graduate in the Divinity School but there is no record that he ever obtained the divinity testimonium, the qualification without which he would never have been accepted for ordination into the Church of Ireland. No lecture attendances are recorded against his name; instead, the word *'off'* is written in pencil on the appropriate line of the first year register. In the following years his name does not appear at all. Further, what purports to be his signature showing attendance at the BA degree Congregation, in March 1848, does not match that of his later signature as it appears on authoritative documents.

So, sometime between the date when he completed his first degree course, in the Summer of 1847, and the date of the commencement of the postgraduate Divinity course in the Autumn of the same year, he left Trinity College; not, as he suggested, when he was on the point of being ordained. This is only one of many pieces of evidence that Eyre Shaw had a good imagination but a poor memory; or was careless in the accuracy of the facts he gave about his life.

CHAPTER TWO
SAILOR, SOLDIER, FIREMAN

"I took a good house, furnished it in a sumptuous manner far beyond my means, and thought I should never move again"

Cobh was the principal Irish port for America. Eyre may well have watched the SIRIUS, the first steamship to cross the Atlantic, set out when he was about ten. He would certainly have seen many sailing ships leave for the same destination.

When in his seventies, he wrote:

"Young men of the present day . . . may think it a stupendous measure to change the comfort of a genial home for the rough forecastle of a sailing vessel in the North Atlantic; but in my day, and especially in my county, young fellows led a very hardy, healthy life, doing their two and sometimes three days' hunting a week on a . . . horse, which they led to the meet, perhaps miles away, rode all day, jumping off at the heavy fences, and hopping over in company with the steed, and then jumping on again . . . and after the run again leading the horse home, perhaps eight or ten miles, and themselves giving him his bran mash before coming into the house . . . a very different proceeding from what is customary at Melton Mowbray or Market Harborough, but for those brought up to it an enjoyment simply without alloy . . .

"In short, the mode of life then common in the South of Ireland, making an indulgence in the intense pleasure of sport compatible with very limited means, was no bad equipment for that in the forecastle of a sailing ship, and I have no doubt that there are many of my own class still living who can speak with interest and without regret of some dozen or more voyages in timber-laden vessels between Quebec and Cork."

The references to the forecastle suggest that when Eyre went to America he did so as crew; it is also implicit that he made several trips. The Quebec timber trade was still important about 1850, though less so than it had been. But even if Eyre made only one journey and went as a passenger, he is still likely to have travelled via Quebec; it was cheaper that way.

He spent some time in the United States. One writer has said that he led the life of a sailor for two years on leaving Trinity College; if so, he may have spent four or five years ashore in the New World, from about 1850. He told a House of Commons Select Committee, in 1862, that he had been in America five or six years previously, but he was probably under-estimating the time he had been away from there: another example perhaps of his indifference to accuracy when talking about himself. This same Select Committee questioned him about fires he had seen in the States and he claimed, in reply, to have witnessed them in New York, Philadelphia, Washington, Boston and *"great many"* other places. He referred particularly to one that he had seen on Broadway in 1852 when, so he said, a large church and a large hotel adjoining had both been burnt down. He remembered it particularly because the hotel he had been living in was destroyed. But again, research throws doubt on his statement. The New York Public Library can find no reference to a fire of any consequence on Broadway in 1852. There was one, in March 1851, which destroyed a church; but there were no hotels nearby. There was a much larger one in April 1854 which destroyed a clothing store and killed thirteen people. The Astor House, a large and elegant hotel, was a few doors away but was not damaged by the fire and neither were any churches. Eyre Shaw seems to have had a remarkable capacity for embellishment as well as a somewhat hazy recollection of dates.

What he was up to when he was ashore, we do not know; and we would perhaps be disinclined to believe him if he had told us. But we may accept his account of what happened to bring him back home. *"A mistaken family,"* he later wrote, *"often interferes with natural careers, and mine supposed that I was fit for better things, and put me to . . . soldiering."* This they did by obtaining for him a commission in the North Cork Rifles, a militia unit of little note. He probably did well, within three years, to rise to the rank of Captain; he served in the Rifles for six years all told.

In 1855, the year after he became a soldier, Eyre Shaw married. The event took place ten days after his twenty-eighth birthday at Tormoham church, which was at that time the parish church of Torquay. His bride, who was also twenty-eight, was Anna Maria, a daughter of Mordecai Dove.

Dove was 53 years of age when, in 1823, he married Mary Caroline Power Vidal, of Faro, on the Portuguese Algarve coast. She was twenty-two years younger than he, and became a widow after fourteen years of marriage. Mordecai, who may have been the author of a book, the title of which can best be translated as THE KINGDOM OF POETRY: A GEOGRAPHICAL DESCRIPTION IN VERSE, was buried in Lisbon. When he died, he left behind four daughters: Catherine (12) who died eight years later, Anna Maria (10), Elizabeth (9) and Emma Edwards (4). Their mother was a British subject although born in Portugal, and in widowhood came to England to live.

Family stories link the Doves with the port wine trade. There certainly was a substantial wine trade between Portugal and Ireland at about the time Eyre married Anna Maria Dove. Eyre's father — it will be remembered — was a merchant with an office on the quayside at Cork, and there was a firm of wine shippers named Power, Drury & Co. But there, the trail ends.

Even if nothing is known about the way that Eyre and Anna came together, a lot is known about the wedding itself. By 1850 Anna was living with her widowed mother and one or two sisters (Catherine was dead and Elizabeth may have become a nun) at Mount Hermon, a ten-bedroomed house standing in its own grounds, in Upper Lincombe Road, in a fashionable and attractive part of Torquay. The house is now named Oldecourt. The family generally had five servants living in.

In December 1854 two visitors, probably both relatives, arrived at Mount Hermon to stay and about ten days before the wedding they were joined by the Misses Shaw (Eyre had four sisters — Dora, Cornelia, Jane

TORQUAY HARBOUR (circa 1868). It was at a house on the far side of the harbour but slightly more inland that Captain Shaw took lodgings before his wedding in 1855. (Photo: Torquay Central Library).

TOR (or TORMOHAM) CHURCH (1841). A lithograph after T. C. Dibdin and E. Vivian. It was Edward Vivian who gave away Captain Shaw's bride at this same church 14 years later. (Photo: Torquay Central Library).

TORQUAY IN THE 1840s. The house on the right-hand edge of the picture is Woodfield which was occupied for many years by Edward Vivian who gave away Shaw's bride (Photo: Torquay Central Library).

and Maria). There were then between seven and nine ladies (all but two unmarried) staying in the house, with not a gentleman in sight.

Meanwhile, just before Christmas, the bridegroom had taken lodgings at 8 Park Crescent (now, 15 Park Hill Road), down by the harbour. Then, eight days before the wedding, over an inch of snow fell on the very steep unmetalled roads that led down from the bride's home to the church and the ladies at Mount Hermon must have been in a state of some anxiety. But, three days later, the wind changed direction and the snow disappeared almost immediately with, as the TORQUAY DIRECTORY AND SOUTH DEVON JOURNAL reported smugly, *"a bright sunshine which contrasts most agreeably with a fog which usually accompanies a thaw in the inland counties . . . Olive, myrtle, camelia, etc., are wholly uninjured."*

The wedding was on Saturday 27 January, 1855. The service was conducted by the Vicar, the Reverend Doctor Harris, who was later to be a trustee of Mrs. Dove's estate. Anna's father being long dead, she was given away by a close friend of the family and a wealthy and prominent member of Torquay society, Edward Vivian. Magistrate, banker, a Poor Law Guardian and a member of the Local Board of Health, he was also editor of the TORQUAY DIRECTORY AND SOUTH DEVON JOURNAL. He was, too, the Treasurer of the local branch of the British and Foreign Bible Society, a joint-founder of the Torquay Temperance Society, of the Torquay Horticultural Society and of the Torquay Natural History

Society, of which he was to be the Treasurer for almost fifty years. He had presented the Queen with Devonshire cream and flowers when she had visited Torbay and had played a major part in suppressing the 1847 Bread Riots, yet he had let four acres of land to sixteen members of the Chartist Association. The scheme, however, was a failure because, it was said, the operatives were *"unable to bear exposure to rough weather or hard work."*

The guests at the wedding almost certainly included Charles Kitson, Mrs. Dove's solicitor, and his brother, William, the founder of the Torquay Bank. Indeed, Torquay society was well represented and Eyre Shaw may well have reflected how fortunate he was that the cost was falling on his mother-in-law's shoulders, rather than his.

He had made a good match. His bride was a woman of great charm and sweetness and, events would prove, was long-suffering as well. Her mother was wealthy and had no sons to inherit. Shortly before or after the wedding she lent her son-in-law £1,000; and when she died, eight years later, his wife received half her mother's property and money and a half-share in a trust fund presided over by Edward Vivian, by the Reverend Doctor Harris and by Miss Hunsley, one of the ladies who had stayed at Mount Hermon before the wedding.

The Shaws often stayed with Mrs. Dove after they were married. Anna loved Torquay and there survives a lengthy poem that she wrote about it:

"Oh! beauteous, happy, sweet Torquay
Rising like Venus from the sea,
I love to see thy sun's bright ray
Come smiling forth upon the bay —

"I love thy rich luxuriant trees
I love thy cool refreshing breeze
But more than all I love, Torquay
They death-like deep tranquility."

She then goes on to describe how she had crossed the prairies; *"heard the oceans roar/along the rocks of Labrador";* been at sea *"and watched the foaming billows glide/along the storm-tossed vessel's side/and thought as they successive passed/each coming one would be the last".*

Then she continues:

"But though my soul has seen God's form
By day and night — in calm and storm —
In every near or distant scene —
Or bright, or dark, where I have been —
I ne'er have felt His presence more
Than on this peaceful happy shore.

Oh! tranquil, beauteous, sweet Torquay
Emblem of time thou art to me . . ." and so on.

26

Certainly Mount Hermon, where Anna had been living for several years before her marriage, has to this day a magnificent view south over the bay. Torquay must have seemed near-paradise to any Early Victorian who could live there in affluence, even if familiar also with the south coast of Portugal.

By the December following her marriage Anna had given birth to her first child. It was a boy, bearing the same names as his father, Eyre Massey, but always referred to in the family as Massey whereas Captain Shaw used his first name. On this point, Captain Shaw's grandson could not understand why the famous London County Council fire float was named MASSEY SHAW; it was, he contended, a mistake.

Massey lived to be 84 and remained a bachelor until his middle-seventies when he married a widow of 53. He was a disappointment to his father and there was much antagonism between the two of them. So much so that when he finally inherited the family papers, on the death of his younger brother, Clarina, he and his wife destroyed most of them.

As a young man, Massey joined the Royal Navy. He was a sub-lieutenant in 1876 but within four years his name was no longer in the Navy List. He then served with Stanley in the Congo, and the latter wrote: *"Mr. E. Massey Shaw deserves honourable mention . . . for some months of excellent governorship of Vivi during a term which, I fear, gave him more pain and anxiety than comfort and pleasure."* Then, or later, Massey became nearly blind, through blackwater fever.

Very soon after Massey was at Vivi, his father was in Brussels and received an invitation to call on King Leopold II, who said he was *"not wishing to let escape this opportunity of chatting."* Possibly Captain Shaw mentioned his son to Leopold, because six months later Massey received a letter from the banker Léon Lambert, described by Ludwig Bauer in his book, LEOPOLD THE UNLOVED: KING OF THE BELGIANS AND OF MONEY, as Leopold's gilt man-of-straw. In the letter Lambert, who controlled a lot of patronage, wrote:

"I need not tell you how pleased I shall be to be of any use to you.

I am afraid there is no chance for you to be appointed in His Majesty's Cabinet (i.e. the Royal Chancellory) as the King never employs but Belgians in that office. As for the Congo business nothing can be said before the (Berlin) Conference comes to an end which I suppose will be soon. When Colonel Strauch (a prominent member of the Belgian delegation) returns from Berlin I shall certainly place before him your request and in case there is a chance of seeing your offer accepted, I'll do my best to succeed by recommending you warmly to the Committee.

Hoping all your family are well and begging you kindly to remember me to them . . ."

Nothing came of this, apparently, and Massey seems to have done very little with the rest of his life.

He, it will be remembered, had been born in Torquay and Anna returned there for the birth of her second child, Bernard Vidal, in October 1857. But not to Mount Hermon, for six months after the wedding Mrs.

Dove and her one daughter remaining at home had moved into Court Mare, a newly-built house in Middle Warberry Road, in the same exclusive part of Torquay. It was marginally smaller, having only eight rather than ten bedrooms.

Within a few weeks the house had been renamed Castelo á Maré and Mrs. Dove and her daughter, Emma, together with a parlourmaid and a housemaid, continued to live there until June 1862. The house subsequently had a curious history and from the end of June 1897 it remained unoccupied for twenty-five years although no other house in the locality was ever without an occupant for more than a few weeks. The house was said to be haunted after a double murder involving a doctor of foreign extraction, his wife and a maidservant, the doctor sometimes being cast as a victim and sometimes as the perpetrator.

The story is a confusing one. Beverley Nichols and Violet, Lady Tweedale, both referred to it with more enthusiasm than accuracy. The latter visited it with a medium and a soldier on leave and described how the medium had been *"controlled by a violent male entity"* and how all three of them had heard a piercing female cry: *"Terrible doctor — will kill me, has killed master. Help, help"*. But little credibility can be placed on Lady Tweedale's accuracy in reporting, even though she lived locally.

For instance, she said that the murder had been *"some fifty years before"*, which would mean that at least seven families following the Doves, including those of a Royal Naval Captain, a Major-General and two Majors, had lived there undisturbed before the *"violent male entity"* had taken over.

Yet one cannot ignore the story. There must have been some reason why the legends surrounding the house were sufficiently strong to deter would-be occupants for so long; and it is an interesting point that its last tenant before it lay empty was a doctor. Dr. E. P. L. Parrot lived there with his family for two years or more up to 1897. But he was then neither murdered nor charged with murder; instead, he moved to another part of the town where the family lived for a further three years. One possible explanation for the legend is that at Castelo á Maré Dr. Parrot boarded private mental patients and perhaps the noises they made created hysteria among the servants in the nearby houses so that increasingly wild stories circulated about what was going on. Here, is a subject worthy of further investigation.

After many years of decay and dereliction the house was renovated and converted into separate apartments: Norfolk Lodge (1922), Suffolk Lodge (1930) and The Gardens and Grendon (both since World War II). It is not known whether there is still *"a violent male entity"* or whether screams can still be heard.

Into that house, anyway, was born Vidal Shaw, in 1857. He spent his life in the Colonial Civil Service holding successively the posts of Commissioner of Police in the Cape and Superintendent of Police in New Guinea. He was the father of two of Eyre's three grandchildren.

Bernard's birth coincided with the Indian Mutiny and a few weeks before he arrived his father's regiment was embodied. It later embarked at

Cobh for Portsmouth and reached Shorncliffe in early December. Eyre had come on ahead and by 11 November was at Castelo á Maré to see his month-old son. He left at the end of the month, no doubt to rejoin his regiment. Six months later, by which time he was a Captain, the North Cork Rifles had moved to Sheerness to undertake dockyard and garrison duties in company with the Royal Artillery. This posting was to have unfortunate consequences.

On Tuesday 12 October (1858) the SOUTH EASTERN GAZETTE reported that the conduct of the North Cork Rifle Militia was most outrageous. *"Night after night"*, it said, *"soldiers of the regiment — most of them newly-raised men — have gone about in groups of nine or ten, entering public houses, and in some cases shops and private houses, attacking with their leather belts, stones, sticks, etc., indiscriminately, any persons they found, and in some cases civilians have sustained severe injuries."* The previous night, continued the newspaper, a Superintendent of the Kent County Constabulary had arrived in Sheerness with a strong contingent of police and had extracted a pledge from the Commanding Officer of the North Cork Rifles that his men would be confined to barracks for the evening. *"At dusk, however, a body of the militiamen . . . came into the town by Queenborough wall. They first attacked a poor fisherman while going to his boat, which was lying near the wall, and beat him so severely about his head and face with their sticks that hardly a feature remains distinguishable. They then rushed into the town and commenced breaking the windows of the Fountain Hotel . . . A picket of 100 Cork Rifles, under the charge of a commissioned officer (unfortunately unnamed) was drawn up before the hotel (still there, at the corner of West Street and West Lane), and stood silent spectators of the acts of their comrades. The men,"* continued the newspaper, *"then proceeded to demolish the doors, shutters, and windows of a number of other houses; and, as it was found that none of the pickets would act to preserve the property and protect the . . . townsfolk, application was made to the Royal Artillery for assistance."* They despatched a hundred men and the Rifle pickets were ordered back to the barracks. The Artillery, cheered on by the local inhabitants, then cleared the town of militiamen though some of them tried to take forcible possession of houses to evade apprehension. *"They have"*, said the SOUTH EASTERN GAZETTE, *"disgraced the uniform they wear."*

An investigation was commenced and strong Artillery pickets were placed round the fortifications at night to prevent the North Cork Rifles from leaving barracks. But simultaneously, the magistrates issued a notice condemning the local inhabitants for having paraded the streets in a riotous and disorderly manner, and hooting at and generally annoying the military. This prompted *"the most influential inhabitants"* to convene a meeting at the Co-operative Hall at which it was pointed out that the riots *"originated entirely with the undisciplined corps of the North Cork Rifle Militia"*, or alternatively that the quarrels had begun between the military and the sailors. The meeting ended with three cheers for the officer who had commanded the Royal Artillery picket and with the singing of the National

Anthem.

A War Office Court of Inquiry later found that the militiamen could not be considered *"the original aggressors"*. No papers relating to the Inquiry have come to light, but the SHEERNESS GUARDIAN described its findings as being one-sided, superficial and unfair to the townspeople. What part Captain Shaw played in his regiment's only *"battle"* is not known; but we do know that his wife was again pregnant.

Five days after the Sheerness riot the North Cork Rifle Militia were posted to Aldershot where, if their regimental history is to be believed, they *"won golden opinions — even from the voice of Royalty"*. Whilst the regiment was there the Shaw's third child was born. This time it was a daughter, named Anna after her mother. Again, the birth was at Torquay. Anna never married and remained her father's constant companion to the day of his death.

In October 1859 the North Cork Rifles went to Scotland, by sea, the full journey from Aldershot to Ayr and Hamilton taking a week. There, according to the regimental history, the Rifles received great kindness and hospitality, the officers in return entertaining the élite of the area in the same manner. Captain Shaw's meagre financial resources must have been severely stretched, especially at Hogmanay.

Early in 1860 the regiment returned to Cobh, and was disembodied at Mallow on 28 February. Within a month Anna was again pregnant so that Captain Shaw, with no military future, would soon have to support a wife and four children, the eldest only just five years old. But things were happening elsewhere that would change, abruptly, the course of his life.

A disastrous fire in Belfast, in 1859, had caused much criticism of the discipline and competence of the fire brigade there and in November of the same year the City Council resolved to combine the posts of superintendent of the police and fire services, as was being done elsewhere. It was decided to advertise for *"a gentleman of thorough knowledge and qualifications"*. The salary was to be £300 and the duties would include, also, the oversight of the Sanitary and Licensing departments.

There were fifty applications for the post, including one from Captain Shaw. The list was soon whittled down to eight and, in due course, he found himself in the last three. Beyond being a cousin of Lord Massey, and doubtless other candidates could claim similar connections, he had neither qualification nor knowledge. That may have been a common failing of most of the competitors for the post. In his HISTORY OF THE BELFAST FIRE BRIGADE, published in 1935, Alfred S. Moore declared that Shaw was appointed by *"a large majority"* but the NORTHERN WHIG of 10 May 1860 gave the final figures as: Captain Shaw 22, Lieutenant Wilson 14, John M'Cance 13. A second poll involving only the first two candidates could have deprived Shaw of the job.

So, on 1 June 1860, at the age of 32 Captain Shaw took up his new post and moved to 9 Murray's Terrace, Belfast with his family. As Shaw himself later wrote: *"I took a good house, furnished it in a sumptuous manner far beyond my means, and thought I should never move again."* Six months later Anna gave birth to another boy, Clarina. He lived to be 77 and, although regarded by the family as very much *"a ladies' man"*, he never married. Of Captain Shaw's four sons he remained, perhaps, closest to his parents.

The Belfast Fire Brigade had not only been incompetent; it was also very small. When Shaw took it over he had only four engines under his control, a number increased shortly to seven. But he appears to have entered into his various responsibilities with relish. Much later, he wrote of that time:

"The work of a Chief of Police where politics run high as between Orangemen and Papists is most interesting and full of adventure and in some difficult cases, when both sides fought with unusual ferocity, and blood ran freely, I had to act with vigour, and was accused of 'undue violence'; which expression . . . means merely that I had used the strong arm at my disposal without waiting for a magistrate to read the Riot Act — undoubtedly a legal offence, but one frequently repeated by me, and in every case eventually condoned, without apparent opposition from any of the so-called sufferers, who were well aware that but for the prompt action of the police . . . one or other sides would be occasionally annihilated . . . Notwithstanding my position, I was on very good terms with both sides, particularly the (Papists) . . . although I did not belong to their creed, and I began to feel that I had found my proper mission in the world and was settled down for life."

He went on to point out that fires were frequent and property was valuable, *"and much attention was necessarily devoted to this branch of duty."* He described his approach in the introduction to one of his books written many years later, by which time he had become world-famous:

"I immediately set to work to ascertain what knowledge existed on the subject . . . for the purpose of showing others what to do and without any intention . . . of devoting myself permanently to the business.

"To my great surprise I found there was no published information and . . . nowhere the theoretical knowledge without which no . . . profession can keep pace with . . . growing requirements.

"At first a habitude of dealing with men, and a knowledge of the principles and practice of organization coming after a management deficient in these . . . brought some credit . . . but . . . I may now frankly acknowledge that some of the most painful humiliations of my life were undergone at that . . . period. None knew . . . how very nearly the great successes had been great disasters . . . cases in which I had all but sacrificed the whole of my little band in the attempt to do what was almost impossible, and only corrected the error . . . when further delay would have made it irrevocable. Then would follow the explanation in the form of a lecture . . . and by degrees there would creep out from me . . . acknowledgement that such and such a move had been a mistake . . . and then would come from the auditors the condonation — not perhaps in words, as that might have interfered with discipline, but yet clearly . . . and unmistakably expressed . . . There is no order which they will not obey with

alacrity if given steadily by a superior PRESENT WITH THEM.''

In this quotation, much is revealed about Shaw: his almost accidental entry into the job of fireman; his energy; his enthusiasm; his self-criticism; his preparedness, in the absence of existing theoretical knowledge, to compile it himself; and his high regard for discipline combined with education and explanation. If to this, one adds his passion for method and order one begins to see why, in appointing Captain Shaw to control its four fire engines, Belfast Corporation had unwittingly appointed the man who would emerge as perhaps the greatest fireman the world has ever known.

It is that emergence which is described later in this book.

CHAPTER THREE
THE FIRST YEAR IN LONDON
"If a fire happened, you must pull down a part of the house to get the engine out"

Saturday 22 June 1861 was a scorching hot day in London. Shortly before half past four in the afternoon, a passer-by saw wisps of smoke coming from a warehouse on Cotton's Wharf, Tooley Street, just below London Bridge. Hawkins, the local turncock, was sent for. By the time the first fire engines arrived he had the water turned on.

That fire, despite its very ordinary beginnings, was to change the entire organisation of fire-fighting in London; and eventually throughout the United Kingdom. When it was finally put out five weeks later: London's fire chief was dead, eight huge warehouses had been totally destroyed, insured losses amounting to about two million pounds had been incurred, and the body that for the past twenty-eight years had provided London's only paid fire service was well on the way to deciding that it could do so no longer.

The Superintendent of the London Fire Engine Establishment who died that June evening was James Braidwood. He had held the post as long as the Establishment had been in existence, having previously been Firemaster of Edinburgh.

A qualified surveyor and civil engineer, he had been perhaps the first fire chief in the world to weld together a number of small units into one command. Technically competent, strict but kind, he was noted for his composure in difficult situations, and he had created a small, but well-trained, well-disciplined and popular force.

Braidwood's death opened up the way for Captain Shaw. The post was advertised in THE TIMES on two days in August but there was absolutely no response, probably because it was clearly a temporary appointment. However in advance of the advertisement both Shaw and G. H. Birkbeck, a London civil engineer, had already expressed an interest. Birkbeck demanded a salary of £500, a hundred more than the Establishment was prepared to pay; Shaw was more conciliatory, was appointed and a month after he took up post his salary was increased to £500, backdated.

He was incredibly fortunate to be appointed. His command had comprised only twenty-two men and he had been a fireman for less than fifteen months. As he wrote, when offered the post: *"Your Committee has taken me in a great measure on trust"*.

Charles Roetter, in his book FIRE IS THEIR ENEMY, published in 1962, claimed that Shaw took up his London appointment *"with the air of a man who was genuinely surprised that anyone could have managed without him for so long."* But Shaw himself modestly wrote:

"I did not consider myself qualified for the position and, moreover, was grieved at the thought of parting from the friends I had made in Belfast."

So, on 15 September 1861, there arrived in London, as the new Superintendent of the London Fire Engine Establishment, a man who was

described by Sally Holloway in her book, LONDON'S NOBLE FIRE BRIGADES, 1833-1904, published in 1973, as one who came to be:

". . . clearly devoted to the point of obsession to the problems of fire in the world's largest city yet on the other hand could be brusque to the point of rudeness with other experts and his own employers; who was at once loved by the ordinary people of London, admired and criticized by his men and peers, who mixed with princes, advised Queen Victoria herself, yet would go out again and again to fight a fire alongside his men, returning home soaked to the skin . . . (but) ready to set off again in a fresh outfit for the next 'incident'."

He brought with him his army rank of Captain and, from then on, the man in charge of any fire brigade whether paid or not, and however inadequate that brigade might be, gave himself the same title — often for life.

On Shaw's arrival in London he at once realised that the Establishment had two major sets of difficulties to face: one technical, the other financial.

Braidwood had often said that Tooley Street was the greatest fire risk in London. The fire that killed him confirmed that he had been right. The warehouses there were taller than ever before; Scovel's, the one where the fire had begun, was fifty feet high. This made it difficult for the water, passing through inadequate mains and under low pressure, to reach the upper floors. The buildings were loaded indiscriminately with a wide range of goods; the behaviour of these, under heat, was not fully understood and their control was subject to no legislation. Scovel's warehouse had been stacked with hemp, oil, tallow, tar, cotton, sugar, sulphur, chests of tea, bales of silk, and saltpetre. The hemp seems to have ignited spontaneously; the iron fire-resisting doors had been left open negligently and about two and a half hours after the fire began the saltpetre had exploded, blowing out the walls, burying Braidwood under fifteen feet of hot bricks and setting fire to adjacent warehouses with similar flammable and volatile materials in them.

To understand the Fire Engine Establishment's financial problems it is necessary to see how the organisation had come into being.

The separate fire insurance companies had, earlier, had their own brigades but, in January 1833, ten of them had combined to form the London Fire Engine Establishment. This, at first, had nineteen stations and eighty paid men. The stations were mostly in and around the City, and none of them was west of the Parks or beyond Holborn.

The committee of the Establishment comprised either the Secretary or a director of each of the fire offices. The organisation had no charter, no Act of Parliament, no deed of partnership, no legal status, and no power to achieve any of these; and it was in conflict with the generally inept parish brigades which, ironically, did have legal recognition.

The public probably thought that the London Fire Engine Establishment was maintained by voluntary subscriptions; certainly it was a point of principle on the part of the Establishment not to ask, until a fire was put out, whether any of the parties were insured.

The nature of the risk was all the time becoming more complex and the

35

extent of the risk was becoming greater. This was not only because of London's increasing population and the greater height and size of its buildings, but also because of the introduction of gas lighting, the invention of the phosphorus friction match, the widening use of paraffin oil lamps, the nature of women's fashions, and the spread of housing close to warehouses and factories with no planning control and little regard for fire precautions.

It was with this in mind that the fire insurance companies were increasingly resolved to stop running a public fire brigade at no cost to the community. As the Secretary of the Globe Company told a House of Commons Select Committee: *"(It) is no part of the business of a fire insurance office to maintain a fire brigade upon the scale of the present fire brigade in London, any more than it is part of the business of a life office to maintain a staff of physicians, or send people to Madeira."* They would, he said, be happy to transfer the stations and engines to any authority that the Government might appoint.

Faced with this situation, the Government set up the Select Committee already referred to. Its chairman was Thomas Hankey, the Liberal member for Peterborough. The Fire Engine Establishment agreed to carry on until the Committee reported but left the Government in no doubt that some solution would have to be found.

So, less than six months after taking up his post in London, Captain Shaw with only twenty months' experience as a fireman and almost totally unfamiliar with the Capital, found himself called on to give evidence to the Commons and, shortly, to submit schemes for a new brigade for the Metropolis.

The Committee met for the first time on 25 February 1862, it examined forty-two witnesses between then and 1 April, and reported on 8 May. This exceptionally speedy attention to Parliamentary business reflected the urgency and the seriousness with which the Fire Engine Establishment's declared intention was viewed.

Those giving evidence included: the Lord Mayor of London (the retired builder and contractor, William Cubitt); Sir Richard Mayne, the Chief Commissioner of the Metropolitan Police who had been at Trinity College, Dublin, a generation before Captain Shaw; the Commissioner of the City of London Police; the Chief Constable of Liverpool; the Chief Fire Officers of Manchester and Glasgow; and representatives of the Metropolitan Board of Works, the London parishes and vestries, the insurance and water companies, and ratepayer and commercial interests. Many years later Captain Shaw wrote: *"The Committee took the advice of all who were in a position to offer any and many who were not."* Evidence was heard not only about the London Fire Engine Establishment, but also about the parish engines and the Society for the Protection of Life from Fire.

The parish engines were of widely disparate quality. They were operated and maintained, as an obligation, by individual parish vestries, the statutory requirement resting on eighteenth century Acts. There were perhaps, all told, sixteen good parish engines, four or five of these being at

Hackney. And there were ten or so good engineers to look after them.

Stoke Newington had no engine or man. A witness told the Select Committee: *"The parish of Hackney has some sort of combined agreement with Stoke Newington . . . but I don't think they're on very good terms with each other."* At Rotherhithe, there were a number of engines but they were never used because there was no-one to work them. St. George the Martyr, Bloomsbury, had sold their parish engines, and so were in breach of the Acts.

The Clerk to the City of London Union told the Committee that the ninety-eight parishes in that Union contributed about £600 a year towards the cost of the parish fire engines. But, he said, *"you might as well put the £600 a year in the streets, to be picked up by any person who was passing by; it would be just as useful."* He related that one of the engines was bricked up behind a blacksmith's shop. *"If a fire happened,"* he said, *"you must pull down a part of the house to get the engine out."* There was, incidentally, an engineer paid to look after it. Asked if he had ever heard of a prosecution, he replied in the negative. *"The Act,"* he said, *"is looked upon almost as useless as the engines."*

One can see from all this how much London had come to depend on the insurance companies' Fire Engine Establishment. But of course, by its nature and origin, its purpose was to save property, not lives. None of their firemen received proper training in life saving. That was the work of a separate organisation, the Society for the Protection of Life from Fire.

The Hankey Committee had to consider how these various units — the London Fire Engine Establishment of the insurance companies, the statutory parish engines, and the voluntary Society for the Protection of Life from Fire — each created in a different way, each for a different purpose, and each organised and financed by totally different means, might be welded together — with some urgency — to form an efficient system of life and property protection that would meet the needs of a rapidly-growing London.

In the event, the Committee made no recommendations about the Society for the Protection of Life from Fire. It had a reputation for efficiency, it was funded entirely from voluntary subscriptions, and had not threatened to disband. They concentrated, instead, on the future of the London Fire Engine Establishment and on the future of the service provided (or not) by the parishes.

They recommended, in a report that was a model of brevity, that a fire brigade should be created for London which would be under the superintendence of the Commissioners of Police for the Metropolitan area and for the City. But soon, this idea was dropped. An alternative proposal that the brigade should serve under the Metropolitan Police alone was also abandoned, as that body had no powers within the City.

The Government then turned to the newly-founded Metropolitan Board of Works and, after prolonged negotiations, it was agreed that responsibility for the Brigade should in future rest there. The parishes, for their part, were relieved of their largely-neglected responsibilities under the eighteenth century Acts and the Board was given authority to purchase such parish stations, engines and plant as it considered desirable. It was given the duty of protecting life as well as property. There was to be a rapid doubling of the number of fire stations to over forty in an area extending from Hammersmith and Putney in the west, through Wandsworth, Norwood, Lewisham, Woolwich, Bow, and round to Stoke Newington and Hampstead in the north. The number of firemen was to be increased from 129 to 232.

One section of the Select Committee's report that must have given particular satisfaction to Captain Shaw was that which stated that every witness had borne testimony to the high state of efficiency of the Establishment under Braidwood and, it continued, *"it appears to your Committee that it is likely to maintain its reputation under . . . Captain Shaw."*

His future now seemed assured and four months after the publication of the Report his family responsibilities increased with the birth to Anna of another son, Cecil O'Brien, who never married and died, shortly before his 50th birthday, in Suez where he worked for the Eastern Telegraph Company. The Shaws now had five children, the eldest under seven years of age.

CHAPTER FOUR
SHAW IN SOCIETY
"The Prince . . . would prefer a good fire to seeing the printing of the
DAILY TELEGRAPH. Could you not get up one for him on purpose!"

During Braidwood's time, attending fires and even helping to put them out had become a fashionable sport, attracting the bored and the technically minded. Foremost among these aristocratic fire-fighters had been the 14th Earl of Caithness and the 3rd Duke of Sutherland; and Braidwood had allowed them to train with his men so long as they subjected themselves absolutely to his discipline. Both had considerable mechanical knowledge.

The Earl of Caithness (1821-1881) was a Fellow of the Royal Society. He invented a gravitating compass that came into general use, a tape-loom by which a weaver might stop one shuttle without interfering with the action of the rest, and a steam carriage. He drove such a vehicle, with three wheels and iron tyres, from Inverness to his residence near John O'Groats, a distance of well over 170 miles, accompanied by his wife who said, before they set off, that if Caithness blew up she was quite ready to go with him.

Most of his personal papers have been destroyed and it is impossible to say whether he continued to train under Captain Shaw but he was certainly a member of the committee which organised the first fire engine trials at the Crystal Palace, in July 1863.

The Chairman of that committee was the Duke of Sutherland (1828-1892). His engagement books, with their entries in pencil and very difficult to read, show that Shaw had supper with him on 25 July 1863, less than two years after his arrival in London. The engagement may well have been arranged at the Crystal Palace trials, three weeks earlier. References to Shaw continue in the Duke's diaries to within three years of the Duke's death as, for instance, on 16 July 1887, when the Chief of the Fire Brigade dined, with a party, on board the Duke's yacht.

Sutherland was the largest landowner in Great Britain. He could have bought out his friend Bertie, Prince of Wales, many times over and when the Prince and the Shah of Persia were both staying at Trentham, the Duke's Staffordshire palace, the Shah described the Duke as being *"too grand for a subject"* and advised the Prince: *"You'll have to have his head off when you come to the throne."* When the Duke's heir was married, Captain and Mrs. Shaw presented the bride with *"a handsome china basket"* and the groom with *"a centre bowl for flowers."* These must have been coals to Newcastle.

Shaw stayed at Trentham on at least one occasion and at about ten o'clock on the Sunday evening arranged with the Duke a fire drill which resulted in the entire village turning out EN DÉSHABILLÉ. The estate fire brigade was presented next day with ten pounds by the Duke for the smartness and efficiency they had shown.

It would not have struck Sutherland that his friendship with Shaw, whose lack of wealth must have been more apparent than his distant aristocratic connections, was in any way unconventional. The Duke was a

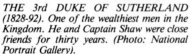

THE 3rd DUKE OF SUTHERLAND
(1828-92). One of the wealthiest men in the
Kingdom. He and Captain Shaw were close
friends for thirty years. (Photo: National
Portrait Gallery).

THE 14th EARL OF CAITHNESS, FRS
(1821-81). He was a member of the
committee that organised the first fire engine
trials at the Crystal Palace in 1863. (Photo:
National Portrait Gallery).

man of strong commonsense and independence of mind. In addition, he had a passion for yachts, driving steam locomotives (he built his own private railway at a cost of nearly a quarter of a million pounds and this remained in private ownership until nationalisation in 1950) and, as has been said, he trained under Braidwood. The time he spent in Shaw's interesting and congenial company may have afforded a pleasant escape for him from his wife who lived in only two rooms of their London residence, Stafford House, mostly lying on a sofa under a silk eiderdown and surrounded by mina birds and parrots which flew about the room or perched on the head of an ancient retriever.

When the Metropolitan Board of Works took over the fire brigade it looked askance at the Duke's presence at training sessions. For instance, in March 1868, the Chairman of the Fire Brigade Committee drew attention to a report in the ILLUSTRATED LONDON NEWS that a drill and inspection of the brigade had taken place on the Embankment at which *"the Duke of Sutherland and other persons were present."* The Chairman complained that he had had no intimation that there was to be a public inspection, to which Captain Shaw replied disarmingly that the event described had been no special inspection, and he *"did not know or observe that the Duke of Sutherland or any other person of distinction was present."*

It was probably through Sutherland that Shaw formed a life-long friendship, also, with the Prince of Wales. The latter was a frequent guest at one or other of the Duke's stately mansions, contrary to the advice of the Queen who warned her son that Sutherland *"does not live as a Duke ought."* Bertie replied: *"I am sure you would like him as he is a clever and most straightforward man in spite of certain eccentricities."* He went on to remind the Queen that the Duke's mother had been one of her *"oldest and most devoted friends"* and added the threat that if the visit he proposed was cancelled *"we should, of course, be obliged to use your name which would not be pleasant."*

Bertie had seen his first fire at the age of eleven when the Prince of Wales Tower at Windsor Castle had been severely damaged. Twelve years later, in March 1865, when the former Saville House in Leicester Square (by then a music hall) was burnt down he, Sutherland and Lord Richard Grosvenor went to the scene, the Prince being attired *"partly in the dress of a fireman."* Then, less than four months after that, the Prince experienced a fire in his own London home. It occurred in a ventilating shaft beneath the nursery of Marlborough House and it gave him the opportunity of organising the servants into a human chain with buckets and jugs of water. He and the guard commander hacked at the floorboards furiously with axes, and used so much water to extinguish the fire that Captain Shaw's first question, on coming up the stairs, was: *"What's all this mess?"* In his official report, Shaw noted the fact that the premises were not insured.

The Prince had shown on that occasion that he had a lot to learn about fire-fighting, especially as he had managed after removing the nursery floorboards to put his foot through to the room below. But it was doubtless as an escape from the boredom of his more orthodox activities, rather than as a desire to improve his fire-fighting techniques, that he soon arranged with Captain Shaw that there should be a complete set of kit kept for him at one of the central London fire stations. Occasionally, too, both he and Sutherland would go along to the Chandos Street station to play billiards, hoping that a call would come in while they were there. A letter in the possession of the Shaw family and written by Bertie's Secretary in June 1879 reads: *"I am desired by the Prince of Wales to thank you for the Fire Brigade Helmet which you have been so good as to send to him, and to add that it fits capitally."* In return for these favours Captain and Mrs. Shaw were frequent guests at Marlborough House.

Fortunately, when at a fire Bertie never attempted to take charge or give orders. He simply did odd jobs and, after the stop (*i.e.* when the fire fighting was finished), was generous with his cigars. Once or twice he found himself in a position of some danger and one can only hope that whatever handicap he was, in distracting attention from the task of fire-fighting, was more than offset by the fillip that his presence gave to the men and the glamour that he caused to be associated with their duties. For several years his attendance at fires was so regular that it ceased to be remarked on by press or public and, when the Hankey Committee asked an insurance company witness what his office thought of the efficiency of the brigade he replied: *"I could not give you an opinion. His Royal*

Highness, the Prince of Wales, would give you a better opinion on that point."

Bertie used fires and fire-fighting displays as a way of entertaining foreign visitors. In February 1871, his Secretary wrote to Shaw: *"The Prince of Wales desires me to thank you for your letter. He thinks your programme a capital one, but would prefer a good fire to seeing the printing of the DAILY TELEGRAPH. Could you not get up one for him on purpose!"*

Most of Bertie's personal papers were destroyed by his Private Secretary after his death. So any evidence from that source for the Prince's friendship with Shaw has disappeared for ever. But there are a few references to him in Queen Victoria's papers, including a brief description of a tour of a fire station arranged for the Grand Duke Vladimir of Russia. Since this also was in 1871, it probably refers to the programme just mentioned. After the almost inevitable opera, the Royal party visited the Fire Brigade headquarters in Watling Street, where Alfred, Duke of Edinburgh and the Duke of Sutherland joined the others. A tour was then made of a number of stations, but no good fires occurred. The party then boarded one of the Brigade's river steamers and went to Southwark Bridge where a *"cohort of engines"* was summoned to *"an imaginary point of distress, ending a late but interesting entertainment with a supper at Captain Shaw's."*

A couple of years later a display was put on for the Shah of Persia, during the visit when he advised Bertie to have Sutherland beheaded. Shaw was presented to the Shah when the exercise was over.

Later, in 1879, a display was given for the benefit of Leopold, King of the Belgians, in the presence of the Prince and Princess of Wales, the Duke and Duchess of Edinburgh, the Duke of Sutherland and the Chairman of the Metropolitan Board of Works. Three fire escapes, thirteen steam fire-engines, five manual engines and about 150 men were in attendance for a formal inspection held on the terrace at the west front of Buckingham Palace. A rescue demonstration was then given and, according to THE FIREMAN, *"so energetic were the men that the stone balustrading gave way and will have to be replaced."*

On at least two occasions Shaw was invited to visit Sandringham. Bertie had it largely rebuilt between 1868 and 1870, and when the work was well under way the Prince's Secretary asked the Metropolitan Board of Works whether Shaw could be spared to advise the Prince on fire prevention in the new building. The Fire Brigade Committee agreed.

When invited there eight years later, however, it was as a guest. The letter reflected a combination of high living and practical advice. Written from Sandringham, it says: *"The Prince of Wales wishes me to say that the best plan on Monday next (1 January 1878) will be for you to come with the other guests by the 2.35 pm train from Pancras to Wolferton and if you like to send on your luggage and servant by the 12.3 train you will find all ready on your arrival. I think they issue weekly or monthly tickets."*

The invitation was an accolade, for only personal friends acceptable to the Princess as well as to the Prince were invited to Sandringham. In some ways the Prince was a model host. He frequently went upstairs with new arrivals on their first visit to make sure that they had all they wanted, even putting more coals on the fire and making certain that the water in the jugs was hot enough. But the east wind off the North Sea blew bitterly cold in winter, keeping up with the host's conversation in a mixture of English, French and German was taxing and living up to his rules for always doing the right thing grew wearying for some after a day or two. Every clock in the house was set thirty minutes fast, a kind of private Summer Time to obtain more light for shooting; and guests were advised to advance their watches accordingly since the Prince demanded punctuality in everyone except his wife. Bertie went to bed abominably late; nobody was permitted to retire before he did. Shaw, however, no doubt found it easier than most to conform to these requirements of a stay at Sandringham.

On their arrival or departure, or both, all guests were weighed by the Prince and the readings recorded in a book presented for the purpose by a Grenadier Guards Colonel in 1874. Shaw weighed in at 13 stone 3 lbs, in uniform. Other guests listed on the same date included: Prince Christian, the Queen's son-in-law (14 stone 11¾ lbs in hunting clothes), Admiral Macdonald, shortly to become Commander-in-Chief in the Indies (13 stone 5 lbs in *"neat morning dress"*), Colonel the Hon. Sir William Colville (12 stone, dressed likewise) and Hélène Standish, the daughter of a French Count (8 stone 11 lbs in a morning gown). Shaw, Colville and Hélène's husband, Henry Standish (who weighed 14 stone when dressed, surprisingly, in *"tea costume"*) were all members of the Marlborough Club, the significance of which is considered below.

In his association with the Prince, Shaw had to guard particularly against one thing. Many of Bertie's associates were led into habits of extravagance, for the Prince was good-natured but thoughtless. When he heard of the social collapse of a friend and it came to his knowledge that the catastrophe had been brought about by the man living beyond his means, it never struck him that his intimacy with the man might have contributed greatly to that end; and no-one ever dared hint at the fact. Shaw, by his own admission, could be extravagant. His salvation lay in his strength of will and, too, in the absorption he had in his demanding work as a fire chief. But one minor extravagance — or at least luxury — that his association with people like Bertie and Sutherland did bring about was his membership of several West End clubs.

He seems first, in 1865, to have joined the St. James's Club, resigning forty years later. This was a surprising choice, for it had been founded on the initiative of a number of members of the Diplomatic Corps, their intention being particularly to provide a meeting place for secretaries and attachés after balls and parties. It may well, as a new club, have been comparatively easy to join without a long wait. It became noted for its cuisine and cellar and, in 1886, was described as *"more than any other establishment of the kind, an international and cosmopolitan rendezvous for gentlemen of position and fashion."*

Shaw's membership was proposed by Lord Richard Grosvenor, a member of the committee responsible for the Crystal Palace fire engine **43**

*LORD RICHARD
GROSVENOR (1837-1912).
Like the Duke of Sutherland, he
trained as a fireman; he was an
organiser of the first fire engine
trials in 1863. He proposed Shaw
for membership of the St.
James's Club. (Photo: National
Portrait Gallery).*

trials two years earlier and present, it will be remembered, with Bertie and Sutherland at the Saville House fire. He kept very full journals and copies of much of his correspondence but, according to his grand-daughter, authoress Elspeth Huxley, all these were destroyed, together with other documents going back to medieval times, by his son and heir (her uncle) when he sold the family home, Motcombe House, Dorset. *"I am told the bonfire lasted a week,"* she wrote. Her mother, writing in her early nineties from Portugal, confirmed that this was the case and went on to recall how her father, Lord Richard, had told her many stories of his travelling to fires with the brigade.

One of Shaw's supporters, in his application for admission to the St. James's Club was Henry Weigall, who six years later submitted for a Royal Academy Exhibition his painting of Captain Shaw, *"a well-executed portrait of a fine manly-looking fellow in full uniform of the Fire Brigade."* Weigall had earlier painted the first portrait of Princess Alexandra after she had landed in this country to marry Bertie. It was probably through Bertie, therefore, that Weigall met Shaw.

Another supporter was Evelyn Ashley. In 1858, he had gone to America with Lord Richard Grosvenor and in the following year he had visited Garibaldi in a private capacity and was given ample opportunity to witness the progress of his campaign. When, in 1864, Garibaldi visited England he stayed with the Duke of Sutherland at Stafford House and was sympathetically received by the Prince of Wales. There is no conclusive proof that Shaw ever met Garibaldi, but we have from these events evidence that Ashley was in contact with Grosvenor, Sutherland and Bertie, all three of whom were on friendly terms with Shaw. Ashley's brother-in-law, Henry Farquhar, was another of Shaw's supporters in his bid to join the St. James's Club.

When he applied he had been in London only about four years. So far as is known, he had virtually no influential friends or relatives, or even contacts. Yet in that short time he had come to be known and highly regarded by men of considerable influence and power who treated him as a social equal.

But even they were not able to secure his immediate election to a second club, the Carlton. In fact, over twelve years elapsed between the time of Shaw's first being proposed (May 1867) and the date when he finally gained admission (February 1880). It must be said though, that it was not unusual for the more popular clubs to have a waiting list extending over such a period of time.

When the membership records of the Carlton Club were searched they were in some disarray but they revealed that Shaw's proposer, in this instance, was Lord Inchiquin. He, the 13th Baron, was related to Shaw by marriage, Shaw's step-mother being a sister of Inchiquin's second wife. In passing, one might note too that Shaw's youngest son, Cecil, was also given the name O'Brien, the Inchiquin surname. Cecil was four years of age at the time of the application.

Another, closer, relative seconded Shaw's application to join the Carlton Club. He was Lt. Col. Sir Robert Shaw, the eldest son of Captain Shaw's grandfather's brother.

Inchiquin died in 1872 and Sir Robert Shaw in 1868, but Captain Shaw's application was supported by Inchiquin's son who became a member of the Carlton in the same year as he became the 14th Baron. Another supporter was Major William Gillett, a much-travelled man who later, in 1881, helped establish and became President of the Bachelors' Club, of which Shaw's son, Clarina, became a member.

When Shaw was finally elected to the Carlton, other members included: Lord Colin Campbell, who was later to claim that his wife had committed adultery with Shaw; Thomas George Fardell, who became a member of the Fire Brigade Committee five years later; James Fergusson, who occasionally dined together with Shaw at the Duke of Sutherland's table and with whom he shared an interest in railways; and Lt. Col. James Macnaughten Hogg, Chairman of the Metropolitan Board of Works and so on its Fire Brigade Committee since 1870, and hence Shaw's master.

A further member of the Carlton when Shaw joined and one who was shortly to have a family interest in the Metropolitan Fire Brigade was the 7th Earl of Egmont. A distant relation of his and heir to the title after a bachelor cousin died was Augustus Arthur Perceval (known as 'Gussy'). Fourteen months after Shaw became a member of the Carlton he was enrolled with the Brigade as a 4th Class Fireman. Two years later he was promoted to the 3rd Class and withdrew from the Brigade in 1887, after nearly six years' service, on appointment as Hall Keeper (i.e. caretaker) at Chelsea Town Hall. A month after his enrolment as a fireman he had married Kate Howell, the daughter of a South Carolina tobacco planter who, according to gossip writers, was working at the time of her marriage behind the counter of Spiers and Ponds, a West End departmental store. Gussy succeeded to the title ten years after leaving the Brigade.

The Carlton Club attracted a different kind of member from the St. James's. It was much more overtly political; and Conservative at that. Shaw, in later life at least, was a Conservative. The Club, in its then comparatively new premises was renowned for its comfort. It was a place for older, staid men than those attracted particularly to the St. James's and it may not be coincidence that although Shaw resigned from the St. James's in 1905, three years before his death, he remained a member of the Carlton to the end.

Shaw was also a member of a third London Club. In 1869, four years after he joined the St. James's and two years after he had applied to join the Carlton, he became a member of the Marlborough Club, in the year of its foundation.

The reason why the Marlborough Club was started has been frequently recited. Bertie, Prince of Wales, finding that White's Club was not prepared to accept his proposal that smoking should be permitted in the Morning Room decided to found his own club, where he could make his own rules and pick his own members. It was conveniently situated just across from Marlborough House.

One of the three original Trustees was the Duke of Sutherland and the founder members numbered four hundred. When the Club closed, in 1952, its records seem to have disappeared. It is not known, therefore, who proposed, seconded and supported Shaw's membership. But the information would in some ways be superfluous since the Prince insisted that his friends should join; and, throughout his life, all candidates for election required his endorsement. Shaw's membership of the Marlborough, like his staying at Sandringham, is firm evidence of the Prince of Wales's close regard for Captain Shaw. It has been said, by Gordon Brook-Shepherd in his UNCLE OF EUROPE, published in 1975, that the Marlborough's first list of members *"gives us the most reliable register ever compiled of his personal friends."* It will be tragic if that list has disappeared.

In due course, then, Shaw became a member of three West End clubs: St. James's, the Carlton and the Marlborough. He also, according to the journal WOMAN in 1891, was a frequent visitor to the Riverside Club at Taplow. All trace of this establishment seems to have disappeared. It is not to be found in the local directories for the period although the houses in what is now River Road, Taplow are, according to the Windsor and Maidenhead District Librarian, *"reputed to have been the scene of many clandestine meetings between actresses and Society gentlemen and could possibly have housed a private club."* The whole of the area adjacent to Maidenhead Bridge on the other side of the river was known as Riverside and the Buckinghamshire County Archivist has located a house, *"presumably in the parish of Cookham"*, bearing the same name but he, too, can find no references to a Riverside Club.

We do not know how extensively Shaw used the Carlton, Marlborough and St. James's Clubs although at the end of his career THE GLOBE described him as *"a great clubman"*. At the Carlton he never, during his twenty-eight years' membership, proposed a single book for the Library; but he was not a bookish person. Nor did he ever propose a member though he did second the application of his son, Clarina, in 1893 when the latter was already a member of the St. James's Club.

He also supported the application, in 1893 again, of Henry Digby Wallis, of Drisbane Castle, County Cork. It may well, however, have represented little more than a good turn on behalf of the proposer, the Hon. Albert Bingham, a son of the 3rd Baron Clanmorris. Any attempt to establish a link between Shaw and Bingham is defeated by the fact that the latter's family documents largely disappeared when Bangor Castle was sold.

This chapter has highlighted deficiencies in our knowledge resulting from the destruction and loss of family and other archives. The personal papers of the 14th Earl of Caithness, of Bertie, Prince of Wales, of Lord Richard Grosvenor and of the Bingham family all seem to have been wantonly destroyed; the records of the Marlborough Club have apparently disappeared. Yet there remains abundant evidence that Shaw rapidly achieved a place in Society that gave him almost daily contact with some of the most influential men of his period.

CHAPTER FIVE
DECISION AND CONFLICT

"I would never have devoted myself to such an arduous profession if I had not expected a much larger remuneration"

All this socialising might suggest that Shaw was a dilettante; a mere figurehead, treating his new post as a sinecure and spending all his time in club and drawing room. But, nothing could be farther from the truth.

Right from the start, he was deeply involved in technical matters, and especially with the increasing use of steamers in the brigade.

At the time of his appointment they were already being widely used abroad and elsewhere in Britain. But Braidwood had largely eschewed them and when he had finally changed his mind and purchased two steamers manufactured by the Blackfriars firm of Shand and Mason it was suggested by some observers that this was because he had fathered a child with the assistance of Miss Shand; a rather complex way of meeting a paternity claim.

Whether or not that was a fact, there were good technical reasons for abandoning manual pumps for ones operated by steam. A manual fire engine was simply a cistern mounted on four small wheels, and equipped with a piston pump operated by two side levers of treadle pattern which a team of men could work up and down. Such an engine could do little more than emit, in jerks, puny jets of water that could hardly reach the second floor of a moderate-sized house. Although a steam pump had the disadvantage that at least half-steam had to be kept up so that the water could be quickly boiled when the pump was needed, it was sixty times as cheap to operate a steamer as a manual engine because of the cost of paying all the men on the levers. Further, as the steam pumps could throw much more water fewer of them were needed and the fire ground remained relatively uncongested.

A major firm in competition with Shand and Mason was Merryweather and Sons, of Greenwich. Shaw made the fullest use of the keen rivalry between the two firms which, in turn, acted as a spur to both of them to make constant improvements. The search particularly was for strength combined with lightness, the problem of weight being illustrated by the fact that one of Shand and Mason's steamers, patented in 1858, had weighed over four tons and needed three horses to pull it along.

Captain Shaw's attempts to get the best out of both firms met with little sympathy from one prolix author, Charles Young, a Chartered Engineer, who produced a book on fires, fire engines and fire brigades in 1866 (even the title of the book ran to 60 words). He claimed that Shand and Mason had a monopoly of the Fire Engine Establishment's orders, *"regardless of the results of practical working or improvement."* But even a superficial examination of the Fire Brigade Committee's minutes shows this to be untrue; and when *"Gentlemen promoting the formation of a fire brigade at Farsley, Yorkshire"* wrote, in 1868, asking which of the two makers was recommended it was resolved by the Fire Brigade Committee that the Metropolitan Board of Works reply should indicate that the Committee was *"unwilling to express an opinion as to the relative merits or to recommend either of them in preference to the other."* The resolution concluded: *"The engines of both these makers are in use in the Fire Brigade and the Board continues to entrust to both of them orders for new engines."*

It is obvious from a study of Young's book that he had an animus towards the Fire Engine Establishment and towards Shaw himself. It is not clear why, unless Young had applied for Shaw's post and had failed to obtain it. But it must quickly have become apparent to Young that Shaw would never be deflected in his judgements or his actions by what might be written in criticism of him.

He had, anyway, little time to spare for self-analysis. From 1 January 1866 he was answerable to the Metropolitan Board of Works and, the following year, the Board also took over responsibility for the duties previously undertaken by the Royal Society for the Protection of Life from Fire. From then on, the saving of life was Shaw's duty at least as much as the saving of property.

The Royal Society for the Protection of Life from Fire was, by the 1860's, maintaining eighty or ninety fire escapes in various parts of central London, chiefly in churchyards or squares. These escapes carried three ladders of different type on a four-wheeled carriage. Under the main escape ladder, which was about thirty-five feet long, there was a canvas chute of stout sailcloth strengthened with copper wire mesh down to within five feet of the ground. People who had been rescued could slide down this, landing on an apron hammock at the bottom. Moving such fire escapes over cobbled streets or worse on a windy night was no easy task. But, despite their design disadvantages, and a total weight of nearly half a ton, all of which limited their effective range to about four hundred yards, fire escapes of this type continued in use in London until 1896.

Each escape was manned at night by a uniformed *'conductor'*, paid weekly by the Society. The ladders were not used in the daytime. When the conductor was warned of a fire he used a rattle to summon the assistance of the police or of passers-by who then helped to trundle the escape, like a pram, through the streets. It was then set up against the burning building, so enabling the conductor to try to reach those who were trapped. By the early 1860's, the seventy-seven men and four Inspectors were saving an average of seventy-one lives a year.

The 1865 Metropolitan Fire Brigade Act authorised the Metropolitan Board of Works to establish fire escapes, either by subscribing to the funds of the Society or by purchasing that body's escapes and stations. The Board took them over with reluctance because of the financial implications. Shaw personally interviewed almost all the conductors and took into the Brigade sixty-seven of them some of the others, as he put it, being *"rather old and heavy for the work."*

At first the Metropolitan Board of Works had no Fire Brigade Committee and responsibility for the implementation of the Act fell to the Main Drainage Committee. When, on 26 September 1865, Captain Shaw attended a meeting of that Committee for the first time he was still Superintendent of the Fire Engine Establishment. There and then, he was asked to prepare a report setting out his views on the future Brigade. Shortly, and not surprisingly bearing in mind how well he had filled the void left by Braidwood's death, he was offered — without competition — the charge of the new Brigade.

Immediately, he came into serious conflict with his new masters. For one thing, he demanded of the Chairman of the Board, Sir John Thwaites, an increase in his perquisites (worth £250 per annum). Then, he quickly seems to have realised that he had perhaps set his sights too high, and wrote again to the Chairman explaining that he had had no precedent of any kind to guide him, that he had not been influenced by selfish motives, and that he was content to put the matter in the Board's hands, *"feeling assured that they can have no desire but to place the officer in charge of so large and important a department in a proper position as regards his emoluments."*

Turning next to the matter of his salary, he pointed out that he had *"laboured in this cause for a number of years"*, but *"had never spared time, money or toil in acquiring an entire knowledge of the profession"*, and that he had studied the working of fire brigades *"in every city of importance not only in England but in all other countries."* He had, he said, *"undergone all this labour and expense for the sole purpose of qualifying myself to take charge of the enlarged Fire Brigade, which I have known for years that London would one day require."*

This slightly arrogant tone then continued with an expression of hope that the Board might name *"such a salary that I may be enabled to take service under them."* He had no doubt, he said, that with strict economy and skilful management it would be possible to produce *"the best and most efficient fire brigade that the world has yet seen."*

His masters resolved to offer him £750 per annum, with a house and other allowances that he had previously enjoyed. He said that he would need a few days to consider the matter, though he must have realised that there was likely to be no other field where he could command such money.

He responded four days later. In a letter to the Chairman of the Board he said that he considered the proposed salary *"exceedingly low"* and, he continued, *"I would never have devoted myself to such an arduous profession if I had not expected a much larger remuneration."* That was of course nonsense, especially when one recalls his statement that he had settled in Belfast with no expectation of ever moving from there.

The letter continues: *"I can, however, understand the difficulties which the Board experience in making these appointments, and I consider that . . . an officer should be entirely in the hands of his masters, and that every advance in his pay or position should depend absolutely on their appreciation of these efforts."* Then having, as he put it, accepted the offer unconditionally he went on to set down a condition of acceptance. Here again, the arrogance shows through. While the remuneration, he said, might be ample for an untried person, he was no novice at his profession. He brought to the post, he said, *"a mature experience in, and an intimate knowledge of, every department of the business."* He had in reality, it will be remembered, been a fireman for less than 5½ years and had served in a brigade of any significant size for only four. He went on to point out that the responsibility resting on the Chief Officer of the new force would be far heavier than that of his present post and that he was accepting the offer only in the full confidence that as soon as the Board became aware from practical experience of the magnitude of the operations and of the skill and unceasing energy and toil needed for their efficient management he would have no difficulty in obtaining their consent to a recommendation that his salary should increase.

He also asked that the £50 per annum that he had previously received from the Trustees of the British Museum *"for looking after the place"* should continue, and he suggested his salary should be free of Income Tax; it had been previously. On the first point, the Committee agreed, so long as the work did not interfere with his other duties; on the second point, the Committee noted that no other officers had their Income Tax paid by the Board and saw no case for making an exception with Shaw. He at once withdrew that demand.

The letter has been treated at length because it tells us much about Shaw and about the relationship that he would have with his new employers, the Metropolitan Board of Works. Contention would often be the keynote. If people were unreasonable he was not afraid to tell them so; if complaints were unjustified he was prepared to fight them, both in Committee and outside. Examples can readily be found.

In May 1866 it was alleged that, at a fire at a cutler's in Goswell Street, sixty or seventy policemen were in attendance and had been given threepence (a little over 1p) for keeping order. Shaw reported that, because their clothes were much wetted by the water thrown from the engines, it had always been the custom to give the police who were present three pennyworth of brandy. The officers got six pennyworth, though whether because they got wetter or were more hardened drinkers or drank better quality brandy was not made clear. He denied that there had been as many as sixty or seventy police present. A fortnight later he had to retract his denial, but added: *"I have invariably found that the Forces in attendance have been only what have been absolutely needed . . . those not required have been sent away at once and therefore not entitled to refreshments."*

A couple of months later he was asked to explain why twenty men, three steamers and a manual engine had all been needed to attend a fire at an 18-roomed house on Beulah Hill, Upper Norwood, which was outside the area covered by the Board. They attended, he said, because of the incompetence of the Croydon engine which was doing a lot of damage by flooding the house with water. This he had stopped, and his men had then tackled the fire with handpumps and buckets of water. It was true that the Board's engines had not been used, but they had enabled his men to attend quickly *"thereby preventing further damage from water which no doubt would have taken place had they not attended."*

Reporting, at the same meeting of the Committee, on a collision between the Paddington engine and an omnibus, he observed that if the omnibus driver had been on his own side the accident would not have happened; in any case, the amount charged for repairs was *"very extravagant."*

The following year, he took to task the Directors of the East and West India Docks Company. In his report on a fire in the brig PILGRIM, he suggested that there had been neglect by the Company in failing to call the brigade for eight hours. This, he stated, was common practice, the Company attempting to deal with fires with their own engines and only calling the Brigade when matters had got out of hand. The Directors made a suitable riposte, whereupon Shaw pointed out to the Committee that, as the insurance rates depended on the number of fires reported, the Dock Companies had a great interest in keeping such incidents secret. *"The Dock Companies,"* he said, *"have no interest in the contents of their warehouses, which are not their property, and which are the risk either of the insurance companies, or of the owners or consignees."*

Sometimes, the dishonest practices were outside the ambit of Shaw's responsibilities. Then, he said nothing though he doubtless thought the more. One such extraordinary occurrence happened in 1868 and is reported in great detail in the Fire Brigade Committee papers. It concerned work on the foundations of a new fire station in Adelaide Road, St. John's Wood. An unsuccessful tenderer, Richard Hackworth, who was also a Hampstead Vestryman, suspected that the contractors, Messrs. Mather and Read, were using unscreened burnt clay and dirty ballast whereas the specification required clean washed Thames ballast. Hackworth wrote an anonymous letter (a frequent Victorian ploy) to BUILDING NEWS and repeated the allegation in a letter to the Metropolitan Board of Works. In a subsequent report, a local publican named Elt, who also was a Vestryman, described how towards midnight on Saturday 2 May, Hackworth had asked him to accompany him to the site to see what was going on. They were joined by Day, a gas fitter, Evans, a cricketting (SIC) outfitter, and Styles, a wine merchant, all of whom were in the pub at the time. They described how, in the bright moonlight, they had looked through chinks in the hoardings and had watched men at work, one in a white smock being seen to tip ballast from a basket onto the site. There were allegations and counter-allegations that both witnesses and workmen were under the influence of drink and the case was further complicated by the fact that the Board's Clerk of Works had disappeared to another part of the country by the time the matter was under consideration. Rather lamely, the Committee reported to the Board that, on the information laid before them, they had concluded that the foundations, although not as specified, were of sufficient strength and solidarity. They did not deem it advisable, therefore, that any further steps should be taken in the matter.

Sometimes, however, the Committee were prepared to take a stronger line with their Chief Officer than they were, apparently, with their contractors. A good, and early, example of this was in the same year as the St. John's Wood case, 1868. Shaw had written a 53-page pamphlet, INSTRUCTIONS FOR THE USE AND MANAGEMENT OF FIRE ESCAPES AND RESCUE OF LIFE FROM FIRE. This document which contained the substance of lectures he had given his men, was printed *'privately'* (which presumably means at his own expense) by Waterlow and Sons, the Board's printers, for distribution among the men. When it was produced he sent a copy to each member of the Board.

The Fire Brigade Committee were offended by this and expressed disapproval of his having the pamphlet printed without their knowledge or authority and he was told he must never do this again.

The outcry had arisen because of one particular passage. In it, Shaw had advised that in the event of unreasonable panic a fireman must use force. *"In short"*, he said, *"he should knock them down if they persist in disobeying his orders; and after once he has shown his power it is not probable that he will have to lose further time in a repetition of the lesson."* This, he concluded, *"may seem rough usage to a peacable citizen suddenly awakened in the middle of the night by the cry of fire . . . but it is, nevertheless, the only safe and proper course to pursue, and in the end the most merciful, as nothing can exceed the disgrace of . . . men rushing wildly out to save themselves, and . . . leaving helpless women and children to perish in the flames."*

This is typical of the no-nonsense approach that Shaw took to his work right from the start and he applied it as much to volunteer firemen, both real and bogus, as to anyone panic-struck at a fire.

CHAPTER SIX

SHAW AND THE VOLUNTEERS
"The acknowledged head of his profession in this, the greatest city the world has ever seen"

The Fire Brigade of the Metropolitan Board of Works gave scant cover to the new suburbs. They were not high fire-risk areas and building was going on too rapidly for the Board to keep up with it. The result was the formation of volunteer brigades by private firms and well-to-do residents.

In 1866, Charles Young listed ten such brigades. But he omitted ones on private estates and any, like that of the Crystal Palace Company, that normally made no attempt to fight fires outside their own confines; also, he made no reference to brigades based on towns or villages (such as Croydon) just outside the Board of Works area but within easy reach in an emergency. Of the ten he named, four were brigades based on industrial premises: two distilleries, Price's candle factory in York Road, Battersea and a works at Millwall where chains, anchors and cables were made. The other six were in the residential districts of Notting Hill, Peckham, Kilburn, Hatcham (New Cross), Holloway and Brompton. That at Notting Hill had been founded in 1841; the one at Brompton was only a year old. The number of men varied from sixty at Peckham to five at Hatcham. Only the Brompton brigade of those in residential areas had a steamer; the Peckham brigade, despite its sixty men, possessed only one manual engine that needed twenty pumpers at any one time.

These brigades varied greatly in efficiency as between each other and from one time to another. The works brigade at Millwall, the True Blue as it was called, was especially reputable. William Roberts, the firm's managing foreman, told the Hankey Committee of 1862 that he was the superintendent of the brigade and his sons were firemen. The engine had been made to his own patent by the company (Brown, Lennox). Asked if he acted in *"perfect accord"* with the London Fire Engine Establishment, he replied: *"Yes, and always have done so"*. As all the firemen were mechanics, he said, they took a pride in keeping the engine in good condition and devoted an hour of their own time each Saturday to drill and to cleaning and maintaining the apparatus.

Charles Young was one of Shaw's bitterest critics in the matter of volunteer fire brigades. He told a later House of Commons Select Committee, in 1867: *"My sympathies are with the volunteers. I represent the voluntary idea of extinguishing fires"*. The Metropolitan Fire Brigade, he said, was very unco-operative, pushing the volunteers out of the way if they reached a hydrant first. There was, he suggested, *"a great amount of skill and science on the part of the volunteers; the paid men only do what they are told"*. Another witness hostile to Shaw, Lewis Becker, told the Committee: *"The volunteers get blackguarded and insulted by professionals . . . the volunteers are gentlemen"*.

On his first two appearances before the same Committee, Shaw ignored what Young and Becker had said. But on his third appearance, he was questioned about their evidence. He had a ready reply. The Board, he told

A NEW FIRE ENGINE AT UXBRIDGE (1881). Shaw had serious reservations about volunteer fire brigades in London and the Home Counties. He saw them as making less likely the appointment of professional firemen. (Photo: London Fire Brigade Museum).

the Committee, held him responsible for having everything properly conducted at a fire. The volunteers come when they like, amuse themselves, and go when they like. He had no objection to them provided they took care not to identify themselves in any way with those who were really responsible. They copied the Brigade's uniform exactly. So, for purposes of identification at fires, he had persuaded the Board of Works to go to the expense of new helmets of a special design, made of brass instead of black leather (except his, which was of silver), even though the earlier helmets were perfectly satisfactory. But very soon, he related, the members of the Holloway Brigade were wearing exact copies.

Becker persisted as a severe critic of the Metropolitan Fire Brigade. About five years after the 1867 Select Committee produced its report Becker was *"Captain Superintendent (Voluntary) and Hon. Secretary (PRO TEM)"* of the West Kent Volunteer Fire Brigade, conveniently based adjacent to the Dartmouth Arms in Forest Hill High Street. From there, he wrote to the Board of Works complaining that the engines of the Metropolitan Fire Brigade had run past the station twice in one week, *"for no apparent purpose"*. He wanted to know from the Board what fires had occurred in the district, as the Metropolitan Police had agreed to advise his force of any such incidents and, he added disingenuously, he was not wishing to lodge a complaint against the Police until the facts had been ascertained. He said that until his brigade had been established two months

55

previously, *"no fire engine was ever seen in this district otherwise than at a genuine fire, therefore one cannot but conclude that these acts are done in a spirit of annoyance".*

Shaw advised his Committee that the men had merely been exercising the horses with the engine to accustom them to drawing it, as it was very different from a cab or any other vehicle. But Becker was not satisfied with this explanation. He claimed that it was not necessary for firemen in practice to be dressed in full uniform nor did they need to shout (the normal method of giving warning of approach when rushing to a fire). He noted, too, that the men had only run about a hundred yards past the station and had then returned, still shouting; further, he said, some of the members of his brigade had been *"coerced by the members of the Metropolitan Fire Brigade, and various threats used towards them".*

Any harassment would have been locally-inspired. Shaw, for all his failings, was not a petty-minded man.

Despite (if one believes Shaw) or on account of (if one believes Charles Young) Becker's leadership, the West Kent Volunteer Fire Brigade eventually became an efficient body, even by Shaw's exacting standards. In 1890, by which time its Hon. Captain was Frederick Horniman, the Quaker tea merchant whose extensive collections later formed the nucleus of the Museum, it sought to persuade the London County Council to licence, as auxiliaries to the Metropolitan Fire Brigade, such volunteer fire brigades as were found to be efficient. Shaw told the Fire Brigade Committee that the West Kent Brigade was *"generally speaking efficient"*; but members agreed that it was inadvisable to licence a volunteer brigade even though they believed it had done useful work in its own district.

One volunteer *'brigade'* that was never likely to be confused with the Metropolitan Fire Brigade was that made up of a gas fitter's family living in the West End. Reporting on a fire in Davies Street, in January 1890, Shaw advised his Committee that the call had been to a small fire in a private house and two men had attended with a hand pump. On arrival they had found that the fire had been nearly extinguished by the fireman in charge of the escape in South Audley Street and by two strangers dressed as volunteer firemen. *"One of these"*, reported Shaw, *"was Mr. Owensmith who . . . lived opposite . . . (and) attended with a hand pump . . . In addition to the hand pump, Mr. Owensmith . . . has also a standpipe, two lengths of hose, and some other small gear, and . . . with the aid of two sons renders any assistance he can at fires in the immediate neighbourhood".* The Owensmith family would have felt at home when firewatching became a duty during the London Blitz.

Attempts were being made nationally, during Shaw's time, to put volunteer fire brigades onto a respectable and reliable footing. To this end, there was formed, in 1877, the Fire Brigades Association. It was started by a chemist, Charles Footit, who was Captain of the Marlow Fire Brigade. He began by circularising about one hundred similar organisations. The aims of the Association were to be: the provision of competent instructors and inspectors; a nationwide system of communication; a benevolent fund; inspection of factories to aid fire prevention; and exemption from jury service for volunteer officers, as a Government acknowledgement of the service the brigades were rendering. Much support and some money were soon forthcoming; and Sir Charles Firth, a government contractor and blanket and rug manufacturer, who had been a volunteer under Braidwood and with the Paris Brigade and who was, by 1877, a power among Yorkshire volunteer brigades, became President. Captain Wykeham-Archer, of the Alexandra Palace Brigade, became Vice-President and Footit, Treasurer.

By that date, inter-brigade competitions were already being held, with prizes provided by the local gentry and by Shand Mason and Merryweather. Unfortunately, these contests sometimes became acrimonious, with large crowds urging on their local *'team'*. Shaw allowed his senior officers to act as judges, but they often received more abuse than thanks. The problem was well described by Engineer William Penfold, in his report on a competition at Watford in July 1877:

"I am strongly of the opinion that these volunteer contests should find judges from their own class, as each competing brigade will always persist in following their own ideas, instead of the rules laid down, and will insist that their own peculiar ways are correct, and that all others are wrong and, as trickery is a great element in nearly all of them, it makes the office of judge for an impartial man a very unsatisfactory office".

It was probably for this very reason that when, four years later, Shaw himself took part in a volunteer fire brigade function for the first time, the proceedings, to quote THE FIREMAN, *"took the form of an inspection rather than of the usual competition for prizes".* The event took place in *"the quaint old town of Colnbrook"* and had a Victorian, and almost a regal, splendour about it.

Shaw was accompanied by one of his daughters, either Anna — by then 22 — or Zarita, who was 18. Also present was Engineer William Port, who acted as a kind of aide-de-camp. The party travelled by train from Waterloo to Wraysbury, three miles from Colnbrook, where it was met by Dr. Alfred Meadows of Poyle Park, Colnbrook, who had been instrumental in persuading Shaw to attend. They drove to Colnbrook, which was decorated with flags, banners and streamers, in an open landau, Captain Shaw resplendent in uniform and silver helmet.

Shaw stood at the gates of the Park as engines from seventeen towns and villages and from breweries at Windsor and Watford passed by. He then inspected them, offering *"several practical suggestions"* as he did so. Photographs were then taken on the lawn after which 260 firemen went to a marquee for a *"substantial luncheon"* generously provided by Dr. Meadows, while the officers of the brigades lunched in a separate tent with the visitors, Dr. Meadows (whose wife and daughters were also present) being flanked by Captain Shaw and the High Sheriff of Buckinghamshire.

There followed drill in the Park, and then a speech by Shaw from a wagonette. He complimented the brigades on their appearance but suggested that, while many had *"worked in excellent order"*, there had in others been *"some slight confusion"*. That, he pointed out, was not a rare occurrence, and was not unknown in his own Brigade. The real difficulty was that some gentlemen had been obeying orders issued by others and not by himself and, as a consequence, *"some little confusion had resulted"*.

In the vote of thanks that followed, Superintendent Green of the Oxford Brigade saw the event as *"the inauguration of the time when all the brigades will unite, wearing one uniform, doing one drill, and acting under one chief, the one who has this day done us honour"*. In the event, it would be another sixty or so years before a National Fire Service would come into being, and then only temporarily.

In its account of the events at Poyle Park, THE FIREMAN concluded kindly: *"As some misapprehension seemed to exist with a section of the firemen regarding the object of the manoeuvres . . . some little confusion was inevitable"*. They were held after lunch too.

Shaw had not, apparently, been invited to assist in the formation of the Fire Brigades Association and was not even invited to their first Annual Banquet. But a couple of months after the Colnbrook display, he was the subject of a presentation, at his residence, by a number of volunteer fire brigade captains. This was in appreciation of his attendance at the event and he received a testimonial on vellum, the Association's ten years' service medal and a copy of a photograph that had been taken on the day. Miss Shaw received a brooch. Dr. Meadows, in his speech, referred to Shaw as, *"the acknowledged head of his profession in this, the greatest city the world has ever seen"*. He had been specifically asked to express to Captain Shaw the hope that the latter might give some practical encouragement to, or even accept some official connection with, the volunteer fire brigade movement.

THE FIREMAN, in its next editorial, took up this theme. *"For some years past,"* it said, *"Captain Shaw was thought to be opposed to volunteer fire brigades . . . We have no doubt that Captain Shaw was never favourable, and never will be, to a volunteer fire brigade existing in a town large enough to require the services of firemen always at their posts."* But, it continued, *"we are confident that when our volunteers prove themselves to be . . . efficient . . . neither Captain Shaw nor any other professional fireman . . . will withhold either encouragement or support"*.

The journal went on to suggest that the active intervention by Shaw in the affairs of the Association could only be for the good. He was known to have a hatred and detestation of all sham firemen. *"The influence of a man of this stamp,"* it concluded, *"is just what is wanted to remedy the present great defect of the Fire Brigades Association: namely, the absence of much that is practical, and the presence of much that is mere show and sham"*. In the event, the Fire Brigades Association had faded away within another seven or eight years.

Even if Shaw was increasingly well-disposed to volunteer fire brigades outside London, he still had no time for them in the Metropolis. He advised his Committee to reply to one correspondent, in 1887, to the effect that *"the Brigade would be weakened by the introduction of assistance, undisciplined and only half-trained"*. And when, shortly afterwards, the London County Council took over the Brigade, it too showed a distinct antagonism to amateurs.

Indeed it may have detected a somewhat ambivalent attitude on Shaw's part for, as we saw earlier, he accepted and even encouraged specific individuals like the Prince of Wales, and Sutherland, and Lord Richard Grosvenor to join in the action, whilst remaining antagonistic to amateurs in general. The first London County Council, however, was the last body that would accept that kind of élitist stance.

When, in May 1891, shortly before his retirement, Shaw was asked by the London County Council Fire Brigade Committee to say how many volunteer firemen were told about the existence of fires and how much they were charged for the information, he replied that he knew of not one case. But then a member of the Committee, Nathan Moss, who was a constant critic of Shaw, said that at a fire in Newgate Street he had seen two auxiliary firemen in black helmets at work with the Brigade. One of them, a house surgeon at St. George's Hospital, had told him that they had premises in Farringdon Street to which notification of fires was sent. The Chairman added that he, also, had seen auxiliary firemen at work, at a fire at Messrs. Courage & Co. Referring to the latter case, Shaw said that one was a Mr. Guinness, who was connected with the brewery and was in the habit of attending fires with the Salvage Corps; the other, a Mr. Lawson, a house surgeon at St. George's, had paid exceptional attention to the men of the Brigade and their families at that institution. The Committee resolved that, in future, auxiliary firemen were not to be allowed to assist at fires.

Even when the volunteers were formally organised the London County Council Fire Brigade Committee looked askance at any offer of help. When, for instance, in 1890 the Metropolitan Police Commissioner advised the Committee that the Finchley Volunteer Fire Brigade had asked that its station should be linked by telephone to the nearest police station the Committee resolved to inform the Commissioner that the Metropolitan Fire Brigade *"does not stand in need of any assistance from volunteer firemen"*.

One of the many problems with a voluntary fire brigade was that it might, of course, begin as an efficient well-run organisation but later fall into bad ways. The South Metropolitan Volunteer Fire Brigade was certainly in that category. When it was founded, in 1874, by a number of gentlemen at Sydenham there was even sufficient money raised for the purchase of a steamer. Then subscriptions fell off and a Mr. Cucksey took it over. He sold the steamer and bought a manual engine. He engaged three assistants as collectors, by which time the Brigade must have been far more heavily engaged in collecting money than in extinguishing fires so that when Cucksey made his will he found it worth his while to leave the Brigade to his widow. She in due course sold it to an ex-policeman, named Seals, who was already running it on her behalf. Seals had been receiving thirty shillings (£1.50) per week as Engineer and the collectors were entitled to 25% of all subscriptions. As a condition of the sale, Mrs. Cucksey would receive from the profits £1 per week, for life.

When, in 1884, one of the collectors was charged for frudently collecting subscriptions (he was dressed at the time in a Metropolitan Fire

Brigade uniform) the magistrate commented that if the public were stupid enough to subscribe there was nothing he could do about it since the Brigade was actually in existence. Not only was it in existence, it still had an engine for it was mentioned in court that the entire brigade except the annuitant, that is Seals and the three collectors, had recently been locked up for being drunk in charge of a horse and fire engine.

Volunteer brigades were especially prolific in the middle-class suburbs of North London and in 1877 a loose amalgamation was attempted. The inaugural meeting, attended by representatives from Alexandra Palace, Barnet, Hendon, Tottenham, Wood Green, Hornsey, Willesden, Kilburn, Highgate and Tufnell Park, met at the Tufnell Park Hotel. The purpose was the formation of a joint committee. The moving spirit was a Captain Shean of the Tufnell Park Brigade; and, since one of the committee members was Captain Wykeham-Archer (Alexandra Palace) who at about the same time was elected as Vice President of the national Fire Brigades Association, we may assume that it was a respectable organisation.

But some of these brigades, even if very active were also extremely short-lived; and they were certainly not helped by Shaw or his Committee. Four months before the Tufnell Park Hotel meeting Shean had written to the Committee asking for financial support; but he was advised that the Board had no power to give it. Nine months later, Shean asked whether the Tufnell Park Brigade might be linked to one of the Board's stations by telegraph; Captain Shaw told the Committee he could see no advantage in such an arrangement. The following year, the excellently-printed 36-page Annual Report of the Brigade claimed that it was the only volunteer brigade authorised by the Board to attend fires under the Chief Officer; this, the Fire Brigade Committee decided was incorrect and must be put right.

The same report pointed out that Mr. H. A. Tufnell (Hon. Captain and President) had lent the brigade £500 but that, in 1877, 203 subscribers had contributed only £66 19s (£66.95) whereas adequate protection for the neighbourhood could only be guaranteed if the annual income were £250.

Soon Mr. Shean had cause to write to the Committee once more. He complained that, at a fire at Pratt Street, Camden Town, he had arrived with his engine and men, and being most scrupulously careful to avoid interference with the Metropolitan Fire Brigade, had called at a shop near the fire to obtain information about it. From thence he had been, he claimed, *"most roughly and rudely ejected, in fact literally thrown into the road"* by one of Shaw's officers. By the time Shean's complaint reached the Committee Shaw had already replied, pointing out that Shean had no cause for complaint and that he could not be too careful about entering into conversation with the officers of the Brigade when they were engaged in their work. Shaw suggested to the Committee that as Shean considered he had been assaulted, his best course would be to take out legal proceedings.

The next Annual Report, covering 1878, showed that the number of subscribers had increased from 203 to 998, and contributions from nearly £67 to a little over £184. The following year the contributions exceeded

£200, but expenditure for the year had been over £508 because: a new fire escape had been bought, an additional conductor was on duty at night, and new hose reels made by Shand and Mason *"from plans drawn by Captain Shaw"* had also been purchased. Shean offered to demonstrate his reel to the Fire Brigade Committee, but Shaw pointed out that it was of a type which the Metropolitan Brigade had ceased to use.

At this point, the Tufnell Park Brigade's Accountant took issue with Charles Loch, the Secretary of the Society for Organising Charitable Relief and Repressing Mendicity. Loch had written to the DAILY NEWS warning its readers about people, *"usually dressed up as firemen"* asking for contributions for suburban fire brigades *"of a doubtful or fraudulent character"*. The Accountant challenged Loch to state in writing *"AND BY RETURN OF POST"* whether he regarded the Tufnell Park Brigade as one of the fraudulent ones. Loch replied in rather vague terms, whereupon Shean weighed in, pointing out that the letter had been published *"in the middle of our collecting season"*. He went on to demand a disclaimer to the effect that the comments did not apply to the Tufnell Park Brigade. Loch, however, answered that he could not possibly comply unless his Society first examined the Brigade's books.

The correspondence ceased at that point because within a month, and after only three years' existence, the Tufnell Park Volunteer Fire Brigade ceased to function. It had spent £1,800; it had received only £700. But even if the Brigade would never be heard of again, Shean would.

Rather less than four years after the Tufnell Park Volunteer Fire Brigade ceased to exist, an article on Captain Shean appeared in the journal, THE REFEREE. It is a reminder of how unkind the Victorian press could be. It began:

> *"Mr. Arthur W. C. Shean, FRGS, FZS, etc. assures me that while Captain Shaw, whose place he evidently thinks he could well fill, is away in Berlin trying to find out the latest things in connection with the prevention of fires, thousands of people in London are nightly running the risk of meeting the most awful of deaths. I am exceedingly sorry to hear it . . ."*

It ended:

> *"It will be a happy day for England when Shean is made King. Ten thousand . . . readers have hastened to say that (this) probably can never be realised, seeing that Shean . . . is engaged as a Clerk in the Bank of England Postal Warrant Office, from half past nine to four and that, were he to accept the Crown, the Old Lady of Threadneedle Street would be so distressed and disorganised that she would have to shut up her shop. The only thing to be done so far as I can see, in this grave emergency, is for Captain Shaw and Captain Shean to exchange places."*

The article was quoted at some length in THE FIREMAN and this brought a letter of complaint from Shean. Anonymous letters of a most abusive character, postcards with indecent writing and newspaper cuttings *"of a character tending to bring me into ridicule and contempt"* were being continually addressed to himself and others at the Bank. He was telling readers this, he said, so that they might learn *"the bitter animosity and malignant hatred it is possible to create by an honest endeavour to render service to a public cause"*.

Such abuse, and the danger one would have thought of the publicity resulting in his dismissal from the Bank, did not deter Shean's enthusiasm for fire fighting. In May 1889, very soon after the London County Council took over the Metropolitan Fire Brigade from the Board of Works Shean wrote offering his services as *"Consulting Fire Brigade Engineer"*.

Unfortunately, his detailed supporting letter was not accurate in every particular. For instance, he said he had commanded the Tufnell Park Fire Brigade for five years (it seems to have existed for only three); and that it had disbanded because of *"the increase of radius and general augmentation of the Metropolitan Fire Brigade"* (at best an indirect cause: it ran out of money). Much of what followed looked impressive but was really very superficial: he had commanded a Guard of Honour of 150 firemen at the opening of a Life Saving Appliances Exhibition at Alexandra Palace; his hose reel had been awarded a *"diploma of merit"* by the Prince of Teck and had been bought for the Czar of Russia's Palace at St. Petersburg (but not, it will be remembered, by Captain Shaw); he had been consulted by H.M. Inspector of Explosives *"on a matter referred to him by the Secretary of State"*; he had submitted to Prince Leopold a system for the better preservation of works of art from fire; he had also conducted him over the scene of a fire at Hampton Court Palace; he had had numerous letters published in THE TIMES; and so on. It all proved he had been busy, but little else. He was advised, perhaps not surprisingly, that the London County Council did not propose to appoint a Consulting Fire Brigade Engineer.

However, the most curious group of *'volunteer firemen'* in Shaw's time must have been six women who went to France from London in 1889. They travelled on the same boat as a party of English firemen and had the same destinations in view: an International Congress of Officers and Sub-Officers of Fire Brigades in Paris, to be followed by a competition and manoeuvres at Vincennes and a Festival Review at Neuilly-sur-Seine.

THE FIREMAN told its readers that each of the six women was attired in *"a becoming blue dress, with red facings and brass buttons, consisting of a tight bodice and short (relatively) skirt disclosing well-fitting patent leather top-boots. Their headdress was a kind of polo cap of red silk, adorned with a white cockade bearing a cross and the words: 'LIFE-SAVING BRIGADE'"*.

THE FIREMAN considered their presence on the ship an outrage, the majority of the men having been unaware of their existence until they had left Dover. The women were, it was pointed out, connected with the theatrical profession and were to exhibit and advertise a special life-saving apparatus. The fire officers on board disavowed any connection with the women, despite which nearly all reports of the proceedings gave the impression that they had some official status.

THE FIREMAN took a sexist approach. A ladder was needed, it said, to assist them to mount to the top of the omnibus taking them from Paris to Vincennes. *"Then"*, it continued, *"as the horses moved an inch whilst the first of them had her foot upon a rung of the ladder, the young lady uttered a heart-rending shriek. It was with the greatest difficulty,"* concluded the article, *"that some of them could attain the roof by means of the wheels, steps, straps, handles, bars and whatnot duly provided to that end"*.

Another article, in the same journal, described their appearance in the competition. *"As they tripped along the high scaffolding which, with French gallantry, was placed at their disposal, the spectators shouted 'Bravo', and cheered lustily. Miss Mortimer led the way up the ladder, and when she had reached the fourth stage, which was as high as a modern Paris house, she descended to the ground by a rope"*. Finally, continued THE FIREMAN, *"the six women descended by the canvas shute. As they reappeared, legs first, the people cheered more loudly than before"*.

Readers of THE FIREMAN were later assured by a letter from ONE WHO WENT TO PARIS that the ladies were *"quite respectable despite insinuations to the contrary"*.

London County Council had decided, on grounds of cost, not to send a contingent of firemen but Captain Shaw had advised the Fire Brigade Committee that he would be going in a private capacity. He would, one may be sure, have approved of Miss Mortimer and her troupe, but certainly not of their being mixed up with the serious business of fighting fires and saving lives.

CHAPTER SEVEN
CHARITY AND FALSE PRETENCES
"The escape had only been out once in the five years of its existence and it had then broken down"

In taking over responsibility for saving lives, from the Royal Society for the Protection of Life from Fire, the Metropolitan Fire Brigade greatly increased the chance of its men being killed in the course of their duty.

The first victim was Second Class Fireman Joseph Ford, and his death had important repercussions on the question of compensation for firemen's widows and orphans. He had been in the brigade over five years, was twenty-six and, according to Shaw, steady and trustworthy.

Early one morning in October 1871, when on duty with an escape, he was called to a fire over a chemist's shop in Grays Inn Road. By the time he arrived, the Police had already rescued some people using a builder's ladder; but others were trapped on the third floor. Ford pitched his escape ladder and with great difficulty and skill, for several of the victims were very old and crippled, he got out five who were crowded at one window. Having sent the last of them down the escape chute, he started to climb down the ladder. Suddenly, flames and smoke burst from a first floor window and, coincidentally, he became entangled in his gear. He was severely burned before he fell to the ground. He died in hospital.

The Fire Brigade Committee, on hearing that Ford had left a widow and young children, granted her the unusually large sum of £1 per week (about three quarters salary) for six months, at the end of which time the case would be reviewed. Ford's death had received much publicity and within four months £1,795 had been donated by the public. Captain Shaw arranged for Mrs. Ford to be given £275, and for the remainder to be invested. The Board of Works gave its approval to this arrangement, but stopped the pension.

The ill-feeling that this created was exacerbated when Third Class Fireman Stanley Guernsey (or Gurnsey, his name is spelt both ways in the Official Report) was killed at a fire at a flour mill in November 1872. He was single, had died in far less dramatic circumstances than Ford, and there was no public subscription of any significance on his behalf. His father claimed some dependence on his earnings, but the Board considered this was not a case for assistance. It had discretionary powers to award compensation for injury, or pensions for dependents and the retired, but there was no mandatory requirement.

The next year (1873), Captain Shaw and his officers asked the Board to lay down a scale of pensions; the request was rejected. Then the firemen with Shaw's full support submitted a further superannuation scheme. For two years it was ignored by the Board, which then produced its own proposals. These were rejected unanimously by the men. Shaw not only agreed with their action; he complained that it had been made to look as though he had accepted the scheme in committee, as the men's representative, whereas he had received no details of it until they were passed to him five minutes before a vote was taken.

A case that created further ill-feeling was that of Engineer Charles Radford. He was invalided out with consumption after 17 years' service, the Brigade Surgeon certifying that his condition was due to his work in the Brigade and that he had less than a year to live. Shaw said he had been a very strong man and a very valuable officer, and that he had a family to support. The Board granted him only sixteen shillings (80p) a week pension, less than a third of his wage. When the firemen claimed that there was great destitution in his home and that the nature of his illness made medicines and delicacies a necessity, the Board would not even reconsider the case. Radford died six months later; his widow received merely a gratuity, eventually, of £10.

It must have been clear to the Selwin-Ibbetson Committee, which considered Fire Brigade matters in 1876-77, that the members of the Board were divided. Some favoured paying the firemen well to encourage thrift and self-reliance so that they could provide for themselves or their dependents when illness or misfortune, retirement or death occurred. Others believed that firemen, like policemen, followed a dangerous calling for which allowance should be made. When one Board member described to the Committee how the men had turned down *"a most liberal and advantageous scheme"*, its Chairman retorted that the rapidity with which a scheme had been drawn up once the Select Committee had been appointed was in strong contrast to that which had gone before. The Board ignored the Committee's advice that a proper superannuation scheme was essential; likewise, it still took no steps to regularise compensation for injury or death.

By then, there had been yet another fatality. This time it was Fourth Class Fireman George Lee, who died in August 1876 of injuries received earlier at a fire in West Smithfield, when he was rescuing two people who had been trapped. He left a sister, for whom the Board did nothing. His funeral cost £9 10s (£9.50), but the Board made only the standard allowance of £5. So the position of dependents of firemen killed or injured on duty remained uncertain: there would be no fixed scale until 1887. It is true, however, that in the meantime the Metropolitan Board of Works was to become much more generous. That was due partly to public pressure and partly to increasing indifference to the control of expenditure.

It meant that when a regular scale of widows' and orphans' benefits was finally introduced, it was found to be less generous than the best of recent AD HOC practice, even though the Board finally adopted for firemen the most liberal scale already in force, that used by the Metropolitan Police. The Chairman of the Fire Brigade Committee explained official thinking in a letter to the DAILY TELEGRAPH. The principle in all the public services, he said, is that *"a widow who is . . . young and strong should not receive such a large annuity from the public funds to dispense with the necessity of any future exertion . . . but rather that what she can obtain by her own exertions shall be supplemented by a fixed and permanent annuity which she can always rely upon, and which will at all events keep her from want".*

Lord Charles Beresford, in the House of Commons, attacked the assumption that policemen and firemen should be regarded as being equally at risk. It might be that ten policemen and the same number of firemen had been killed over a given period, but the ten firemen were from a single Brigade of only 600 men whereas the ten policemen were from a force of 15,000.

But not only was there a fear in some quarters that too generous a widow's pension might make the recipient unwilling to exert herself further. There was also jealousy about the payment of superannuation. In 1889, for instance, the Chairman of the London County Council received a letter from a Mr. Heathman, whose firm made fire appliances. It complained that First Class Engineer George Duck had been discharged seven years earlier with a pension of £2 2s (£2.10) per week — in fact it was only £1 17s 8d (£1.89) — yet was earning £50 per annum for looking after the fire hose at Post Office buildings, £5 per week as foreman of works for the Spanish Exhibition and also remuneration as a director of a firm of fire escape manufacturers, and as a drill instructor to fire brigades in the provinces. This was a particularly mean attack for, as Shaw pointed out, Duck had served for 25 years with zeal and fidelity before he lost the sight of an eye when it was struck by a jet of water at a fire, and medical advice was that if he continued in the fire brigade he would go blind in the other eye as well. Shaw commented, pointedly: *"I am given to understand that the writer of the letter is a discharged shop man of Merryweather's, and is engaged in the same kind of work which Duck has taken up"*.

It can be seen then that throughout his career as Chief Officer his men were uncertain as to their position if they became disabled, and anxious about the welfare of their dependents if they were killed. Even if there was occasional jealousy about the size of some of the awards there was wide public sympathy for disabled firemen and for the widows and children of firemen killed in the course of their work. These two factors, the uncertainty and the public sympathy, gave great scope to unscrupulous rogues and, throughout his career, Shaw had to fight a continuous and not very successful battle against collectors who claimed that they were helping fire brigades and also firemen in misfortune. The law, as we shall see, did nothing to help. If a group of people possessed a fire engine or escape ladder, however decrepit it might be, it was difficult to prove that a collection for that 'brigade' or 'society' was being made under false pretences, even if most of the money was then taken by the collectors as commission. If a prosecution was successful the operation could always be resumed after a short prison spell. The Board of Works was accused of *"masterly inactivity"* in putting right these abuses; but it was beyond its power to do so. Warnings were frequently issued to the public not to be beguiled, but the public was still duped and then wrote to Shaw complaining that it had been. Matters were made worse by the fact that malfactors were not working alone; it was not organised crime on a big scale, but whenever a court case occurred the defendant appeared with others who were known to be involved in similar deeds.

Reference has earlier been made to the South Metropolitan Fire Brigade which started off as a well-intentioned and well-organised body and then fell into bad hands. But others were bad from the start; and not only does one find an inter-linking of names, one also finds a predisposition for particular families to make a living by this means.

For example, the Skevingtons, father and son, comprised for many years the entire staff of the North London and Suburban Fire Brigade. Based on their house in Canonbury they were a genuine brigade in that alongside the house there was a shed with a red door, containing an old manual pump and a horse. When a fire took place in the locality they turned out but disappeared again as soon as a genuine engine arrived. Their attendance, however ineffectual, made any subsequent canvassing for subscriptions quite legal.

Then there was Samuel and George Titlow. In 1866, when the Board of Works had taken over the machines of the London Fire Engine Establishment and was empowered, also, to buy up other brigades it received a letter from Samuel Titlow. He claimed that he had a part share in the Kentish and Camden Town Fire Brigade, a fact that was denied by solicitors acting for other claimants to the title. One of these was a greengrocer, Edmund Reaney, about whom Samuel made several statements to the Police. Reaney, he claimed, had entered into partnership with him to buy an engine, most of the finance coming from voluntary contributions, but Reaney had then sold the engine without consultation as a result of which, he (Samuel) was £70 out of pocket. Reaney, he alleged, had then hired an engine for twelve months and had solicited for subscriptions for what he described as the Western Brigade. After that, he had founded the North Western Fire and Escape Brigade for which he was collecting subscriptions under the pretence that it was the, perhaps more respectable, Royal Free Escape Brigade. Samuel Titlow also informed the Police of a man named Wood who had told him that, while working for Reaney, he had collected £6 for the widow of Fireman Ford. Wood had handed the list of subscribers and the money to Reaney in a public house, whereupon Reaney had torn up the list and put the money in his pocket. Wood himself was little better if, as seems likely, he was the H. Wood who, seven years later, was Superintendent of a highly dubious South London Fire Brigade at Weardale Road, Lee.

George Titlow was committed for trial with two other men in 1885 for soliciting money from shopkeepers in the Borough. He was said to be the proprietor of a volunteer fire brigade at Lewisham. In the previous year they had collected £286. Three years later, the Society for Organising Charitable Relief and Repressing Mendicity warned that caution was needed in any dealings with the Local Fire Escape Brigade which, it said, had been set up by George Titlow in 1886 and taken over, on his death, by a man named Ponsford.

This was Henry Bazeley Ponsford who, under an earlier name of Fenton, had been convicted for vagrancy at Brighton in 1883 when he had claimed that the money that he was collecting was for the fire brigade there. He had been sentenced to three months' hard labour. On his release, he had assumed the name of Ponsford and then worked for one of the Skevingtons.

In January 1889, Ponsford went over to the offensive. He took out a summons against Anthony Rogers, a Penge auctioneer and estate agent, whom he claimed had illegally detained a collecting book. Ponsford, in this instance, said he was a member of the Knight's Hill Fire Brigade at West Norwood; Rogers belonged to the West Kent Volunteer Fire Brigade at nearby Forest Hill (the respectable one captained by Frederick Horniman). Rogers was legally in the wrong and was ordered to return the collecting book or pay for its value, estimated at one shilling (5p) and for the cost of the summons. But the magistrate commented that Rogers *"deserved thanks for the trouble he has taken, which at least has resulted in the matter being brought before the public"*.

Four months later Ponsford made another court appearance, this time as witness for the prosecution at Sevenoaks. Two men were charged with obtaining sums of money there with intent to cheat or defraud, or by false pretences. Ponsford, in evidence, said that he was in charge of a fire brigade at Norwood. The men had been authorised to collect for his organisation up to 23 April (sixteen days before the alleged offence), but not after that.

He was supported by Mary Ann Orchard, a widow, who said she was the proprietress of the fire escape brigade, Ponsford being the Superintendent. She was also Ponsford's mother-in-law.

Two years later (in April 1891) Ponsford was called as a defence witness in a case at Bromley. The defendant was described as being a Norwood volunteer fireman and at the time of the alleged offence was collecting for that organisation, but at Blackheath and Eltham. The magistrates asked him how he would get his escape from West Norwood to either of those places — a not unreasonable question as both were a good eight miles away. Ponsford replied: *"They would do their best to get there — they would walk"*. He later admitted that the escape had only been out once in the five years of its existence and it had then broken down. The magistrates committed the man for trial and had Ponsford arrested on a charge of conspiracy.

More despicable than the collecting of money for non-effective fire and escape brigades was that purporting to be for disabled firemen and their dependents.

The most notorious perpetrator of this kind of fraud was Samuel Simpson Seccombe. Born in Devon in 1812 or 1813, he later lived at Bude in Cornwall for some years and four of his children were born there between 1848 and 1860. During that time he was a draper and grocer; and a police informant later said that he had travelled for a Bristol house (he was away from home on the night of the 1851 census). His sister kept a draper's shop in the same place. At the time of the next census ten years later he was in Bude and was described as a *"retired draper and householder on pension"*.

Then some time between 1861 and 1867 he moved to London, for in the latter year he became an assistant to a professional charity collector, a man named Ellis, of Barnsbury. One of his duties was to collect for the Fitzroy Market Ragged Schools but, after two years, Ellis dismissed him when he found that Seccombe had deputed the collecting to another man who had given no receipts to subscribers or had entered amounts on the counterfoils much smaller than those on the receipts. Seccombe explained that the other collector was one of his brothers to whom he had given the work *"as a little practice for him"* so that he, too, might eventually be given a job by Ellis.

Readers of THE FIREMAN, some seventeen years later, were treated to a long letter of self-justification from Samuel Seccombe. In this there was quoted a confession by his wayward brother, who said he had made the false returns because his wife was an unreclaimable drunk who pawned or sold everything she could lay hands on.

But Samuel Seccombe himself was far from blameless. When working for Ellis he collected not only for the Fitzroy Market Ragged Schools but also for the Dressmakers and Milliners Association. Ellis sent him to Brighton to collect for the latter cause, at about the same time as the Ragged Schools deception, giving him 6s (30p) in advance to cover his train fare. Hearing nothing from him for some days, Ellis found out from Seccombe's brother where he was staying and ordered him to return to London. Seccombe replied that he had only managed to collect thirty shillings (£1.50) and had spent it all. He was dismissed, after which Ellis discovered that he was still collecting for the Ragged Schools and had him arrested. He was locked up over a weekend, the Officer at the Station regarding it as too serious a charge to let him out, but the magistrates dismissed the case as he should have been charged with embezzlement, not fraud. The Chairman added that if Seccombe were brought up on the correct indictment he would be pleased to deal with the matter. Ellis, however, discovered that the officers of the Dressmakers and Milliners Association refused to support him, taking the view that he (Ellis) as their agent was solely responsible for any defalcations. The case was dropped.

Samuel Seccombe next found employment with the Christian Men's Union Benevolent Society but they quickly dismissed him when they discovered he had collected between £13 and £14 and had only paid in twenty-five shillings (£1.25).

It was at this juncture, apparently, that he turned his attention to fire brigades and so first came to Shaw's notice. From then on, his activities were a constant source of irritation and inconvenience to the Fire Chief. It has been said that over the following twenty years or more Seccombe's income was £2,000 a year — double that of Shaw's and presumably untaxed.

He first founded the Disabled Firemen's Pension and Relief Fund. Shaw soon began to receive anxious enquiries about it from the public and asked the Police to investigate. They came up with little information but, in December 1871, Shaw was able to report to his Committee that he had managed to obtain a leaflet about the Fund from a private source. One of the listed officials was Edmund Reaney whom, it will be remembered, was alleged by Samuel Titlow to have sold the engine of the Kentish and Camden Town Fire Brigade when he only owned it in part and to have pocketed money collected for the widow of Fireman Ford. Shaw told his Committee what he knew of Reaney and then continued: *"Of the man who appears as Secretary (Samuel Seccombe) and to whom subscriptions are to be paid I can ascertain nothing, except that his name is not in the Directory"*. Shaw would, in due course, learn a lot about him.

The leaflet that Shaw obtained and which is still filed with the Committee papers looked most impressive. The Fund, it said, numbered among its contributors the Duke and Dowager Duchess of Grafton, four earls, a countess, a viscount and a baronet. There was a committee of six, an honorary solicitor and three honorary surgeons (one of whom lived a few doors from the Fund's offices). Reaney, Superintendent of the North Western Fire Brigade (for which, it will be remembered, he was collecting subscriptions under the pretence that it was the Royal Free Escape Brigade) was described as *"Visiting Inspector"*. Seccombe was not living at the office address earlier in the year, at the time of the census; it was probably little more than a POSTE RESTANTE although, according to one writer, a man sat outside dressed in the uniform of the Metropolitan Fire Brigade and with his leg in a splint and his arm in a sling.

By May of the following year (1872) the Fund had, no doubt under pressure, changed its aim from *"the relief of firemen"* to *"the relief of volunteer and private firemen"*. The contributors were said by this time to include H.R.H. Prince Edward of Saxe-Weimar, several further peers and baronets and a sprinkling of admirals, generals and captains R.N. The Honorary Solicitor had been replaced and the local doctor no longer served as Honorary Surgeon. One can read what one will into these changes, but two others can perhaps be readily explained: one Committee member, W. Gosling, had changed his address from Barnsbury Road to the Fire Brigade Station in Pimlico Road; and Edmund Reaney had been replaced as Visiting Inspector.

Gosling's move was connected with the fact that Samuel Seccombe had recently started a fire brigade, the London and Suburban, with a new and powerful engine *"built expressly"* by Messrs. Merryweather. The brigade was also soliciting subscriptions, Gosling being the Collector and Seccombe the Secretary. It shared the office address of the Disabled Firemen's Pension and Relief Fund.

The disappearance of Reaney's name as Visiting Inspector was probably due to the fact that he and Seccombe were no longer on good terms. Certainly, some four months later they had a most curious exchange of letters, copies of which are among the Fire Brigade Committee papers.

On 15 September 1872 Seccombe wrote from the London and Suburban Fire Brigade to *"Mr. Edmund Reaney, Superintendent, North Western Volunteer Fire Brigade"*, as follows:

> *"I have to inform you that by an order of the Committee you are duly appointed Superintendent of the London and Suburban Fire Brigade."*

Three days later another letter was sent to Reaney, this time from both Seccombe and a George Harrison. It reads:

> *"I hereby give you notice that at a Meeting of the Committee held at the office, 7 Everett Street, Russell Square, on Monday the 16th day of September 1872 (only one day after the previous letter had been*

written) your appointment as Hon. Superintendent of the London and Suburban Brigade was formally withdrawn."

On the Board of Works Fire Brigade Committee copy the word *"Committee"* in the letter has been crossed out and replaced with the phrase, *"do not try to make me sick"*; and a marginal comment, doubtless by the Board's Clerk reads: *"An obliteration of 'Committee' and the interlineation was evidently the work of Mr. Reaney, 'Superintendent'"*.

The next day, 19 September, Reaney sent a revealing reply. It reads:
"Sir

Your letter of yesterday is to hand . . .

*I wonder you should address me in this stilted style knowing as much as I do. Where were the **Committee** when I received the appointment and from whom did I receive it, if at all? Your negociation (SIC) with me was for a partnership and you went with me and exercised several acts of authority as a partner with also giving further instructions . . . about the joint taking up of the site for an Engine House at Brixton. I intend to proceed tomorrow to Brixton accompanied by my Secretary and give notice to the Proprietor of the Engine House that I have no further connection with you or your imaginary brigade, insert the same as an advertisement in the two local papers and cause a cautionary handbill to be distributed throughout the Neighbourhood. Accompanying this you will have a request to give up my books etc. to which I require your immediate compliance.*
Yours etc.
Edmund Reaney"

The letter was not actually written by Reaney. It had neither his pungent style nor his unorthodox spelling. The author was probably a man named Younger, perhaps the Secretary referred to. On the same copy letter in the Metropolitan Board of Works archives is a comment written on the same day:
"Sir

My business is with Mr. Edmund Reaney and not with you — therefore I trust you will not address me again in any way whatever.
Yours
S. S. Seccombe
*It was Mr. Reaney's place to treat with me **not** yours"*

A sideline comments reads: *"No name at foot of this, but it was evidently sent to Younger"*.

That same day, 19 September 1872, Seccombe wrote also to Reaney:
"Dear Sir

While Mr. Younger is with you we cannot possibly do business together.
I am yours obediently
S. S. Seccombe"

This time, it was nine days before a reply was forthcoming. It came from the pen of Edmund Reaney himself:
"Fire Station, Rochester Road, N.W.

Dear Sir

You object to Mr. Younger writing on my behalf, who is Mr. Harrison who write to me from you.

*How does your so **calld** committy withdraw my appointment as seupt which they did not make and on what date appointed you **Captain**. When we joined in Partnership we had no Committye as i gave you the title of **Captain** and you gave me that of Superintendent now if you had a committye they could sack you and you ought to know that writing such humbug to me should not have taking place as we know too much of Each other, i have sent you two letters asking when i could see you but you did not deign to answer either, will give you a call as soon . . ."*

Here the letter ends abruptly.

These copy letters accompany a report to the Fire Brigade Committee on the Disabled Firemen's Relief and Pension Association, by a Sergeant Peck of Scotland Yard. He stated:

"I have ascertained that Mr. Samuel Seccombe, the Secretary, a man of doubtful character, was the sole proprietor of the affair and that the Committee is a myth, the parties named in the Prospectus knowing no more about the affair than that Seccombe asked them to be Members and they consented, but were never present at any meeting, everything being done by Seccombe, whose Collectors, Gregory Seccombe, William Seccombe (his brothers), Henry Wood and another man named Girling (a mis-transcription, perhaps, of Gosling) who also acts as Office-keeper, having been collecting money all over the West and North of London, and have no doubt collected large amounts.

"Seccombe has also started a Volunteer Fire Brigade of which he appears to be Captain, Superintendent, Secretary and Treasurer as well as Committee, and there can be no doubt that Seccombe and his brothers and the other Collectors are entirely getting their living out of the subscriptions of the two things and that therefore the whole business is morally a conspiracy to defraud; — but although I have used every endeavour to obtain legal evidence to establish a charge against them, I find it quite impossible to do so, as I find that Seccombe is actually keeping a small staff of pensioners, and also occasionally gives Gratuities to those Volunteer Firemen who are, or pretend to be, sick or disabled . . ."

The extent to which Shaw became involved in the trail of deceit left by Seccombe can be seen in two statements made to the Fire Brigade Committee in 1872 and 1873.

The first was from Arthur Fremantle, a middle-ranking army officer destined eventually to become a General. He described how a young man had called on him at his West End address asking for a subscription and flourishing a receipt book. The Collector told Fremantle that his Society *"worked with Captain Shaw who entirely approved of them"*. They had, he said, as yet published no accounts but would be doing so shortly and, meanwhile, anyone was at liberty to examine their books at 7 Everett Street (the address referred to by Seccombe and Harrison in their letter to Reaney of 18 September). In this statement, the Collector was reflecting Seccombe's braggadocio which had shown itself for instance when, in the previous year, he had written to *"the Rt. Hon. Lord A. Churchill"* assuring him not only that the first Report would be out at Michaelmas but that, in the meantime, *"should you, my Lord, desire any further particulars I shall be pleased to wait upon your Lordship at any time you may please to name"*.

The second statement was dated February 1873, and was from *"A.L.R."* who can be identified as A. Lockhart-Ross, a retired Indian Army Colonel. He wrote, as follows:

"Early in December . . . I had a Dinner Party at my House, 38 Lowndes Street, S.W. As we were sitting down to Dinner my Butler informed me that there was an alarm of fire in the House, that two firemen in costume insisted on entering the House, and that the area was filled with a mob trying to enter the lower storey of the House. I desired to let the Firemen in, and send a Servant all over the House with them . . . They went all over the House and left saying there was no fire. One servant defended the basement of the house from the mob, while another went for the Police. On leaving the house he was accosted by two men who said they were Policemen in plain clothes and that there was no danger. I have no means of knowing whether they were Police or not. There was no fire. The mob were kept out by force, and all was soon quiet. Next day a fireman in uniform called on me, he said, about the fire the previous evening. I said there had really been no fire in my House . . . I asked who was his Chief, was it Captain Shaw? He replied no — Captain Seccombe . . . He did not ask for money, though of course that was his object in coming. I believe the whole affair was a plant to create a disturbance. It seemed to me a very good (one). It was very nearly successful. Its object was my spoons. All this was reported to Captain Shaw and to the Police. I received a simple acknowledgement, but I am not aware of any steps having been taken to prevent a recurrence of the trick. I have not given a dinner party since."

The Fire Brigade Committee, having received the statements and having earlier called the attention of the Board of Works to the need to warn people against giving money to such Collectors, concluded that there was no more they could do.

The London and Suburban Volunteer Fire Brigade went into voluntary liquidation three years later — in 1876. But it was soon resuscitated for at the end of the following year a man appeared at Westminster Police Court charged with obtaining five shillings (25p) by false pretences *"on behalf of the West London (late London and Suburban) Fire Engine and Escape Brigade"* whose Secretary was named as Samuel Seccombe. A police inspector said that the Brigade had no fire engine, that there had been 250 letters of complaint about the collection of subscriptions for it, that whenever he called at the advertised office Mr. Seccombe was not there and nothing could be found out about the Brigade. In his view, the whole thing was a fraud.

In his own defence, Seccombe said that at one time the London and Suburban Brigade had had 75 volunteers, three horses, a steam engine, two manual engines and a fire escape. It had attended 700 fires in five years. Then subscriptions had fallen away. But now, he claimed, it was in business again. All that was lacking was an engine and one was expected from America the following month. The magistrate was obviously suspicious and asked about the Disabled Firemen's Pension Fund which, he observed, had its offices at the same address as the West London Brigade and was served by the same Secretary, Samual Seccombe. Defending solicitor advised the Bench that the two affairs were *"separate although under the same management"*. Since the Brigade was being made up and an engine was, apparently, on its way from America the Collector was found not to be in breach of the law and was discharged.

The same issue of THE FIREMAN that contained the report of the case just described, carried also a letter of a kind not uncommon in Victorian times. It was from J. J. I. of Clapham, and read:

"May I ask whether the Mr. S. S. Seccombe, who is the Secretary of these concerns . . . is the same Mr. S. S. Seccombe who formerly collected for the Fitzroy Market Ragged Schools, for the Dress-makers and Milliners Association and for the Christian Men's Union Benevolent Society; who established the London and Suburban Fire Brigade, respecting which a statement was made at the Greenwich Police Court, on 14 November 1874; whose brother was sentenced to three months' hard labour at the Greenwich Police Court on 29 December 1875 for obtaining subscriptions to the London and Suburban Fire Brigade and the Disabled Firemen's Pension Fund; and who went into liquidation at the end of 1875 or the commencement of the following year?

"I ask these questions in good faith and shall be glad if they enable Mr. Seccombe satisfactorily to remove any unfavourable impressions which may exist respecting his societies."

Seccombe obviously considered that his best defence was attack, or perhaps one should say threatened attack followed by silence. In the next edition of THE FIREMAN he acknowledged the letter, promised *"a full reply"* in time for insertion in the next number and said that if it were not published he would issue it in circular form to every fire brigade in the kingdom. The editor promised, in a footnote, that Seccombe should have every reasonable opportunity of explanation. Two months and therefore two editions later, the editor complained that Seccombe had not sent *"the explanatory letter he promised some time ago and which we are both willing and anxious to insert"*.

A year later THE FIREMAN referred to a hoax, a notice of death that had been inserted in the DAILY CHRONICLE. This had prompted Seccombe to proclaim from the offices of the London Suburban Fire Brigade Association that the notice had caused him much astonishment. *"I am not only alive,"* he wrote, *"but have never enjoyed better health"*. The editor of the THE FIREMAN, whilst deploring the stupidity of the hoax, reflected that it had given Seccombe an opportunity to compile the *"full reply"* which he had promised, but which had never been forthcoming.

The Disabled Firemen's Relief, Pension and Award Association, its title having become rather more comprehensive, continued to find a place in the newspapers as when, four years later (in 1883), Fenton (later Ponsford) received his three months' sentence for vagrancy at Brighton. Although claiming he was collecting for the local brigade, THE FIREMAN noted that he was connected with *"that rather questionable society"*, The Disabled Firemen's Association.

Complaints both about Seccombe and the Association were still being received by Shaw and by the Fire Brigade Committee six years later. Indeed, for the last twenty years of Shaw's thirty-year reign in London Seccombe's name was rarely missing from the Committee's minutes for long. Sometimes, as in the case of T. Howell Williams, of Idris & Co., *"pure mineral water makers, manufacturing chemists and export merchants"*, the complainant sent the Committee a copy of the handbill he had received. On that occasion there was another slight alteration in name, subscriptions this time being invited on behalf of the National Disabled Firemen's Institution. The privileges, pointed out the leaflet, were not confined to any particular brigade, but were open to all firemen throughout Great Britain and Ireland. That comprehensiveness must have made it even more difficult to prove improper practices. The Institution now named, as its supporters, a couple of Dukes, four Earls, two Barons, six Reverends, a Duchess, a Dowager Duchess and four Countesses. The Secretary was *"Mr. S. S. Seccombe, Captain in Command of the London and Suburban Fire Brigade"*. On paper, it all looked respectable; but we do not know how many of the people had given permission for their names to be used. Further, even though the Collectors wore *"a special uniform with the initials 'D.F.I.' on the collar and a gold Phoenix upon the cap"*, and carried *"a printed authority signed by the Treasurer and Secretary"*, subscribers had no way of telling how much of their money was eventually put to proper use.

In 1890 Seccombe finally produced his long-promised defence in THE FIREMAN. He quoted two declarations. One was by Ellis, the Chief Collector of the Fitzroy Market Ragged Schools and the Dressmakers and Milliners Association, regretting the charges he had made against Seccombe *"who has acted in a most honourable way"* and been *"so crudely wronged"*. The other, by Frederick Cox of the Christian Men's Union Benevolent Society declared the Seccombe had *"discharged his duties with exceeding satisfaction and honesty"*. These declarations, claimed Seccombe, had been signed in the presence of a Commissioner of Oaths, in 1883 and 1889, respectively. Whether the letters really existed and, if so, whether or not they were forgeries will probably never be known.

What is certain is that Seccombe spent his last years making a substantial living, sailing very close to the wind, and working with some rather dubious colleagues. One writer has claimed that a group of fire offices offered to buy him out and that he asked only £250 for his organisation, *"as a going concern"*, but demanded vast (unspecified) compensation for loss of his own post. Yet he claimed, in his 1890 letter to THE FIREMAN: *"The Committee of the Institution is composed of clergymen, physicians, solicitors and other gentlemen of character and reputation, whilst its books and accounts are annually audited by a high-class chartered accountant. I do not think you would suspect these gentlemen of conspiring to defraud the public"*. But even if they weren't, he still was.

By this time he was in his late seventies, and Captain Shaw, if not he, was about to retire. So it is appropriate to end the saga of Samuel Simpson Seccombe with a case that first came before the Brentford Police Court two months before Shaw retired and was then tried by jury a month after he had gone.

It concerned a man named Allen who had obtained a shilling (5p) from an Ealing shopkeeper *"for the Excursion Fund of the Ealing Fire Brigade"*. He had admitted, however, to a detective that he was collecting for the London and Suburban Brigade. The Chairman of the Bench claimed that the latter body was itself a fraud, since it said it was established for those districts of the Metropolis that were otherwise unprotected when, in fact, there were none such.

Seccombe defended his Brigade as a genuine one. It had an engine and other appliances worth £400, he said, and a number of firemen were always on duty. The jury found Allen guilty but recommended him to mercy on the grounds that he was Seccombe's dupe.

He received six months' imprisonment. As one of the hostile witnesses was leaving the court a man was heard to say to him: *"You ought to be burnt"* and was at once taken into custody and committed to prison for seven days. The offender was described as *"Seccombe junior"*; doubtless the heir to the family business.

CHAPTER EIGHT
SHAW AND HIS MEN

"We very seldom interfere with Captain Shaw in any way; he is an absolute-minded man and does not like interference of any sort"

Despite the distractions of having to give evidence before House of Commons Select Committees, of a busy social life, of volunteer fire brigades and bogus charity collectors, Shaw never forgot that he was London's chief fireman. That he was, in other words, the instructor, the leader and the inspirer of hundreds of men who had the exciting, dangerous, unpleasant and often boring task of giving fire protection to the people and property of the capital.

From the moment of his appointment, Shaw left his men in no doubt that they were privileged to serve under the greatest living fireman. But they found also that although he bore himself like a general in charge of a military campaign, he never hesitated to join them in the most exposed positions if he felt they needed encouragement. He was completely indifferent to personal danger, and over the years was seriously injured on a number of occasions.

He was known alternatively as *"the Skipper"* or *"the long 'un"*. The latter nickname was because of his tall slender frame; the former is a reminder that he accepted only sailors into the Brigade. His reasons for this were: one, they were accustomed to living on the job and to confinement for long periods; two, they were used to being called out at any hour, and to night watches; three, they could (so he asserted) be trained in a quarter the time required for men without seafaring experience; four, they had already been taught to obey orders; five, they were generally hardy, practical, strong and agile; and six, they had a good head for heights.

The 1876-77 Selwin-Ibbetson Select Committee on the Fire Brigade was told by an earlier chairman of the Fire Brigade Committee that it was well known that young men going to sea were *"of a fickle mind and disposition"*; and the Committee's report recommended that it was unnecessary to confine recruitment to sailors. But Shaw never wavered in this policy.

Discipline in the Brigade was severe. For a minor offence a fireman could be fined, by the Chief Officer, a sum equivalent to one week's pay. Shaw, and other officers, also had power of suspension for up to one week.

An article in THE WORLD perhaps summed up Shaw's philosophy accurately: *"Captain Shaw does not object to . . . (the) epithet (martinet). He maintains vigorously that a state of discipline under whtch every man knows his work exactly and performs it punctually is perfect freedom"*. So, when the Fire Brigade Committee was considering the possible employment of supernumeraries (men employed on a day-to-day basis) he reported: *"It is impossible in London to find men who can be trusted to carry out satisfactorily such duties as ours unless they are subjected to most strict discipline"*.

A TURN OUT. The men on duty were in full uniform, except for helmets; the water in the boiler was already near to boiling so that steam for the pump would be immediately available. (Photo: London Fire Brigade Museum).

Yet this military attitude was tempered with commonsense. He advised the Committee, for instance, that their instruction that firemen should not attend in uniform the funeral of a colleague, as the event was then a public spectacle, was conducive to their still being there but looking very shabby. In the Fire Brigade, he reported, *"there are many men who have no clothes except their uniform and many others who have only such clothes as are unfit for . . . a funeral"*.

Likewise, commenting on the untidy appearance of the windows of the living quarters at some stations, he advised his Committee that the firemen considered it a hardship that they should have to provide their own window blinds especially since, when the men transferred to other stations, the blinds rarely fitted. Often, as a result, old pieces of sacking were used and this looked very disreputable. The Committee resolved that, in future, Venetian blinds would be fitted at all stations.

He could indeed be fiercely protective of his men, as when a Doctor Godfrey, of Ormonde House, Regent's Park, used *"the most abusive, threatening and disgusting language"* against two firemen attending a chimney fire at his home. Shaw told the Committee that an example should be made of Godfrey, not only to prevent a repetition but so that the men knew they had protection without having to resort to violence. The Committee heard the evidence of the firemen and resolved that Godfrey should be brought before the magistrates, but the Board's Solicitor subsequently advised that neither the Board nor the men had a case.

In 1876 Shaw wrote:

"Every man must obey, without a moment's hesitation, all orders he may receive from his superiors". But, he went on, *"discipline alone is not enough, there must also be that confidence and fellow-feeling between all ranks, which makes the failure or success of individuals a source of regret or congratulation to the whole body"*.

In an interview, he was reported as saying:

"My men know perfectly well that if they are remiss in answering a call or . . . slow in getting out an engine, the offence will be visited by fine or reprimand, and will be written against their names in . . . the service book . . . containing almost a biography of every man since he joined the brigade . . . Each engine has also an account opened against it showing at once its age, prime cost and cost of maintenance. All is conducted on this principle of accurate attention and registration of detail . . . You can arrive at nothing without facts carefully collected and properly arranged . . . and facts are easily collected with proper method. (Here at Headquarters) are just as many hat pegs as there are men, so that I can see at a glance how many men are out and how many at home . . . For want of seeing things at a glance, the absence of rapid calculation, and the consequent firm grip of the business in hand, has led to the greatest fires of modern times."

He also wrote perhaps the earliest statement of what is now a cliché in personnel management: *"Real efficiency cannot exist . . . unless the seniors of each rank are competent to perform, not only their own . . . duties, but also . . . the duties of the rank next above them"*.

For those who inexcusably fell short of his own high standards, he had little time or patience. Sub Engineer William Perdue, he told his Committee in November 1866, was *"lazy . . . without energy . . . totally unfitted for general command"*. Perdue was by-passed for promotion a year later, *"being unfit for the position"*, and six months after that was reported as having been drunk on duty when in charge of Chandos Street Station. For that he was reduced to the bottom of the list of First Class Firemen. He resigned a fortnight later.

On the other hand, Shaw encouraged those who failed but made the effort. For instance, he advised his Committee in 1867 that Sub Engineer Thomas Sharp was not being recommended for promotion in his normal turn. He was, said Shaw, a respectable, intelligent and trustworthy man who thoroughly understood every branch of a fireman's business. Unfortunately, he was such a bad scholar that the station books could not be put in his care. But, continued Shaw, *"from the efforts which Sharp has made within the last three years and which I know from his own assurance and other sources he is steadily persevering in, there is every reason to hope that in course of time he may succeed in qualifying himself for promotion"*. Fifteen months later Sharp, still a Sub Engineer, was placed in charge of the Southwark Bridge Road Station but could not cope and, after eighteen months, reverted to the rank of First Class Fireman at his own request. He died three years later of heart disease after over seventeen years' service in the London Fire Engine Establishment and the Metropolitan Fire Brigade.

Despite his autocratic manner, Shaw also showed a desire to inform and consult with his men. For instance, in the very early days of the Metropolitan Fire Brigade Committee he requested additional copies of the minutes of the meetings of the Board for the use of the firemen at the various stations and for reference at Headquarters. But the Committee decided this was *"not advisable"*. Also, when considering the anomalies that were likely to arise from the absorption into the Brigade of the former Parish Engineers he called together *"the seniors of each of the ranks"* and explained the problems. He was able to report subsequently that as a result the men would be satisfied with whatever course was adopted. Similarly, when the men of the Society for the Protection of Life from Fire were being interviewed for transfer to the new Metropolitan Fire Brigade, he told them he was always available at Headquarters if they had any matter on which they needed further information. Some did in fact take him up on this, concerning money that they had voluntarily saved while in the employ of the Society.

Conditions of service in the force were arduous, especially as it was too small for the increasing tasks imposed upon it. A former Chairman of the Fire Brigade Committee told the 1876-77 Select Committee that it was Shaw's strict discipline that drove the men out of the Brigade. On being asked whether he had ever considered Shaw should be told that the Board thought he expected too much from his men, the reply was: *"We very seldom interfere with Captain Shaw in any way; he is an absolute-minded man and does not like interference of that sort"*. Shaw himself, however, on being asked if he considered his discipline was unnecessarily stringent, replied: *"I do not, or I should not insist on it"*.

Shaw never hid from his employers the pressures that his men were under because there were not enough of them. He told his Committee in 1868 that the firemen's hours were longer than those of any other workers, including soldiers, policemen and sailors. He also pointed out that the hours were irregular and their rest was frequently interrupted.

The men were on a continuous duty system which was organised — if not interrupted by fire calls — on a three-day cycle. In the daytime the men were engaged on station work, cleaning and maintenance, and drills. On the first night of the cycle, a man stayed in the watchroom, but could sleep with his head close to the telegraphic instrument. On night two, in the early days of the Brigade, he was on duty at a street station equipped either with an escape or a hose cart; at such a station he was allowed to sleep in the watch-box and was provided with one blanket, though in winter he probably had to spend much of his time walking or stamping around his box to keep warm. On night three, he was allowed to undress and go to bed, but he was still liable to be called out.

Except for this concession on night three, he remained fully dressed all the time wearing uniform, boots, belt and axe. The third night concession could be withdrawn without compensation if there was a shortage of personnel through sickness or other cause. Occasionally, a man would have a hundred and twenty hours continuously on duty; and a succession of large fires could cause intolerable strain. The 1876-77 Select Committee heard that a good many men had broken down in health because of the severe and continuous work.

Even the officers and men who compiled the Annual Report for the Fire Brigade Committee worked on it for two successive nights right round the clock. This was merely, so it would seem, so that the report could be presented at the very earliest opportunity. Shaw pleaded, in 1867, that for this they should receive a gratuity as they had in the past. But the Committee decided it would be *"inexpedient"*.

The Board of Works, as we have heard, did not interfere with Shaw in any way over matters of duty or discipline; and the firemen, with their naval traditions, made no attempt for some time to form or join a trade union.

In the 1860's and 1870's, all the men did was to make written representations about their conditions from time to time. A former Chairman of the Fire Brigade Committee told the 1876-77 Select Committee that the conditions of service were the responsibility not of the Metropolitan Board of Works, but of Shaw himself.

"If Captain Shaw," he said, *"were inclined to spare his men and give them rest . . . it was in his power to do it . . . If he chose . . . that the men coming off the fire escape fatigued and tired should go upstairs to bed instead of being engaged on station work all morning, he could do so. No other engines were cleaned and polished up as these were . . . It is not for the Committee to interfere with Captain Shaw's discipline, but I consider it is putting a man through purgatory to insist on his keeping his hatchet and boots on all day and night, and it is not necessary"*

Having heard the evidence of one fireman that he had been a whole week on duty without taking off his clothes, the same former Chairman of Committee commented: *"That is a very cruel arrangement for Captain Shaw to have made. I am quite sure he had the means of obviating it and, if he had not, he should have told the Board of such a circumstance"*. But the Board bore a lot of the responsibility for the situation. Some eight years before, Shaw had drawn attention to the desirability of giving *"every man in the Force one night in bed each week"*. But, he reported, *"with the existing number (of men) such an arrangement is impossible"*.

Any leave, beyond a few hours in the daytime, and any involving absence after ten in the evening could be granted only by Shaw himself. In the Manchester and some other provincial brigades, by contrast, men were entitled to a day's leave every fortnight. In London, as a First Class Engineer told the 1876-77 Select Committee: *"A fireman has not one day a year to call his own"*. The men, he said, were asking for one night a week off duty. It was, he said, particularly hard on young men who were courting; *"and we don't allow females to come to our stations"*, he reminded Members. The Committee, however, seemed to have little sympathy for frustrated romance, but was concerned that the men had little or no opportunity to go to church.

The situation was described graphically in a letter that Third Class Fireman William Wheeler wrote to his masters when he resigned to better himself, in February 1876. It was a very circumspect letter for, as its author pointed out, *"circumstances may arise in which I might be under the necessity of applying to you for a recommendation for another berth"*. Wheeler had, too, a good record as a fireman. He had served six years in the Brigade, had saved six lives at a fire in Albany Street, Regent's Park and a further three at Hampstead Road. But he wrote of *"the continual strain of duty both physical and mental"*.

"I myself", he continued, *"have gone out four consecutive nights in the depth of winter on escape duty and each morning on my return from my night duty (which has lasted 13 hours) I have had the general work of the station to do which consists of cleaning engines, gear and the station itself. Such work lasts invariably until dinner time, and I have made a point of taking my clothes off and lying to sleep like a rational being. Such rest, I am sorry to say, is not often of long duration for often before I have been in bed ½ an hour my bell has been rung for me to attend a chimney fire which perhaps lasts until tea-time which having had I have had to get ready to go out on the streets for another 13 hours and after that has expired I return to my station and find myself booked on duty for the day to take charge of the telegraph instrument . . . a duty terminating at 7 o'clock when I have found myself relieved from that duty to go out with an escape for the night again, thus making 36 hours consecutive duty. The following night (my night in bed) we have turned out to a fire with the other men and been hard at work all night — but no allowance can be made for that it **must** count a man's night in in order to allow other men who have been on escape duty to go to bed the following night in their turn . . ."*

Yet within a framework of rigid discipline and incredibly hard conditions Shaw looked after his men with considerable humanity.

This showed itself in the instance of Samuel Helps. During the first nineteen years of his service with the Brigade he had achieved the rank of First Class Engineer, had saved numerous lives and had been injured six times. Not once in that period had he been charged with misbehaviour. Then he took to drink and was reported to Shaw three times in eighteen months; on the third occasion he used threatening language to another officer. Shaw appealed to the Committee on his behalf. He conceded that Helps could not remain an officer or in any position where he might command men, but suggested that because of his previous record he should be reduced to the bottom of the list of Second Class Firemen rather than be dismissed. Four years later he was sufficiently rehabilitated to be promoted to the First Class, a year before he was pensioned off through infirmity being by then over fifty years old.

Shaw's general concern for the welfare of his men, and the working efficiency of the Brigade, is illustrated by his provision of a *"Diarrhoea Mixture"* for the men. Braidwood had first introduced it, the prescription coming from Apothecaries Hall. It comprised chalk powder with opium, aromatic confection, sugar powder, gum arabic powder and cinnamon water. Its effect, he reported to his Committee, was *"most satisfactory"*. The ingredients used are, with the exception of a few details, those still in use today. The need for such a mixture may have resulted from the large amount of impure water likely to be drunk from local pumps when the firemen were hot and thirsty; or to counteract tension diarrhoea.

To summarise Shaw's attitude to the men he commanded: as ex-sailors they were used to a hard life and found their work in the Fire Brigade was no soft option; discipline was strict, even by the standards of the period, but it was fair; the demands on the men's physical and mental stamina were great, probably unreasonably so; and, if Shaw had been less demanding or the Board of Works more generous with manpower, those demands would have been unnecessary.

Shaw saw an iron discipline as being necessary, not only for efficiency but for the safety of his men, both collectively and individually. He obviously did not suffer fools or rogues gladly, or indeed at all; yet he was sympathetic and supportive to those who tried but failed to achieve or maintain positions of responsibility. He also showed great loyalty to those who had served well in the past but were now in decline, so long as they were respectable and continued to do their best. For a man who was hard, overbearing and arrogant he was remarkably sensitive and what is especially striking, when one reads his reports to Committee, is that he was a natural manager of men. If that had applied only in his later years one might attribute it to experience, but he displayed this particular quality from the moment he came to London when his only previous responsibilities had been limited to his short period of service in the North Cork Rifles and his even shorter spell in Belfast.

His achievements are all the greater when one appreciates that he had to work within the confines imposed on him by his Committee and by the Board of Works. Some writers have given the impression that his employers gave him a totally free rein or were browbeaten into submission by him. But even a superficial examination of the Committee minutes shows that his advice was frequently disregarded, sometimes misunderstood and rarely taken without consideration of the minutest details.

This last, is well illustrated in the case of Luke Green's girl friend. When Green, a Third Class Fireman, took Maria Gillis, *"a woman of doubtful character"*, to the single men's mess room, Shaw wanted to have him dismissed. But Green claimed that she was respectable and was, furthermore, his fiancée, at which the Committee instructed Shaw to find out more about her and report back. Shaw was thus put to much time and trouble that might have been better expended in firefighting, but characteristically he did the job with great thoroughness and honesty.

By the date of the next Committee meeting, a fortnight later, he had obtained letters (i) from her landlady of the past seven weeks who claimed she had seen nothing amiss in Maria's behaviour; (ii) from a fellow tenant, who described her as *"an industrious sober young woman"* and as *"a fit and proper person to become the wife of Luke Green"*; and (iii) from her mother, who said she was a *"Hard Working endustries woman"*, and who continued: *"I . . . fell very sorry to think that they sHould speak disrespectful of her CHarctor knoweing that I never see any thing wrong with her".*

Despite this evidence that Maria was a paragon of virtue, Shaw told the Committee that she had been in the habit of having Green and other men in her previous apartments, sometimes all night, and that she was *"nothing better than a loose woman".* He produced, as witness, Maria's former landlady, but when Green was invited to speak he said she was aggrieved because Maria had left as the house did not have a good character in the neighbourhood.

The Committee, having taken much time in hearing all the evidence, resolved that the Board be recommended to dismiss Green. An amendment was then put that he should, rather, be reprimanded and when the voting was seen to be 4-4, the Chairman cast his vote against the amendment. Then another amendment was put, proposing that Maria should be summoned to attend next time, though no consideration seems to have been given as to what power the Committee had to issue such a summons. Eventually both that amendment and the original proposal were withdrawn and it was agreed to reprimand Green, despite a proposal to that effect having earlier been defeated.

Previously, Green had been both reprimanded and fined for being drunk on duty. A few months after the Maria Gillis incident he was suspended for being under the influence of drink and threatening a superior officer when on duty; he was then fined twice more for drunkenness and was severely reprimanded for not entering a call in the occurrence book. Eventually, he was dismissed, so vindicating Shaw's earlier belief that he should go. But what is significant is not that Shaw was right and the Committee was wrong; rather, it is the amount of time that was wasted by the Committee in resolving a matter that could have been dealt with in half an hour by, say, Shaw and his Chairman and Vice Chairman.

The claim made before the House of Commons Select Committee that the Fire Brigade Committee very seldom interfered with Captain Shaw hardly rings true, yet it was made only seven or eight years after the Luke Green case.

CHAPTER NINE
LEADER AND HERO
"Often a whistle awakes him from his slumbers in the middle of the night, for there is a speaking tube right over his pillow"

The long day that Shaw demanded of his men was almost matched by his own, even if in his case some of it was spent in socialising.

He claimed that in his early years in London he had risen at three in the morning and had then walked from Headquarters, at that time in the City, to perhaps Rotherhithe or Kensington to drill the men and train them in the use of their appliances. After a couple of hours he would walk back to Headquarters. Later in his career, he did not commence drill until seven o'clock.

His mornings were spent receiving or writing reports, after which he would visit the drill yard at Headquarters. Later he would make a round of inspections, during which he might drive forty miles. At night, he was about the Metropolis, moving from fire to fire; or, if there was a particularly large one, remaining at it to take command.

Twice a day — morning and evening — he received a report from each district headquarters. This detailed every man, every engine, every ladder and every hose cart available for operations. Noticing on one occasion that an escape supposed to be on duty at Whitechapel Church had been omitted, he telegraphed the Superintendent to enquire its whereabouts. He was assured that it was in working order and was manned, despite which he sent a stand-by escape from Headquarters, by then at Southwark, and had the men wheel the errant escape from Whitechapel to Southwark so that he could inspect it. They then had to wheel it back.

He created a Turnout Board which made spot checks on stations and appliances. But he was also liable to do so himself, without any warning. On one occasion, he arrived at one station from another speedily enough to intercept a telegraphed message: *"The Long 'un is out visiting. Look out. He may give you a look up"*. He telegraphed back: *"Thanks. I have your message. Chief Officer"*.

His speed in reaching an incident was greatly helped by his domestic arrangements. One writer said that he had *"a private and particular bedroom of his own — from which even Mrs. Shaw is excluded, and a regiment of uniforms to change about with after each . . . soaking. All is orderly and methodical. On the floor is a row of jackboots standing erect, shoulder to shoulder, like a well-drilled regiment, and over them hangs raiment without end all ready to hand at a moment's notice"*. The DUBLIN ADVERTISER wrote in 1890, the year before his retirement: *"Captain Shaw . . . sits at a table practically surrounded by innumerable speaking tubes. These communicate with every part of the building, and the Captain is continually stopping in his work to answer a whistle from one of the numerous departments for there is scarcely a thing done save under his supervision. If you went into his private house you would find a tube in every apartment. Often a whistle awakes him from his slumbers in the middle of the night for there is one right over his pillow"*.

CAPTAIN SHAW (circa 1879). Shaw's strength of character comes through in this drawing made when he received his CB. He was by then fifty-one, was about to celebrate his Silver Wedding Anniversary, and had over the previous eighteen years built up a world-wide reputation as a fireman.

This raises a question that is very difficult to answer: did he delegate adequately? There is evidence both for and against.

For twenty years he had no deputy. There is no evidence before 1879, when he had been with the Board thirteen years and had been London's fire chief for eighteen, that the Fire Brigade Committee ever discussed the matter, though doubtless they would have done if he had raised it. And when it did come up, it did so in a report of a sub-committee appointed to investigate a quite different matter. It pointed out that if Shaw were away command devolved on the most senior of the four Superintendents (or Foremen as they had, earlier, been called). But whilst they were well qualified by experience to direct the force in fighting a fire they could not be expected to advise on policy matters.

Eventually, after much delay, what would now be called a job specification was drawn up for a deputy to Shaw. This was done jointly by Shaw and the Clerk to the Board but many elements were almost certainly at Shaw's insistence. The postholder was to be under 35 (later amended to *"at least 30 and not over 40"*) because, *"owing to the special character of the organisation and work of the Brigade there would be much to learn before he could attain the knowledge and experience necessary to control and direct the operations of the Brigade in the Chief Officer's absence".* This requirement at once ruled out almost any provincial fire officer of any standing.

Further, since he would necessarily come into contact with *"persons of authority",* he would need to have received *"a liberal education".* Someone was looked for also with a sound knowledge of mechanics and other branches of applied science, of the construction of buildings, and of the strength of building materials both normally and under intense heat. Shaw had, of course, had no experience of any of these technicalities when he had been appointed and some of his critics always regarded this as his weakest asset. As to pay, the Second Officer (which was how the post-holder was to be designated) was recommended to receive £300, rising by annual increments of £25 to £500. This is interesting because the starting salary was only £75 above the top salary for a Superintendent and the terminating figure was only half Shaw's salary. In financial terms, the Second Officer would be little more than PRIMUS INTER PARES among the Superintendents.

There were 105 applicants for the post. No fire officer was short-listed; only engineers and army and navy officers and, ironically with such a wide field of candidates, the choice turned out to be a disastrous one. The man appointed was J. Sexton Simonds, an engineer with Messrs. Carson, oil and colour merchants, of Dublin and he was dismissed for improper financial practices within about five years of succeeding Shaw as Chief Officer.

It is highly improbable that Shaw had any say in the short-listing, let alone the appointment. His relationship with Simonds can be illustrated by the fact that on one occasion when Shaw was on leave Simonds wrote to the Editor of THE TIMES complaining that he was never named as being in charge at fires. The newspaper agreed to rectify the omission, but when

87

J. SEXTON SIMONDS, SHAW'S DEPUTY AND SUCCESSOR. He had an uneasy relationship with Shaw and was largely ignored. He became Chief Officer on Shaw's retirement but was later dismissed for financial malpractices. (Photo: London Fire Brigade Library).

Shaw got to hear of the matter he said that he objected to his officers receiving publicity and, if it persisted, the newspapers would no longer receive his fire reports.

Likewise, when Shaw was to be away in August 1881, he made no arrangement that his deputy would not be away at the same time until so instructed by the Fire Brigade Committee. A report on a fatal fire, nine years later, indicated that Shaw had been away on private business and Simonds had been on leave. So far as Shaw was concerned, Simonds seemed not to exist.

Yet Shaw did delegate a lot of detailed work whilst quite properly remaining in control of policy. He held periodic meetings with his Superintendents and he created a number of Boards composed of station officers: a Supplies Board to draw up specifications for new equipment and to examine goods delivered from contractors; a Correspondence and Accounts Board (he was given absolutely no clerical support); and a Board to manage the stations. He also brought into being AD HOC Boards such as the one formed in 1873 to devise a method of getting hose ashore from river fire floats.

So the evidence about Shaw's ability to delegate is conflicting. He could not have been so involved personally if he had not driven himself so hard and there is circumstantial evidence that his family saw little of him. But he was no desk-bound Chief. Asked by the Hankey Committee, in 1862, whether on hearing that a fire had broken out he immediately went to the scene, he replied: *"If I think it will be large enough to require my attendance, I go myself. As a matter of practice, I attend almost all fires but I am not bound to do so"*. Later, as London — and the Brigade — got bigger, this was impossible; but he attended the major fires right up to the time of his retirement.

Once there, he played an active part. He had strong views on leadership and expressed these in the introduction to his book, FIRE PROTECTION. Any instances of cowardice that had come to his notice, he wrote, *"have been invariably traceable to want of discipline, want of knowledge, absence of organization, indistinctiveness of orders . . . not of the men themselves but of those in charge of them. Men seldom desert a superior who knows his business . . . and who is steady, but if they find themselves . . . working under a man without these qualifications, and are consequently driven to take care of themselves, who shall blame them?"*

This philosophy sometimes took him into positions of danger since he would never instruct his men to go where he was not prepared to go himself. At least eight times he had narrow escapes from serious injury, disablement or death and on several occasions he was hurt quite badly.

Very early in his career in London, in November 1863, he met with what the London Fire Engine Establishment Committee minutes described as *"a very serious accident"* at a fire in Bishopsgate. He fell from a height onto a ladder that was being carried past at the time, *"striking himself on the Pereneum inflicting a dangerous injury"*. Then, in 1877, on the way to a fire in the Isle of Dogs the horses of the steamer bolted and he was thrown. The wheels passed over his right foot, but he was back in action within a few days. Four years later, at a warehouse fire, a wall collapsed close to where he was standing talking to one of his Superintendents and to his son, Bernard, then a man of twenty-three. The Superintendent and Bernard Shaw were both hurt, but only superficially.

The next year, at a fire off Stamford Street, a huge pile of bags weighing several hundredweight fell near him and pinned down an Engineer. When, in the dense smoke, Shaw missed the Engineer he summoned help and the man was rescued, burnt and injured. Then, only fourteen months later, Shaw himself was badly injured at a fire at Kesterton's carriage factory, in Long Acre. The blaze had spread to the roof of an adjoining Co-operative store and to check the position of his men Shaw climbed an awkward ladder. The wet hoses had made the rungs slippery and when half way down he fell to the bottom, hurting his back. Almost immediately, a Superintendent fell from top to bottom of the same ladder and was knocked unconscious. The latter was taken to King's College Hospital in an ambulance and Shaw followed in a hose van, accompanied by the Second Officer. He was not detained but, uncharacteristically, he had to take to his bed through shock. Two days later he was permitted to receive visitors, *"of whom great numbers called"*. Such was Shaw's fame by this time, that among those to go to his bedside was the Princess of Wales who was accompanied by her daughters Louise, Victoria and Maud. Also in the party were her niece by marriage, the Princess of Saxe-Meiningen (Kaiser

89

Wilhelm's sister) and the Grand Duchess of Mecklenberg. They drove to Shaw's house, in Southwark, in three open carriages, to the cheers of the crowd. He was up and about three days after their visit but needed a week's convalescence out of London before he was fit to resume duty.

The very next year he just missed a heavy fall of wall in the City and, in his last year of service, had two similar narrow escapes at a large fire in Great Tower Street.

It could be said of course that such incidents were evidence not of Shaw's bravery but of his recklessness. But that cannot be said of the occasion when, in the course of duty and for the future well-being of his men, he allowed himself to be the subject of a dangerous series of tests of a smoke respirator designed by John Tyndall, the Superintendent of the Royal Institution.

These can best be described using Shaw's own words in his subsequent report to the Fire Brigade Committee:

"In the early part of last year (i.e. 1871) Professor Tyndall . . . gave me a respirator which enables a man to breathe in dense smoke and poisonous vapours. The efficacy . . . was proved . . . by practical experiments of the most searching kind . . . I remained myself on one occasion about 10 minutes in a cellar completely full of vapour of the most poisonous kind, one breath of which taken direct would have caused instant death. The cellar was specially prepared by Professor Tyndall all doors, keyholes and openings of every kind being carefully stopped and a red hot stove or furnace being placed in the middle, loaded with the necessary chymicals (SIC). So strong and pungent was the vapour that the opening and closing of the door for my admittance was not without danger to the Professor and his assistants.

"The result was entirely satisfactory and I have now for upwards of a year been engaged in endeavours to adopt the invention for our use.

"When the experiment was made in the cellar it took the Professor and his assistants fully a quarter of an hour to prepare me. They fitted up a pair of round glasses or goggles on the eyes, drawing them tight with a band round the back of the head and stuffing the edges and rims with small pieces of the finest wool. They did very nearly the same with the mouth, and closed the nose altogether with cotton plugs inside and a strong spring outside."

He went on to describe how he and other officers had subsequently tried to use the same principles to devise a respirator that could be quickly fitted by a fireman and he believed that finally he had succeeded.

"Our part of the work", he continued modestly, *"has involved much trouble and loss of time, but there is no special merit in it. The whole credit of the apparatus is due to Professor Tyndall for the invention of a combined mechanical and chymical air filter for enabling men to work in places which without it they could not enter or live in."*

Who can doubt Shaw's bravery after reading that?

CHAPTER TEN
INVENTORS' CORNER
"The extinction and prevention of fire are a mystery"

Shaw's work with Tyndall is a reminder of the extent to which he was called on to test and give advice about a vast range of fire appliances, means of escape, building design and materials specifications. He had, of course, no scientific training and so had to rely on his practical mind, his commonsense, his charisma and, increasingly, his experience.

Sally Holloway has suggested that Shaw must have felt half London was sitting up until the small hours racking its brains to produce gadgets. These included a brass helmet containing a cistern of cold water which could be sprayed on a fireman's face when he ran through flames, spring-heeled boots for jumping safely from great heights, and scaling steps that could be fastened to a wall with large suction pads. Shaw himself wrote: *"Inventors are doubtless important persons and have contributed largely to the advancement and prosperity of the world; but in connection with fire brigades they have added fearfully to the expenses"*.

Naturally, he was in constant demand to advise on fire prevention. Bertie, Prince of Wales, it will be remembered summoned him to Sandringham, and the Lord Chamberlain's Office asked him in 1868 to look generally at the Royal Palaces. Then, in 1883, after several stately homes had been damaged by fire, the Queen invited him to report on Osborne House. With relief, she wrote: *"Captain Shaw . . . thinks Osborne one of the safest houses he knows, which is a great thing, and was intended to be so when it was built. He has made several suggestions for future precautions against fire"*, adding rather inconsequentially, *"he has 500 men under him, all sailors"*. For his services he received a massive ebonite clock with a suitable inscription. Osborne now has no record of his recommendations, but a cast iron water tank was installed in the south wing in the year of his visit and a drawing at the Public Record Office entitled *"Drainage and Fire Mains of the Kitchen Block 1883"* is no doubt another consequence of his inspection. THE FIREMAN of October 1891 referred to a scheme of protection for Osborne devised by Shaw and carried out by the Estate Surveyor of Works.

Four years later, the Queen's son-in-law, Prince Christian, was asked by the House Committee of the Governors of Royal Holloway College to invite Shaw to inspect there and report. After eight years the building was nearing completion and Shaw was very unhappy about what he found. He noted that its size (it was nearly 170 metres by about 115 metres) and its absence of party walls would make a complete system of protection so expensive as to be virtually impossible. But he did recommend: (i) a common round thread for all the outlet screws of the hydrants and fire cocks; (ii) the purchase of a manual fire engine and its positioning within a hundred yards of the main entrance; (iii) the distribution through the building of twenty-four corridor engines; (iv) the purchase of forty one-hundred-foot lengths of rubber hose; and (v) the making of arrangements with the water company for a constant supply at a pressure sufficient to

Above: PROFESSOR JOHN TYNDALL (1820-1893). Shaw asserted that Tyndall was largely responsible for the successful development of the smoke respirator. Like Shaw, Tyndall was largely self-taught. He became Superintendent of the Royal Institution. (Photo: National Portrait Gallery).

Right: TYNDALL'S SMOKE RESPIRATOR (1880s). Shaw described this as "a combined mechanical and chymical (sic) air filter for enabling men to work in places which without it they could not enter". (Photo: London Fire Brigade Museum).

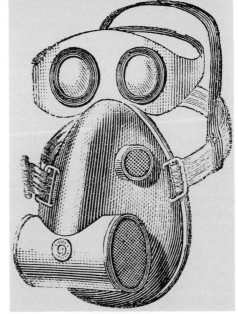

ROYAL HOLLOWAY COLLEGE. Prince Christian, Chairman of the Governors, invited Shaw to report on the fire protection arrangements when it was nearing completion. Shaw was horrified at what he found. (Photo: Mr. A. F. Kersting, AIIP FRPS).

reach the highest point of the building (the east and west wings each had six storeys and the towers were even higher). Shaw pointed out that all this would be expensive, but he could see no other way of giving anything like reasonable protection.

The Governors were much concerned about the report and recommended that initially only a part of one side of the building should be occupied and that about a quarter of the recommended appliances should be ordered. Prince Christian wrote to advise Shaw of the outcome of the meeting. *"We told the architect (W. H. Crossland, a pupil of George Gilbert Scott) to communicate with you about several things which are not very satisfactory. I hope he will be able to explain them to you, but I am bound to say that he failed to do so at our meeting"*.

The subject of dissension was the recommendation about the threads. The architect had provided V-shaped threads, partly at least because they were compatible with those of the nearby Egham Volunteer Fire Brigade. Shaw found the V-shape unacceptable, with its knife-edge that could be accidentally damaged if it hit anything hard and with the attendant difficulty of joining up in muddy conditions or on dark nights. The Governors sided with the architect on this and agreed to contribute £20 to the Egham Brigade on condition it drilled at the College at regular intervals. Shaw said he was not prepared to alter his recommendation. The round-thread screw was *"the screw of the future"* and, in any case, those

93

in residence at the College (the students were women) *"would have to depend more upon their own exertions than upon help afforded by local brigades"*. Ironically, at Girton the Lady Superintendent had tried to persuade Shaw to train the students in fire fighting, but he had refused.

Shaw received a continuous flow of requests from institutions for advice. When they were in London this was readily given, but when the Clerk of the Peace for Leicester invited him to advise on fire protection for the County Lunatic Asylum he offered to do so only if someone travelled to London with the plans. Two months earlier he had made the same response to Dr. Butler, the Headmaster of Harrow, but on being pressed to go there he reported to his Committee that *"as the Harrow School is one of the great public institutions of the country and it may be the wish of the Committee to oblige the Managers I think I can make arrangements to do what is wanted"*. The Committee assented.

Commercial organisations also sought his help. In 1868 he inspected the Princes Street premises of the Union Bank of London and was sent a cheque of ten guineas for his trouble. This he promptly returned, telling them: *"I never accept payment for services of this kind except through my employers . . . and in this case could not think of asking their permission . . . As my business is to reduce losses by fire to the minimum I always consider my time well bestowed when occupied to that end"*.

Charrington's Mile End brewery, the Royal Agricultural Hall, the Office of H. M. Works, the Royal Arsenal at Woolwich, the Royal Army Clothing Depot and the Royal Small Arms Factory at Enfield all used his expertise. He was also called in to advise the Royal Engineers who had been given the job of fire protection at the English part of the Paris Exhibition of 1867 and clearly had no idea what needed to be done. And, on New Year's Day 1886, when he was on a short visit to Brighton he inspected the Police Fire Brigade there, accompanied by Mrs. Shaw, gave them a favourable verdict and received three cheers for his trouble.

On a grander scale, the Viceroy of Egypt in January 1871 sought Shaw's advice on *"the protection of Cairo from fire"* — a tall order by any standards. Two years earlier, Shaw's friend the Duke of Sutherland had been in Egypt and had probably suggested the idea. In 1875 Shaw went there: the minutes of the Fire Brigade Committee suggest that he was out of the United Kingdom for nearly eight weeks. The Viceroy of Egypt clearly had more influence than the Clerk of the Peace for Leicester.

Occasionally Shaw showed an uncharacteristic modesty, as when a Mr. Clyatt, of Brixton, proposed in 1874 a new type of lightning conductor. Shaw reported to his Committee *"I do not understand enough about electricity to be able to say whether there is any necessity for lightning conductors on our buildings"*. But eight years later he did know enough about electricity to recommend to the Committee that the offer by the Edison Electric Light Company to provide the Brigade's headquarters with *"incandescent electric lighting"* for about £2,400 should be taken up. He advised that it would be *"a great advantage during the long nights of winter and also during foggy seasons"*, especially as the running costs would be only about £400 per annum compared with the charge for gas of

£466. The letter from the company, dated 31 October 1882, is the very first in the Committee's associated papers to be typed (entirely in upper case) and was accompanied by a 38-page booklet giving a complete technical description of the lighting system.

All the time, Shaw's mind was being exercised by the rapid advances being made in the development of materials. He often depended then on analogy, as when asked in 1871 to report on the inflammability of asphalt paving. He wrote:

"Even if it were in itself inflammable . . . no danger could arise from its use in the streets as clearly exemplified in the case of the wooden pavement in Chicago . . . which is absolutely uninjured (by the fire three months earlier that had laid waste four square miles), the part destroyed being only the side-walks which were made of light planking and raised on small joists above the ground."

But Shaw's technical knowledge was perhaps most severely tested by a constant succession of inventions concerned with fighting fires once they had broken out.

These included: *"a mixture of earth and water"* (W. H. Brown, Lyme Regis, 1873), which Shaw described as *"not at all practical"*; steam (T. H. Dunham, Boston, Massachusetts, 1877), the correspondent being advised that if he came to London to exhibit, the Board would be interested to attend; compressed air from a portable engine (Messrs. Vinning and Anderson, 1882); and the purification of air and so the extinguishing of fires without water (Dr. R. Neale, 1883) about which Shaw wrote that the principles were quite correct but *"the difficulties of carrying them into practice are much greater than Dr. Neale seems to suppose and . . . in the case of large buildings would be virtually impossible"*. Trinity House, having solicited his view on the efficiency of the Harden Star Hand Grenades for extinguishing fires (1885) was told that some experiments had seemed *"fairly successful"* but *"at the recent fire at the Inventions Exhibition . . . they appeared to have no effect whatever"*. Mr. Glover (1890) suggested that warehouse floors might be flooded with water when fire broke out; but Captain Shaw pointed out that there was no authority to require or even recommend such an idea and he could not express an opinion on its practicability. Mr. Sorby, of Copthall House, in the City, was advised that his idea that fire spread could be prevented if absorbent material such as blankets was thrown over the woodwork of the property adjoining a fire and then kept well-saturated with water would, at large fires, be quite impracticable.

One inventor, Robert Atkin (Wandsworth, 1891) claimed that his invention was dual purpose; it extinguished fires and exterminated vermin simultaneously. He was, he wrote, a master mariner of 47 years standing *"with varied experience in command of vessels over a large part of the globe"*. He had, he claimed, never been shipwrecked (presumably, the ultimate accolade). But he had been paralysed by *"hard Brain Work"* and had been an invalid for the past sixteen months. His patent involved the generation of carbonic acid when all windows and doors were closed to exclude oxygen; and people could be trained, he said, then to open the window and defy the gas because it was heavier than air. He claimed that by this means one man could do more to put out fires than a hundred men of the Brigade using conventional methods. He offered to sell a one-twentieth part of his patent to the London County Council for £25, the party purchasing having the option of becoming a director of the company when it was promoted. Shaw acknowledged that carbonic gas destroyed both fire and life but suggested *"the arrangement is not one suitable to the requirements of a public Fire Brigade"*.

Some correspondents were hard to put down. E. Hawkins (Bow Common, 1890) advocated the use of Monogram Blowers and Exhausting Fans as made by the Sturtevant Blower Company of Queen Victoria Street. These, he claimed, would extract smoke or draw the fire away from the building into the open air. On being invited to produce a working model he replied that he could not afford to do so. He continued:

"i am now 55 Years old and i Do not see that the Fire Brigade are any more able to extuinguish a fire than they were 40 years agoe . . . i would like you to consider wether is is a goodwaye to allwaye to keep useing the same old things and never to look for anything else to help or witch the best thing to do to Run all Over the Building after the flames or to Draw or Exaust the flames out of the Building and into the Oven (open?) air whare ther is nothing for them to feed on. If any Gentleman wd like to have a moddle macheine to give an idea of what air would do i know whare there is a capital working Model worth 30 shillings to be bought for 10 shillings it would stand on the table and can be worked by hand."

More complaisant was R. Topham (Kentish Town Road, 1883) who drew attention to a liquid which would *"extinguish fire, destroy the explosive power of gunpowder and render wood uninflammable"*, but then asked that any demonstration might be deferred as *"at present my discovery is a failure, but if I should be able to perfect the discovery I will communicate with you"*.

Shaw showed more interest in a proposal by Messrs. Atkins & Co. (1873) for impregnating water being pumped onto a fire with a gas that would not support combustion. Shaw told his Committee that the process had been tried many times and in many countries with only partial success, but that Messrs. Atkins' representative claimed that their proposal involved a new gas made on scientific principles which could not fail. The firm worked at the idea for another five years and then sought to demonstrate it, explaining that the apparatus was a small stove-like vessel that could be attached to any part of the fire engine, its contents were ignited and the products of combustion were then drawn into the pump and ejected, in the right proportion, with water from the hose branch. On contact with the fire, it was claimed, *"the gases expand and . . . surround and envelope the burning materials . . . and by . . . cutting off the supply of oxygen the combustion ceases. The water . . . is only used as a carrier"*. However, on trial, Shaw found that the gas broke up the jet of water and he had to disconnect the system.

Other inventors with perhaps an engineering rather than a chemistry bent assumed that water would continue to be used for fire fighting and concentrated their energies on its more efficient use.

New types of couplings proved especially difficult to design effectively because they needed to be inexpensive, efficient and easy to connect. On nozzles, however, Shaw had no doubt. When asked to comment on the Prosser Spreading Nozzle (1873), Shaw reported: *"All nozzles unfortunately spread the water, and I once devoted my best energies for nearly a year to a series of experiments for the purpose of ascertaining the form of nozzle which would spread least, and that form we now have in use, but it is only under favourable circumstances that this completely serves its purpose of delivering a solid stream. The least jerk or shake of the branch or the smallest obstruction of any kind instantly converts the solid stream into a film or spray . . . The spreading of the stream . . . is one of the difficulties we are always endeavouring to avoid and not an object which we would wish to accomplish."*

A curious instance where Shaw's advice was disregarded was in connection with the purchase of respirators: paradoxically in view of his own testing of them in conjunction with Professor Tyndall. A Mr. Applegarth persuaded Shaw (1875) on behalf of Messrs. Denayrouze of Cannon Street and of Paris, a firm that made diving equipment, to look at a respirator they had produced. But Shaw reported that until the respirator *"was improved in some of the most material points"* and also reduced considerably in cost he could not see it being brought into general use in the Brigade. After further tests a couple of months later, the firm was asked to quote for 120 sets, which they did at £2 16s (£2.80) each, and were requested to provide one for thorough examination so that the men would know all about it and have complete confidence in it. George Edwards, a member of the Committee and its Chairman-elect, pressed that the 120 sets should be bought at once, but more prudent counsels suggested that only twelve sets should be purchased until they could be tested in operational conditions. Captain Shaw went further. He said that the Denayrouze respirators were no improvement on what was already available. The Committee accordingly deferred making a decision pending a further investigation. When this had been undertaken, and at the next meeting, Edwards said that another member of the Committee, William Newton, wished to be present but was engaged at the House of Commons on the Metropolitan Board's Gas Bill. Curiously, it was agreed for this reason to adjourn the matter until the next meeting, an especially odd decision as Newton had attended only three of the last fifteen meetings of the Committee. At that next meeting Shaw again advised strongly against Denayrouze's apparatus. He considered that the chamber and facepiece were worth only one-fifth of the value of those made within the Brigade. There were design objections as well, he said: the nose as well as the mouth needed to be fully available for breathing when heavy work was being done, but it was not; a part of the apparatus would rest in the mouth, thus causing an injurious accumulation of saliva and mucus; the whole apparatus should be capable of being put on and taken off in one piece, but it was not; and the materials and workmanship gave little confidence.

97

DENAYROUZE'S SMOKE RESPIRATOR (1880s). Against Shaw's advice 120 sets were bought by the Brigade. He regarded them as badly-designed, poorly-made and much over-priced. He refused to use them. (Photo: London Fire Brigade Museum).

Despite these firmly stated professional and technical objections, Newton moved and Edwards seconded that 120 sets should be bought and it was resolved accordingly. But that was not the end of the matter for when, nine months later, the Admiralty enquired of the Fire Brigade Committee about Denayrouze's apparatus Shaw reported that they had not been used at any fire and that until certain alterations had been made to the design he was *"unwilling to order the respirator to be used by any man under my command"*. The apparatus continued unused, because five years later Shaw reported that one of his own Engineers had designed a head covering with valves and other arrangements which would probably enable the Board to utilise the pipes purchased seven years previously from Messrs. Denayrouze.

The enthusiasm of the Committee to purchase 120 sets of an apparatus that Shaw had advised was unsafe to use contrasts with their action when, in 1879, he recommended the purchase of twelve smoke-excluding masks (made by Messrs. W. J. Barrow & Sons) which, he claimed, would be *"a valuable addition to our present appliances of this kind"*. They agreed only to purchase six.

Some of the most bizarre inventions (and inventors) that Shaw had to investigate and report on were, however, concerned with rescue and escape from fire.

G. Elsden (Lincoln's Inn Fields, 1867) designed escape ladders. Shaw reported:

> *"He is a very poor man and lives on an upper floor of a small house . . . At the door there is a board . . . 'G. Elsden — repairs to boots and shoes neatly executed'. He has no workshop of any kind, but he states that if he gets an order he can give satisfactory security for its proper execution, and as this estimate is obviously the work of a man who understands something of the business, and as many new Fire Escapes must be provided . . . I recommend one be ordered from him."*

Shaw showed less enthusiasm about a self-lowering domestic fire escape, the invention of a Dr. Bennett Gilbert (Gipsy Road, Lower Norwood, 1870) and manufactured by G. Shrewsbury (of the same place). The leaflet Shaw was sent described it in these terms:

> *"The appearance is that of an elegant sunshade or verandah placed over any window . . . In the case of a fire a small cord which hangs down inside the bedroom is pulled, thereby lifting a large collapsing bag (capable of holding 2 or more persons) from within the verandah, and allowing it to fall into position so that anyone can easily enter it from the window."*

Shaw reported wearily that it had nothing to distinguish it from thousands of others that had been submitted to him during the previous ten years; obviously any that were really self-acting would make access to a house as easy as egress from it; this particular one would anyway require skilled labour to operate it; and if one had to be put up at every window the cost would be very heavy. A not entirely dissimilar idea from D. Pattison (Limehouse, 1885) was described by Shaw as seeming to be more suitable for the removal of goods than the saving of life.

Later, a more sophisticated version of Dr. Bennet Gilbert's idea was put up by E. Weavers (Diss, Norfolk, 1889), with his Acme Fire Escape and Life Saving Apparatus. For this, a tramway of iron rods, bracketed to the house, was fixed right round the building just above the topmost windows. On this tramway there ran an escape, enabling one to transfer from one part of the building to another. Additionally, there was a lift built into the wall of the house. In this, people could lower themselves to the ground. It normally rested at ground floor level and had a locked door (the key being with the nearest policeman) to prevent illegal entry. Unlocking the door activated an alarm bell in the house and at the fire station. The lift, it was pointed out, could also enable firemen to carry escape ladders to any window. The apparatus could, at other times, be used for cleaning, painting or repairing the building. Shaw pointed out, as he had so often, that such an arrangement would be at the discretion of the private householder and was of no service to a public fire brigade.

Much simpler, though expensive to construct and certainly outside the authority of the Fire Brigade to insist upon, was a system of continuous iron balconies outside the windows of all bedrooms of tall buildings. The idea was put to the Fire Brigade Committee, with great humility, by Madame Alexandrine, Principal of the Millinery Department at Messrs. Jay's Mourning Warehouse in Regent Street (1888). She said that she wrote hoping that the letter would be read *"although only from a woman"*. What she had to say is horrifying in its implications.

"Mr. Jay", she said, *"in whose desirable employment I am, has a magnificent building in Swallow Buildings, Oxford Street, of 5 floors supposed to be Fire-Proof — the sleeping accommodation for young people in his Establishment. I being the principal of one of the departments and wishing to confer on me a great favour — a room on the first floor was selected for me. Unfortunately it was situated over a shop . . . occupied by a Chandler — the room was so impregnated with the smell of Petroleum and the doubt in my mind so great from an explosion coupled with the knowledge that the premises were locked at night after the young people were in and the keys taken away — that I became seriously ill — and . . . have been obliged to take a room out where I go to sleep . . . If the proposition of a balcony could be arranged . . . it would bring tranquility to the minds of **thousands** not only to those that are actually in Houses of Business but to Parents and Relatives."*

She concluded her letter, which must have been the most humble one ever written to the Fire Brigade Committee: *"With many compliments — and praying you to pardon the very great liberty such an insignificant person as myself has dared to take in addressing you — I respectfully remain your most obedient servant"*.

Thomas Nugent, a Walthamstow schoolmaster (1880), favoured a quite different approach to the problem of escape. He suggested a tank that could be taken to the scene of the fire in two parts, screwed together, and then filled with water. Into this, anyone who was trapped might jump. The

Committee suggested, gently, that what was proposed was *"not so convenient and suitable"* as the fire escapes currently in use. R. Rayner (Stepney, 1881) advocated sheets of sailcloth being kept in locked boxes at corner houses but the Committee pointed out that every fire escape already carried a jumping sheet and that it would be difficult to educate the public in the use of such a facility. Somewhere in between the two extremes of lowering oneself beneath *"an elegant sunshade"* and simply jumping into a sheet or a tank full of cold water came the suggestion of Alfred Jones (Islington, 1886) that pieces of wrought iron should be cast into the water or gutter pipes, and left projecting about six inches on either side. His extremely crude drawing shows them, running like a series of steps the full length of a downpipe; an open invitation to burglary one would have thought.

More AVANT GARDE perhaps was a rocket life-saving apparatus (Woolven, Ede & Co., West Brighton, 1887). This required from two to four staff drilled in its use so had no value to a householder but could, it was claimed, deposit people some distance from the burning building with great rapidity but no jolting. It could also be used to raise a person from the ground to the top of a building. There was a cradle that could hold two adults or four children; and from the figures given the speed of descent must have been about 8½ miles per hour. Shaw saw it demonstrated, but claimed he had seen similar before and it was not, anyway, suitable for use by the Brigade. Thomas Nugent (Clapton Park, 1888, but presumably the Walthamstow schoolmaster of 1880 who had suggested the water tank form of escape) had perhaps something similar in mind to Woolven, Ede's rocket apparatus when he solicited Shaw's interest in what he said might be called a parachute. But he failed to appear before the Committee to demonstrate it when invited to do so.

It can be seen that Shaw needed a more than superficial knowledge of chemistry, hydraulics, building structures, engineering, electricity, ventilation and human nature. Then, too, there were during his thirty years in London considerable advances in the methods used to summon the Brigade to fires, although in this field he was very much in the hands of organisations and firms that were advertising their products not specifically for the Fire Service but for more general use.

At the time of the Fire Engine Establishment, messages about fires had been carried by runners, who received a reward if they were first with the news. In addition to these runners the brigade had depended on watch towers. Every station had one, and the firemen took turns of duty looking out for fires. Each tower had a compass; and the engines would often be ordered to a fire on a compass bearing.

In this connection, the River had presented a particular problem. One could get the direction right, but be on the wrong bank. For example, a call in 1871 was given at Headquarters by a policeman from London Bridge, for a light showing eastwards. Stations covering both banks of the River were asked by telegraph where they thought it was. Several engines were despatched along the north bank but a few minutes later a message was received from the south side that the fire was at Bull Head Dock,

Rotherhithe. Having thus established how to get to the fire Shaw was then able to despatch a very large force that was standing by, and reported, subsequently: *"I went myself . . . with the first party. The road being clear, the engine must have travelled at very nearly . . . 20 miles an hour".*

The first British fire brigade to use the telegraph had been that of Glasgow, in 1861; but Braidwood had refused to permit it to be used in London. He was justified in this in so far as the system was fraught with problems. It was in the hands of private speculative companies, engaged heavily in advertising against each other, and lacking the technical staff to fulfil effectively their extravagant claims. The instruments themselves were complicated in their construction, uncertain in their action, and difficult to operate; their cost was, initially, almost prohibitive. The agents for the companies ranged from *"needy broken-down merchants' clerks"* to commercial Members of Parliament and even speculative peers.

But, as Shaw later commented: *"Progress can only be DELAYED by stupid persons, it cannot altogether be stopped"*; and the day eventually arrived when telegraphic communication with alphabetical instruments was established between each District Superintendent and all stations in his District. After that, from 1880, many of the stations were surrounded with lines of call points from which anyone could call an engine without having to rush to the station. This proved a tremendous benefit, despite the inevitable hoax calls.

There were however unexpected difficulties. For instance, the Drapers Company insisted that they had a freehold from the centre of the earth to the canopy of heaven, so that wayleave was necessary for any telegraph wires. Then, too, the first great span over the Thames sagged and was carried away by the masts of barges and so had to be replaced with a stronger and lighter wire.

Sometimes, the arrangement for calling engines even when the telegraph was in use was most complicated. For instance, when fire broke out at High Street, Sydenham, the Sydenham engine arrived in thirteen minutes but the Lewisham engine took forty-three. This was because there was no telegraphic communication between Sydenham and Lewisham; so, a telegram had to be sent to Lothbury, from there a messenger to Watling Street, then a telegram from Watling Street to Kennington, another from Kennington to Greenwich, and another from Greenwich to Lewisham — four telegrams and one runner in all.

In 1877, Alexander Graham Bell demonstrated a new invention, the telephone. Its first showing in England was to a marvelling audience at the Queen's Theatre when a pianist played HOME SWEET HOME and THE BLUE BELLS OF SCOTLAND over two thousand yards of wire. Indeed, the original use of the telephone seemed to be as the basis for a public broadcasting system rather than as a means of person-to-person communication. The following year the India Rubber, Gutta Percha and Telegraph Works Company was claiming to the Board of Works that it had been appointed sole manufacturer of the telephone, a statement that left the Board quite unmoved. Almost coincidentally the National Telephone Company was formed and, a year later, was operating in

London, being taken over eventually by the General Post Office.

Reporting to his Committee on a letter from the General Telephone Agency Company, in October 1879, Shaw wrote:

"There has . . . been placed before me . . . a proposal to establish a really trustworthy means of communication by means of a loud-speaking telephone . . . I was not myself in the house when the machine was brought, but my assistants . . . inform me that everyone in the watch room could hear what was said. We shall know very soon whether this was the ordinary practice or merely the result of accidental circumstances . . . From what I have heard and seen there seems to be no room for doubt that within a very short time we shall be able to use the telephone for our purpose; but we must make sure of getting a clear sound."

So quickly did the phone prove its effectiveness that less than five years later Shaw was obtaining estimates from the Post Office for the cost of replacing all the existing telegraph lines throughout the Brigade (43 in all) with telephonic communication. Only the parlous state of the funds allocated to the Metropolitan Board of Works prevented that happening immediately.

More generally throughout his period of service in London, few meetings of the Fire Brigade Committee passed without Shaw being asked to report on some new invention or idea. Many had great potential but lacked the right design details or awaited the invention of new (perhaps lighter or less flammable) materials before they could be effective; others were copies, being posed as new ideas; others were of use, perhaps, to a householder or a factory owner but not to a fire brigade; others were ineffective or monumentally impracticable. Sometimes the inventor or his representative could afford only to make a scale model of what he had in mind and then solicited (unsuccessfully) the wherewithal to make a life-size one. Just occasionally, Shaw was pestered by people who were wasting public time and money or were even on the fringe of lunacy.

A person who came into one or other of these last categories was Matthew Callaghan. He first came to notice by writing to the Lord Mayor in January 1883, from Saltoun Road, London SW. That personage returned his letter and Callaghan, nearly three years later, sent it with a covering note to the Fire Brigade Committee. It drew attention to the huge financial losses incurred by fire and continued: *"To prevent the destruction of property by fire would be a benefit second to none confered (SIC) on England which without the fear of failure I can do"*. Much later on in his very long letter he suggested that a Jury of twelve (the Lord Mayor, 2 Merchants, 3 Insurance Directors, 3 Bank Directors, 1 Wholesale Manufacturing Chemist and Druggist and 2 Police Commissioners) should determine two questions: *"First the merit of what I confidently and without the fear of faction state to do, viz to save the property of Merchants and Manufacturers from fire; second, the Jury being satisfied as to this fact, that I should as a public benefactor get full and ample compensation"*.

Eight months later, in May 1889, by which time the London County

Council had taken over the Fire Brigade and Callaghan was living in Palace Road, Upper Norwood, he wrote offering for sale a *"secret to ensure the preservation of merchandise from fire"*. It was agreed that the letter should lie on the table, but five months later he again wrote asking if he might attend Committee to express his views on fire prevention. Shaw was asked to report and, at the next meeting, it was resolved that Callaghan's request should not be met.

Within a few months, in February 1890, he had written again, this time from Oakfield Road, Croydon. On this occasion he intimated that unless the Council agreed to pay him an acceptable sum for his remedy for preventing fire his discovery would not be divulged and would be *"for ever closed"*. Again, the Committee was unmoved.

Finally, Callaghan named his price. Writing from New Street, Jersey, in April 1891, he again deplored the huge fire losses which, he had been told by a gentleman in Jersey who was an importer and exporter, amounted over sixty years *"with interest and compound interest"* to a sum sufficient to extinguish the National Debt. Having, he said, been told previously that he would get no compensation he had given up the question but, having now heard the extent of the country's loss, he had decided to make *"a final appeal"*. Captain Shaw and his fine body of men, he wrote, are not to blame, for *"the extinction and prevention of fire are a mystery"*. His secret discovery could be theirs for £500,000. The letter was received without comment and, so far as is known, Callaghan took his secret to his grave.

CHAPTER ELEVEN

AT HOME WITH THE SHAWS
"Captain Shaw is EN RAPPORT with the firemen of the whole world"

There seems to be only one photograph of Shaw with his children: it shows him being rowed, possibly on the Serpentine, by his two daughters. He was essentially a man's man and there is no evidence that he showed any particular interest in his children or, more broadly, in family life. His children's upbringing was no doubt left to his wife and to whatever nursery staff he could afford.

His offspring later showed a marked reluctance to marry. The eldest child, Eyre Massey, was seventy-four before he ceased to be a bachelor; Bernard Vidal was thirty-two; Anna, Clarina and Cecil never married at all; only Zarita was married when still in her twenties. Many references to Fire Brigade events refer to *"Miss Shaw"* and this may be taken as meaning Anna, although Zarita had sufficient admiration for her father to compile two massive scrapbooks of newspaper cuttings about his resignation.

There were three grandchildren: Bernard and Eyre Massey, both sons of Bernard Vidal; and Geraldine, who was Zarita's daughter. This Eyre Massey died of wounds when a Lieutenant in the Middlesex Regiment in World War I; Geraldine died in 1975. Bernard is still alive and in his nineties. None of the three had children so that, in spite of his having six children himself, Shaw had no great-grandchildren.

Of Captain Shaw's wife, Anna, we know little except that she was quite wealthy and very kind-hearted. She must also have been long-suffering: her husband's massive dedication to his work, at all hours of the day and night, must have left him with little time to devote to her or the children. Also, having lived in Torquay which she loved so much, Anna must have found London irksome in any season. In winter, the fog and the cold must have been quite alien to her Portuguese background; in summer, as we shall see shortly, the neighbours were troublesome. Further, *'living over the shop'* meant that she was surrounded almost continuously with the paraphenalia and the noise of horses, men, firebells and communications systems.

When the Shaws first came to London in 1861 the Headquarters of the Fire Brigade Establishment were in the City, in Watling Street. The site comprised four houses which served as an engine house, a stable, a watchroom, an office and apartments for the Chief and a few of his staff. There was no workshop, no drill ground, no space for examining or testing engines and no lecture/reading room for the men. Repairs to the engines were carried out in an old warehouse, drill on a rough piece of common land, engine-testing in the street before daylight, and instruction of the men in a loft, or in the open air or in Shaw's private apartments. These apartments were old-fashioned and cramped and there were complaints of leaking roofs, dirty ceilings, a kitchen range out of order and gas fittings that were defective.

At the time of the 1871 census, Shaw was registered as living at 66 to 69

CAPTAIN SHAW'S WIFE (1827-1897). She was a successful hostess to all (including Royalty) who came to Brigade Headquarters and was noted for her kindness and generosity to the firemen's families and to the poor of the district. (Photo: Sir Bernard Shaw).

Above: 'LA REINE' (1885). Shaw relaxes whilst the ladies (presumably his daughters Anna and Zarita) row. It is the only surviving photograph of him with his family. (Photo: Sir Bernard Shaw).

Below: CAPTAIN SHAW'S CARRIAGE(1880s). The Shaws had only a small number of female domestic servants but of course had access to almost unlimited man- and horse-power. (Photo: London Fire Brigade Library).

Watling Street, between 65 Watling Street and 11 to 13 Bear Lane, that is at the Metropolitan Fire Brigade's Headquarters. In the census he described himself, simply, as *"fireman"* and twenty years later, at the time of his retirement, the DAILY TELEGRAPH said of him that he had been as proud as his men to call himself a fireman, and it was that pride in the Brigade that had made his men love him.

To the census enumerator he gave his correct age of 43. Also at home that night were his wife, Anna, who was the same age and children Bernard 13, Anna 12, Clarina 10, Cecil 8 and Zarita 7. Eyre Massey, the eldest son, was presumably away at boarding school. There were only three servants, all spinsters. They included a cook of thirty and a housemaid of twenty-six; as both of them had been born in Torquay, we may reason that they had been recruited from or through the Dove household there. The third servant, a nurse of twenty-four, was a German. The complete absence of male servants suggests that many tasks (as groom, coachman, gardener, valet) were undertaken by firemen. Much later the Shaws had the services of Florrie, Millie and Beatrice Farrow. These seem to have been *'looked after'* when Shaw died and later they presented various Shaw items to the Fire Brigade Museum. One of the Farrows, Millie, was left £10 by Shaw's daughter, Anna, for every complete year she had been in Anna's service or in that of Captain Shaw; and Clarina referred to both Millie and Beatrice in his will. This was witnessed in 1937, so the Farrows must have served different members of the family for very many years. In retirement, they lived in Sussex.

The 1871 census also named four firemen and their families who were living in married quarters at Watling Street. Three of them had a daughter apiece and one a niece. Alfred Holmsden became a Superintendent six years later; Sidney Fogden became an Engineer in 1875 and, thirteen years later, was one of nine officers and men commended for their skill in saving twelve lives at a fire at the Bay Tree Tavern, St. Swithin's Lane; William Thomas Smart, a Sub Engineer, was totally incapacitated after being badly injured at a fire at a large flour mill in St. George's-in-the-East just before Christmas 1876. Also living at Headquarters were two coachmen and twelve bachelor firemen, one of them being William Chalkley who would become a Superintendent by the time Shaw retired in 1891.

In the search for more suitable and spacious premises than those at Watling Street, it was Shaw's hope that they would be at the water's edge, between the Temple and Southwark Bridge on the north bank, or between Waterloo and Southwark Bridges on the south. Then, with a floating pier, it would be possible for fire floats to exploit the river more fully than in the past when, at some stages of the tide, it had taken half an hour to get the men on board. For his private use, he told the Committee, he required a house of about twenty rooms (including hall, kitchen and cellars). Further his residence needed to be near the workshops so that he could supervise the work closely. His residential requirements for his officers were much more modest: four rooms for the officer-in-charge of the station, three for each of three Second Class Engineers and two each for six married men.

The site of the Fire Brigade workshops in Queen Victoria Street was looked at, but was thought to be inadequate. An acre of land on the Albert Embankment was discarded because it was insufficiently central. There was in fact considerable and powerful opposition to the removal of Headquarters out of the City at all as it was felt that the valuable risks there might then be neglected. But a move somewhere was inescapable.

Eventually, a site was found in Southwark Bridge Road. It lay outside the City, it was on the *'wrong'* side of the River and it was not at the water's edge. But it made up for these deficiencies by its spaciousness. It had been part of the Winchester Park estate and, about 1770, a Thomas Finch had opened up a pleasure garden on the land claiming that there was a spring with medicinal properties. That project failed after a few years and St. Saviour's Parish then erected a workhouse there. In due course, Rawlinson Harris, MP for Southwark, bought the workhouse and converted it into a hat factory. To the east of it he built, in 1820, a pair of semi-detached town houses of considerable size, one for himself and the other to be leased to his two brothers. The houses had a lawn in front, but any pleasure must have been diminished by the presence of open sewers, one of which was where Southwark Bridge Road now runs. Then, or later, the building was named Winchester House.

It was Alfred Pocock, a new member of the Fire Brigade Committee, who first drew attention to the site in early May 1876. The Board of Works architect, George Vulliamy, reported that the property was worth £35,000 and that some houses and cottages on part of the land might fetch £8,000. Conversion of the buildings might cost between £8,000 and £10,000. Shaw went to the site to inspect it and reported back that if a riverside site was impossible this would be the next best thing. He was doubtless attracted to the pair of semi-detached town houses which, if combined, had the makings of an excellent residence, with a kitchen in the basement, a hall, drawing room, dining room and space for a private office on the ground floor and eight bedrooms on the two floors above. The north wing (part of the former workhouse) would provide a room for four Superintendents, a waiting room, a watch room and lecture room; and the west block (the remainder of the former workhouse) contained eighty-three rooms above basement level. It was proposed to add to this, at the southern extremity of the residence, a new engine house, stables and workshops, facing onto Southwark Bridge Road.

Negotiations were soon completed in the sum of £35,000, plus a further £100 for preventing the property going to auction. Conversion and new building work soon commenced and the new engine house (now B23 station) still bears the legend *"MFB 1878 MBW"*. The lowest tenderer, Messrs. Hook and Oldrey, came up against various site difficulties, not least of which was the presence of an unforeseen burial ground, and the discovery that the north and west blocks rested on piles that had decayed whilst the house itself had been partly and insufficiently underpinned. This increased the cost of the building works from a tendered figure of £27,798 to a final agreed figure of £35,000. On completion, the Fire Brigade Committee agreed to carpet the Chief Officer's study and to provide carpets, curtains and blinds for his hall and dining and drawing rooms. The new station was formally declared open on 1 June 1878. It remained the Fire Brigade Headquarters until 1937.

The Shaws were no doubt delighted with the spaciousness and elegance of their new home. But they soon discovered that the locality left a lot to be desired. Less than a month after the official opening, the Architect reported to the Fire Brigade Committee that the inhabitants of nearby Durrant Place were causing great annoyance to the Brigade by climbing the perimeter walls and throwing stones and filth into the yard at the rear of the building. This seems to have been a local custom, for the police station at Stone's End, less than half a mile to the south, had had similar trouble; and there it had been found necessary to raise the wall to a height of eighteen feet. The Committee agreed to have the Headquarters wall built up to fifteen feet and to have broken bottle glass set in the coping, at a total estimated cost of £95. Much of the wall (and glass) is still there.

Six months later it was reported that the locals were using the gateways into the escape yard as a public urinal, especially after they left the public house opposite. This was alleviated at a cost of £40 by the provision of light iron gates and railings. Then, four months after that, Shaw sought the Committee's support in persuading the Police to stamp out behaviour *"of the most revolting and disgusting kind"*, the cause being ascribed, particularly, to the public house on the corner of Orange Street (since renamed Copperfield Street) and Southwark Bridge Road (the building remains but it has ceased to be a public house).

The local Police Superintendent's report was not encouraging. The houses in Orange Street and Pepper Street on one side of Southwark Bridge Road and the district known as The Mint, on the other, were occupied *"by some of the lowest class of persons whose language and demeanour one to another generally is objectionable, and often offensive to the ears of respectable people"*. During the summer months, he continued *"the doors and windows are usually open, in addition to which the occupants of the Common Lodging House, many of which are of the lowest description, congregate and lounge about the doorsteps . . . in the evening, and frequently the greater part of the night"*. He pointed out, however, that the Police could not interfere unless some specific act of disorder was committed. The Committee suggested that the matter might be helped if the public house licence were not renewed.

Two summers later, it was the offensive smells from the houses that caused Shaw to complain. He suggested that the Board might buy all the property on the fire station side of Orange Street, pull down any houses that were a nuisance and select tenants for any that remained. The properties had lately come into the hands of the Ecclesiastical Commissioners and, shortly, the St. Saviour's District Board served notices for the nuisance to be abated. The houses along the frontage of the former Orange Street between Pepper Street and Southwark Bridge Road, on the fire station side, still remain. They are named Winchester Cottages.

It is extraordinary that Bertie, Prince of Wales, could take foreign princes to supper at Winchester House and that his wife and daughters could visit the Shaws' home in such a locality. It is a reminder of how close, cheek by jowl, affluence and utter poverty could co-exist in Victorian towns. It is not even as though the Board spent money lavishly on home comforts. It refused, as was said earlier, to have electricity laid on; it also turned down Shaw's recommendation for the adoption of *"Dr. Clarke's process of pumping water to prevent deposits accumulating in the hot water pipes"*, presumably some kind of water softening. The argument that this would greatly diminish expenditure on soap and soda was disregarded.

The principal rooms of the house, the dining room and the drawing room on the ground floor, both had an area of about 46 square metres (the size of a typical school classroom of the present day). The dining room was oblong in shape, being about 8½ metres long and 5½ metres wide, and with windows on both long walls since the house is only one room deep on this floor. This room, and the drawing room in the north-east corner of the house, must have been overshadowed before long on the east side by a huge block of men's quarters erected parallel with Winchester House on the Southwark Bridge Road frontage. But this block was bombed during World War II and subsequently demolished so that there is, once again, open space between the front of Winchester House and the road. In what was the courtyard between the house and the now-demolished block there stands an AILANTHUS GLANDULA, one of six such trees imported from Japan in the 1840's. On the west side of the house, the dining room windows look down on the drill yard, beyond which is the main block of the old workhouse. These windows must have provided an excellent vantage point for any visitors to the house wishing to watch the men at drill; from a specially constructed balcony there was an even better view.

The hall and staircase (the latter with cast iron balusters) are modest in size but, it must be remembered, they were built to serve only half the present house. They led up to ten rooms on the first and second floors, the main bedrooms being of about 25 square metres.

The house was therefore reasonably spacious and certainly had sufficient rooms for the numerous Shaw children and for the servants. But its limitations are obvious. It was in the heart of a very impoverished neighbourhood and in the immediate vicinity of at least one really disreputable public house; it was overshadowed on both sides, east and west, by tall buildings occupied by the Fire Brigade; it was immediately adjacent to the drill yard and within a few hundred feet of an engine station, with all the attendant noise; and it was really a pair of semi-detached town houses that had been converted into one dwelling. But, as one might expect of him, Shaw contrived to live there in some style whilst, at the same time, surrounded by memorabilia connected with fires.

A contemporary visitor noted:

"In the drawing room is an admirable statuette of Captain Shaw by Count Gleichen, the centre of a group of agreeable testimonials of regard from distinguished personages. Even this sacred refuge contains photographs and drawings of conflagrations. The dining room is lined with pictures of similar character: ships like the BOMBAY, burnt to the water's edge in an incredibly short space of

"TO THE EXTINGUISHER FROM SOME OF HIS CHUMS. 1870". This statuette, by Count Gleichen, stood in Captain Shaw's drawing-room at Headquarters. Gleichen was another amateur fireman. (Photo: London Fire Brigade Library).

time, and other records of colossal disasters. The study, occupied by Captain Shaw alone, is a storehouse of maps and plans, recording the introduction of his system into foreign cities, notably Cairo and Alexandria, both organised by himself in person. Overhead, too, is a library of the literature of fires — figures, plans and reports from the big cities, for Captain Shaw is EN RAPPORT with the firemen of the whole world."

There is something of a mystery surrounding the subsequent movements of the statuette. The above description indicates that is was at Winchester House in Shaw's time. But in 1921 Count Gleichen's daughter, Feodora (also a noted sculptor) offered, to the London Fire Brigade, *"a statuette of the late Captain Shaw which was made by my father . . . a good many years ago and which has now returned into my possession"*. There is only one Gleichen statuette at the Fire Brigade Museum and it might be that after Shaw's death the piece somehow reverted to Count Gleichen's family and was, in 1921, being offered back once more to the Brigade. However Feodora, in her letter to the Fire Brigade Committee, said that the Brigade might already have *"a replica"*, in which case her offer would be of no interest. But the Brigade accepted the item and the statuette was delivered to Hammersmith Fire Station by Feodora's nephew who was living nearby. She thought that the statuette might have been made about 1879 or 1880 (it is dated 1870) and said that it was in the hands of Lady Dalton-Fitzgerald, who herself described it as *"a copy"*. Feodora said she had intended to obtain £5 for *"each"* of the statuettes but would be glad to give the Brigade this one, so there must have been a number in existence. The piece bore the explicit inscription: *"The Extinguisher from some of his chums"*. Feodora told the Committee that her father had taken part a great deal as an amateur fireman, *"accompanying Captain Shaw to many fires"*.

The Fire Brigade Museum, in Shaw's former house, also has the clock presented to Shaw by Queen Victoria in 1883 for the advice he gave on fire prevention at Osborne (presented to the Brigade by his daughter, Zarita, in 1938); and a handsomely-carved swagger stick in ebony, topped with Shaw's own likeness (donated to the Brigade by the Farrow sisters, and restored by the Victoria and Albert Museum, also in 1938).

Descriptions survive of Christmas festivities at Headquarters with Captain Shaw descending from the mountain to address his flock rather than, so far as we know, from his reindeer to play the part of Father Christmas. In 1891, for instance, the festivities were spread over three evenings, one for children and the other two for the members of the Brigade and their friends. The children had music, sweets and food, and about 300 toys distributed by Miss Anna; the adults a more substantial diet of music, songs and dances and a brief address from Shaw. *"The expense"*, pointed out THE FIREMAN, *"comes not from the rates but from the contributions of friends of the Brigade, and the Chief Officer and his family are among the most liberal donors to the fund"*.

It may be said, then, that the Shaw family lived in quite spacious and even elegant accommodation, adequate enough to enable them to entertain British and foreign Royalty, despite the poverty and roughness of the immediate neighbourhood; that they normally had only about three servants living in but that much work customarily done by male servants was doubtless carried out by firemen detailed to do it; that Shaw was almost certainly more interested in fires and fire-fighting than in his children; that Mrs. Shaw created a considerable social life for herself with her Wednesday afternoon 'at homes'; that she and her daughter Anna showed much kindness to the firemen and their families; but that family life was dominated by the presence and the sounds of firemen being trained, of engines being summoned, and of maintenance work being carried out on the numerous appliances located on three sides of the family home. It was, for Mrs. Shaw, a far cry from Torquay or the Portuguese Algarve. She may well have been lonely, despite all the activity around her; and perhaps no more so than when her husband came to be a leading figure in a nationally famous divorce suit.

CHAPTER TWELVE

THE COLIN CAMPBELL DIVORCE CASE
"Sounds were heard from the dining room which caused remarks among the servants"

In 1886 Shaw was cited in a much-publicised divorce case. It was a society affair, the husband being the son of a Duke, and the other co-respondents a Duke, a General and the wife's own medical adviser.

Shaw must have realised the dangers. The publicity would be embarrassing, the legal costs not insignificant, and his shadowy reputation as a ladies' man might prejudice the jury against him. Further, he was not sufficiently high in society to share the benefits of immunity from condemnation. As Anita Leslie has written in EDWARDIANS IN LOVE, *"marriage was the cement which held up the whole social edifice. To sin in secret was one story, to shake the home by getting into the newspapers or law courts another"*. The middle classes had become, increasingly, the dominant force in Victorian MORES. Sexual misdoings, reported in a by-and-large hostile press could mean complete social undoing. Further, divorce suits received great prominence because they were so uncommon. Only 7,321 divorces were granted between 1858 and 1887 and, although increasing, the divorce rate was only 15 per million in 1880, and in that year only 116 divorced people remarried.

The couple at the centre of the case were Lord and Lady Colin Campbell. He was the fifth son of the 8th Duke of Argyll and was thirty-three years old. Tutored for the Indian Civil Service (his father was Secretary of State), he became a barrister and, at the time of his marriage five years earlier, had been MP for Argyllshire.

His wife was Gertrude Elizabeth, the younger daughter of Edmund (or Edmond, it is spelt both ways in the reference books) Blood of County Clare and Thurloe Square, South Kensington. Educated in Italy and France, she was well-known in society and was referred to during the divorce hearing as *"a very popular, attractive and accomplished lady"*. She was a person of undeniable attainments: she had written an illustrated story book for children that had reached seven editions, had worked as a *'lady journalist'* on the society magazine THE QUEEN which supported the Rational Dress Society and the election of women to the London School Board, and had contributed articles on scientific subjects to the SATURDAY REVIEW and other publications. She also sang for charity (forty concerts in 1882 and 1883 alone), was associated with night classes for factory girls at Nine Elms, and made regular visits to Stepney on Wednesdays and Sundays to help at a soup kitchen, visit the poor and sing in a church there. She fenced, swam, rode, painted, played a good game of lawn tennis, smoked cigars and cigarettes, and was described in one book as a *"glamorous nymphomaniac"*. She frequented Whistler's Sunday morning breakfasts and was the nude model for his *"beautiful portrait of a beautiful woman"* which she submitted for the Society of British Artists Winter Exhibition of 1886-87 when he was currently President and when coincidentally, more or less, the divorce suit was being heard. As the painting was unfinished, members were able to demand its removal from the display. It seems unlikely that her relationship with Whistler was any more platonic than that of Lily Langtry's. Shaw admitted visiting her; she may have been hard to resist.

The case came before Mr. Justice Butt. It lasted from 26 November to 20 December 1886, with hearings on eighteen days, to the great distress of the jury who pressed for and latterly were reluctantly given a guinea a day each in expenses because of its exceptional duration.

Lord Colin Campbell sued on the grounds of his wife's adultery with the Duke of Marlborough (when he had been heir to the Dukedom and bore the courtesy title Marquess of Blandford), with General (then Colonel) Butler, with Thomas Bird, her doctor and with Captain Shaw. She in turn sued on the grounds of her husband's adultery with Amelia (or Mary) Watson who had been their housemaid.

Lady Colin Campbell's counsel was Sir Charles Russell. The Attorney General represented the Duke and the Solicitor General Mr. Bird. Captain Shaw's case was in the hands of William Court Gully. He had specialised in commercial cases in Liverpool but had a sound general knowledge of the law. He had recently contested Whitehaven as a Liberal, later became the Member for Carlisle and was Speaker of the House of Commons from 1895 to 1905. On retirement, he was created Viscount Selby. He has been described as *"a most agreeable, genial and highly-informed person"* and as being *"handsome, dignified and courteous"*; but his great-grandsons, the 4th Viscount Selby and Lord Mowbray Segrave and Stourton, have no papers in their possession that might indicate why Shaw chose him. Most of Gully's papers were, apparently, scattered to the four winds during the lifetime of his son, the second Viscount.

The Campbells had first met at a deer drive, in August 1880, when Gertrude was staying with a family who were the Duke of Argyll's shooting tenants. She had accepted his offer of marriage within two or three days but the ceremony had to be postponed several times because of what Lord Colin Campbell's counsel described as *"a fever contracted in Greece or Turkey"* and what was otherwise referred to as the result of *"an indiscretion when a youth"*. Several operations for perineal fistula and a voyage to the Cape of Good Hope achieved little success, but the bride-to-be's mother began to press that either the marriage should go ahead or the engagement be cancelled. Neither party had substantial financial assets, Lord Colin bringing into settlement a meagre (by Ducal standards) £10,000 and Gertrude being worth £6,000. The marriage was not of the groom's father's choosing but he acquiesced in it, Gertrude having insisted that he should be told of the engagement. The Duke had never called on Mr. and Mrs. Blood.

The wedding took place at the Chapel Royal, Savoy, in July 1881; one of Shaw's daughters was a bridesmaid. The unhealthy groom was 28 and the bride, described later as being then *"in robust health"* some five years younger. They had a five-day *"melancholy honeymoon"* in the Isle of Wight, the groom having been advised against co-habitation too soon. Then they settled down in London, Lord Colin being attended by hospital

Left: CAPTAIN SHAW IN THE 1880s. This photograph is a copy of one in a collection at Windsor Castle.Throughout his time in London, Shaw was a favourite of Bertie, Prince of Wales. (Photo reproduced by Gracious Permission of Her Majesty the Queen).

Below: WILLIAM COURT GULLY, VISCOUNT SELBY (1835-1909). Gully successfully defended Shaw in the Colin Campbell divorce case. He later became Liberal MP for Carlise and, in 1895, he was elected Speaker. (Photo: National Portrait Gallery).

nurses and his wife *"who had a great affection for him"*.

Three months later, at Bournemouth, the marriage was consummated and, within a few weeks, Lady Colin's health began to deteriorate. She also began to live an independent life and, it was alleged, when well enough dined out and returned home late at night, sometimes accompanied by gentlemen. In September 1882, Lord Colin needed another operation and this was carried out at Leigh Court, near Bristol, the home of Lady Miles who was Lady Colin Campbell's cousin. Lord Colin was attended after the operation by Thomas Bird and, since Lady Colin was unwell, he attended her as well.

By the following February Lady Colin found it intolerable to continue living with her husband though she was prepared to continue to act as *"friend, companion and nurse"*. Her husband alleged at that point that she had a miscarriage, the father of the child being Doctor Bird; he withdrew the claim after a heated family conference, but it was resurrected at the time of the divorce hearing. Then, in August of the same year — two years after the wedding — Lady Colin petitioned successfully for a judicial separation on the grounds of legal cruelty and she left the family home at 79 Cadogan Place. This petition was to be important, because a wife was not entitled to a divorce for the adultery of her husband if he had not committed an additional marital offence.

She spent part of 1884 with her parents, with whom she was on affectionate terms, in Paris and Florence. Her husband, suspecting that she was sleeping with Lord Blandford in Paris, had her watched and obtained a warrant whereby she could be arrested and placed in St. Lazare Prison if she were found IN FLAGRANTE DELICTO. When she returned to England, in June, he threatened divorce proceedings but, on seeking Lady Miles's assistance as a witness, she warned him that she might have to be a hostile one. She had, she said, in June 1882 at his Cadogan Place house seen him in his bedroom with the housemaid Amelia (or Mary) Watson in highly suspicious circumstances. Despite this threat, Lord Colin went ahead with his petition. It was lodged on 7 November 1884. Twenty-four hours earlier his wife had lodged one too.

The allegations concerning Amelia Watson — she was referred to in the Campbell household as Mary because the cook was also named Amelia — were highly circumstantial and Lady Miles was the only witness. She had no illusions about her cousin, Lady Colin. She had written to Lord Colin, whom she knew as *'Coco'*: *"What a pity you ever met such a woman. She isn't a nature to make a man happy. It is a cold, pitiless, cruel nature with no fear of God to guide it"*; and in another letter she had written: *"I think that (Blood) family have run mad"*. But she believed, as she said, that Lord Colin had made his wife's life *"miserable in various ways"*. Then, too, Dr. Bird was an old friend of Lady Miles and it might be expected that she would rush to his defence. So her testimony as to what she had seen in Lord Colin's bedroom was unconvincing even though she assured the court that she could prove the date because she read a psalm each morning and had underlined the relevant part of her prayer book. This was telegraphed for and examined and the underlining was found to be there. But her evidence was demolished by two eminent medical men: Dr. Clement Godson, Physician to the London Lying-in Hospital and the first Assistant Accoucheur at St. Bartholomew's and Dr. Gibbon, Physician to the Grosvenor Hospital for Women and Children. Amelia Watson, they said, was a virgin, a statement commemorated in the rhyme:

"Amelia Watson is my name
And housemaid is my station
VIRGO INTACTA I'm proclaimed
And Godson's my salvation".

The Marquess of Blandford, or the Duke of Marlborough as he was by the time of the case, was no stranger to scandal. In 1869, when twenty-five, he had married Lady Albertha, the sixth daughter of the Duke of Abercorn and a beautiful, refined but bird-brained girl known to her friends as 'Goosie'. He already had a considerable reputation for gaming and whoring and, seven years after his marriage, he had lived openly with the Countess of Aylesford while her husband was in India with Bertie, Prince of Wales. The Earl, on receiving a telegram from his wife to the effect that she was in love with Blandford (who happened also to be Aylesford's best friend) and was going off with him, was despatched home by the Prince, whose indignation matched his hypocrisy in the matter. Faced with social ostracism, she set out to persuade her husband not to institute divorce proceedings using the rather curious method of giving to Blandford a packet of love letters which the Prince had written to her some years before. These were passed to Blandford's less clever younger brother, the irascible Lord Randolph Churchill (Winston Churchill's father) who undertook to use them to bring pressure on the Prince to dissuade Aylesbury from going ahead, compounding the offence by trying to do it through the Princess.

In due course, in 1883 Lady Blandford obtained a deed of separation and then divorced her husband on the grounds that he and Lady Aylesford had lived together in Paris for several years. Lady Colin Campbell had first met him, through her elder sister, when she was still a girl. The allegations against Lady Colin were fairly specific: they had slept together in June 1884 when she was staying in Paris with her parents and they had, two years earlier, spent a weekend together at the Royal Hotel, Purfleet. The Paris allegations were denied by Lady Colin's parents; as to Purfleet, Blandford admitted he had stayed there on the weekend in question but with a Mrs. Perry *"who goes about London"*.

A curious man, Blandford. He was a brilliant chemist, mathematician and linguist and an audacious and self-assured speaker and writer. Morton Frewen, who knew him well, wrote of him: *"Was ever man more agreeable? Nor had anyone such charm of voice"*. Yet he wrote long, angry letters to his father though with some reminder of the Churchill power of expression in prose: *"You have displayed to me an untold cruelty of intention. What can it affect you who I marry and who my children may be? In what manner do they come into the circle of your life?"* And his own son and heir, the 9th Duke, said that he never received a kind word from his father and was *"entirely crushed"*. Despite his constant womanising, it is said that he loved only one woman and that he loved her until the day that he was found dead in bed (at the age of 48, six years after the Colin Campbell case). That woman was his first wife, Goosie, whom he had so badly treated.

General William Butler, another of the co-respondents, was of a different nature altogether. An Irishman, like Shaw, he had an honourable — if in his own mind not very successful — military career. Tall, strong and active, he was quick of observation and full of resource; a genial man yet with much force of character; a ready writer, with a gift of style. By coincidence, he was knighted the day before the case began, having been invalided back from Egypt four months previously.

At the time of the hearing he was about forty-eight and had married, some nine years previously, Elizabeth Thompson, a prominent artist and daughter of the painter T. J. Thompson. She and her sister and husband were all friends of Lady Colin Campbell. Butler did not appear in court, his counsel submitting that he had no case to answer. The Judge suggested that, although the evidence seemed to be weak, that was a matter for the jury.

Thomas Bird was forty-three at the time of the hearing, and was a bachelor. He had known Lady Miles, Lady Colin's cousin, for many years and Lady Colin for twenty. He was known to Lady Miles as *'Cuckoo'*; she, incidentally, was addressed in letters from Lord Colin as *'Muzzy'*. One may be tempted to scoff at these nicknames, Coco, Cuckoo and Muzzy, but they underline the saddest aspect of the case: that the various parties had known each other for many years.

Shaw was no exception to this. He had known Lord Colin since he was a boy and the Blood family since Lady Colin had been a child. She claimed Mrs. and Miss Shaw as *"personal friends"*, and both Lady Colin and Captain Shaw were to deny that there had been any familiarity between them.

Lord and Lady Colin, according to his counsel, were staying at another address in London, in October 1881, whilst their own home at 79 Cadogan Place was being prepared for them. Captain Shaw, he continued, had met Lady Colin at Cadogan Place, when the drawing room was as yet unfurnished. They had remained there together for some time. Lord Colin recalled the incident (though he dated it as September), because when his wife had said she was going there he had elected to stay at home but had then changed his mind and had found Shaw and his wife upstairs together. Lady Colin admitted that it was *"quite probable"* that she had shown Shaw the house while it was being furnished; Shaw himself admitted the visit but assured the court that there had been a light of some kind (candles, he thought) in the room where they had sat.

Amelia Watson affirmed that Lady Colin's former Swiss maid, Rosa Baer, who had been dismissed for gossiping about her mistress, had often had letters to post for her Ladyship and had shown them to her. *"Constantly"* they were addressed to Lord Blandford; sometimes to Shaw. Rosa confirmed that she *"often"* (later amended to *"twice"*) posted letters to Shaw and said she had, on one occasion, seen him walk up and down until a carriage that was at the door had gone away: an incident that Shaw denied. She had only seen him at the house twice. Shaw admitted to having received about twelve letters from Lady Colin but none had survived. He had, he said, probably handed them all to his wife as they referred to matters which concerned her.

The cook, Amelia Murrell, said that Shaw used to call on Lady Colin. She could not say for how long because Lady Colin used to let him out herself whereas, with other visitors, she rang for them to be shown out by the servants. Amelia admitted, under cross-examination, that she had also seen Mrs. and Miss Shaw call at the house, but they had never come with Captain Shaw.

Another servant, Albert Deroche, said he had worked at Cadogan Place for three months (the Colin Campbell servants came and went with great rapidity and so, doubtless, had little loyalty). Nine days after his arrival, he claimed, Lady Colin had told him not to announce Captain Shaw or the Marquess of Blandford in the hearing of Lord Colin. So when either came he wrote the name on a piece of paper, or told Lady Colin that the cook wanted to see her. Lady Colin denied this. Shaw called *"often"*, but not as frequently as Blandford. He had, he said, never shown Captain Shaw out and he had often had to make evasive replies to other visitors when Blandford or Shaw was in the house. Asked whether this made him ashamed he replied, to considerable laughter, that it did not because it was by no means unusual in service.

He also claimed that on one occasion, when he had taken refreshments into the drawing room, he had seen Shaw with his arm in a position which led him to believe that it had been round Lady Colin's waist. Lady Colin denied that this had ever happened.

James O'Neil, another Campbell servant for five or six months in 1882, went much further. Both Shaw and Blandford, he said, frequently called. They always used the area bell; they never knocked at the front door. Captain Shaw called about twice a week and always saw Lady Colin in the drawing room. On one occasion she was out when he called but arrived in a cab as he was about to leave. They returned together. She was told by O'Neil that Lord Colin was in the drawing room so she pushed Shaw into the dining room and instructed O'Neil to tell Lord Colin she had gone out if he enquired where she was. O'Neil joined the other servants in the kitchen and after a while sounds were heard from the dining room *"which caused remarks among the servants"*. O'Neil said he had then gone upstairs. THE TIMES, in reporting this, continued tantalisingly: *"The witness here described what he saw on looking through the keyhole. If it really occurred it would fully establish the charge against Lady Colin and Captain Shaw"*. The full transcript of evidence does not survive.

Cross-examined the following day, O'Neil denied he had been drawing on his recollection of something that had occurred at a brothel in America. He had not, he said, tried the door to see if it was locked; if the key was in the lock *"it must have been turned around"*.

Neptune Blood, Lady Colin's brother, said he had examined the door. If locked on the inside the scutcheon would fall over the keyhole on the outside of the door, and VICE VERSA. If the door was unlocked, *"one could see something, but very little, through the keyhole. Certainly one could not see in the way described by O'Neil".*

Another to give evidence on the keyhole was Thomas Ellis, described appropriately as a surveyor. Through it, he could not see the legs of a chair or the floor of the room. He had placed a bag and a coat on the floor at a distance of ten feet and six feet from the door and could not see them through the keyhole. The scutcheon was stiff, but would only remain up if poised carefully above the keyhole.

The jury agreed that they too would like to peer through the keyhole, the tenants having invited them to do so. The judge had reservations but reluctantly accepted the proposal. Accordingly they all visited the house.

O'Neil had also stated, in his evidence, that no week passed without Shaw and Blandford calling at Cadogan Place throughout the time that he was employed in the Campbell household. If he was wrong, he was perjuring himself fairly seriously. Unlike Deroche, however, he had never been instructed, so he said, to receive Shaw and Blandford any differently from other visitors.

Even if Albert Deroche was complacent about Lady Colin's behaviour, Lord Colin's nurse, Anne Duffy, was not. Described during the trial as being of somewhat malevolent appearance, she said that to some of the things done by Lady Colin she did not attach much importance because she regarded Lady Colin's manner as being different from that of every other lady whom she had known. *"It was not ladylike",* she said. Further, Lady Colin had once spoken to her *"with reference to the prevention of large families".* Such devices as the sheath were not looked on favourably in society, recourse being had to douching or the use of a vaginal sponge. Lady Colin, however, may well have had more advanced views. Duffy, whilst obviously not approving of Lady Colin, helped her case. She had, she said, only seen Shaw at Cadogan Place once. Lady Colin had given instructions that she was *"not at home"* but when she heard that Shaw had called she sent the housemaid after him and he returned. But, said Nurse Duffy, he did not remain long.

Elizabeth Wright, a surgical nurse who attended Lord Colin for six months in 1881, also gave evidence. Shaw, she said, was one of a number of visitors, *"chiefly gentlemen",* who had asked for Lady Colin. On one occasion, Lady Colin and Captain Shaw had driven out together in a brougham. Then there was the bracelet that had been lost by Lady Colin, who had instructed that Lord Colin was not to hear of it. At a later date, Captain Shaw called and Wright heard him say to Lady Colin, *"the lost property is found".* Later she saw Lady Colin with the bracelet again. Lady Colin's explanation to the court was that she had lost a snake bracelet and had told her maid to say nothing to Lord Colin because he had complained previously of her carelessness. It was later found in the skirt of a dress, where it had fallen. Captain Shaw was in no way connected with the bracelet or its loss.

Wright also remembered Lady Colin telling Lord Colin that she, her sister, Captain Shaw, Lord Blandford and one or two others were to dine together. *"Lord Colin looked distressed but said nothing"*, she said. She finished her evidence with the startling statement that Lady Colin was suffering from *"an ailment"* even before her marriage was consummated. But the next day Lord Colin's counsel said that his client, *"as a gentleman"*, wished to repudiate the statement.

The Swiss maid, Rosa Baer, gave evidence that both Blandford and Shaw had stayed at Leigh Court, Lady Miles's home, either at Christmas 1881 or Easter 1882, and coincidentally with Lady Colin. We know, from the minutes of the Fire Brigade Committee, that Shaw was out of London for part of the Easter recess, as he subsequently reported two journeys he had made in connection with an investigation he was carrying out into fires in theatres. He had travelled some 300 miles to visit coal mines in the Midlands to ascertain ways in which smoke might suddenly be raised from below ground level; and 600 miles to ascertain temperatures and draughts in connection with some ventilation proposals that he had made. He did not specify where this second journey had taken him.

Rosa Baer's evidence was contradicted by Elizabeth Evans, a maid at Leigh Court. She said that, although on one occasion Shaw had lunched there, he never slept there during her period of service which was between April 1881 and May 1882. Lady Colin also denied he had stayed there when she had been a guest. Lady Miles said he had stayed there only one night, at the beginning of December 1881, when Lady Colin was not a guest; Shaw himself placed the date as the Autumn of the same year.

Lord Colin said that many of his family knew Shaw, probably through Lord Colin's mother whose brother was the 3rd Duke of Sutherland. But he did not remember ever inviting him to call after the date of the marriage, though he might have done so. He had spoken several times to his wife about her seeing Shaw and had objected to her riding in his brake. Further, in November 1881 (Lady Colin claimed it was March 1882), he had had *"a serious conversation"* with her about the visits of Shaw and Blandford to Cadogan Place. She had promised they would cease and, so far as he knew, they did. Lady Colin said that her husband had not insisted that she should have no social contact with the two men; it was merely that he did not like them calling in the afternoon. She said she had mentioned the matter to both of them, separately, at the launching of the INVICTA on 5 April 1882 and Shaw had exclaimed: *"How ridiculous these Campbells are"*, which Lord Colin's counsel suggested showed a degree of familiarity between her and the man who made it which ought not to exist. After that occasion, she claimed, he never called at Cadogan Place again though she continued to visit his family and to meet him in society.

The evidence crucial to the case against Shaw was contained in the keyhole allegation by O'Neil (who frequently was given a second 'l' to his name in reports of the later part of the case). Gully, when he defended Shaw, admitted that if the story could be relied on the case against his client was conclusive. But the Attorney General said it was *"a story so improbable as to render the witness unworthy of credit"*; and Lady Colin and Shaw both denied the incident absolutely.

Gully ridiculed the idea that Shaw's half hour visit to see the Cadogan

Place house before it was ready for occupation gave any grounds for suspicion of infidelity. He accepted that it was part of Shaw's daily duty to drive about London visiting the various fire stations, and that when near the house he might have called. Indeed, Shaw had admitted to doing so about twelve times but asserted that he always asked for Lord Colin and that there was no concealment about his visits. The servants, said Gully, had said that Shaw visited *"frequently"*. He went on to point out that when frequent visits were mentioned in the Divorce Court adultery was assumed; but not in any other court. If, he suggested, the evidence of Rose Baer and O'Neil was put aside there was nothing to show that Shaw's visits were other than totally innocent. Further, except for a statement by Mrs. Duffy — and that based on hearsay — there was no evidence that Shaw had ever visited Cadogan Place after being advised not to do so at the launching of the INVICTA. Gully concluded by asking the jury *"not to find a verdict damaging to an old public servant like Captain Shaw on the testimony of an untrustworthy witness like O'Neil"*.

Looking back on the evidence and the way Gully tackled the case, one feels he might have argued that casual intercourse was a somewhat impracticable possibility bearing in mind how Lady Colin would have been dressed; but perhaps the issue was too delicate to raise. Shaw's October 1881 candlelight visit to Cadogan Place before the house was ready for occupation, or a shared bedroom at Leigh Court, both seem to have presented more likely opportunities, but of course it was not part of Gully's case to suggest this. Gully really only needed to discredit the keyhole allegation; that was not difficult.

In his reply to the case as a whole, Sir Charles Russell suggested that although Lord Colin was *"kind and affectionate by nature"* the state of his health had made him *"sensitive, morbid and suspicious"*.

As to the case against Shaw surely, said Russell, he could have found a safer place for an intrigue than Lord Colin's own house. Further, he pointed out, Lady Colin was *"a person of such attractions that she could certainly not move in society without attracting attention"* and Captain Shaw was also very well known; yet, the allegations had come only from gossiping servants, not from anyone of their own social class. The case against Captain Shaw, he said, was *"utterly and hopelessly broken down"*. The solitary specific evidence was that of O'Neil.

Mr. Justice Butt, in his summing up, took up this theme. O'Neil, he suggested, had done well out of the proceedings, having received about £60 in expenses for coming back from America where he had gone into service. He had not, therefore, *"carried his eggs to a bad market"*. The jury must not forget the solemn denials of both Lady Colin and Captain Shaw — *"a gentleman who, as far as is known, has led an irreproachable life and been a valuable public servant"*.

The jury retired at 6.45 in the evening. After two and a half hours they returned. The Foreman said they were agreed upon Lady Colin's petition, but not on the charges made against her by Lord Colin. Further, there was no likelihood of agreement. The Judge sent them out again after which, apparently, he left the Court for the night.

They returned at 10.15 and gave as their verdict: that Lord Colin Campbell had not committed adultery with Amelia Watson and that Lady Colin Campbell had not committed adultery with any one of the co-respondents. They added the rider that, in not coming forward to give evidence, General Butler's conduct was unworthy of a gentleman and an English officer (he was actually Irish, it will be remembered) and this was the cause of the difficulty which they had experienced in coming to a decision.

Mr. Justice Butt was told formally of the verdict the next morning. He said that both petitions would stand dismissed and that costs would be awarded to Shaw, Marlborough and Bird. Butler did not seek them.

Lady Colin Campbell continued to write: a farce, BUD AND BLOSSOM, was produced at Terry's Theatre in 1893 and her last book, ETIQUETTE OF GOOD SOCIETY, was published in 1911, the year of her death. She was, by then, still only 53. She had outlived Shaw by three years and Butler by a year; the 8th Duke of Marlborough had already been dead 19 years and Lord Colin Campbell eleven. Her death was ascribed to *"rheumatoid arthritis, ten years or more"*, asthenia (debility and lack of will power) and heart failure. She died in the presence of Lucy Ann Longstaff, perhaps a servant, who also registered her death. Her effects totalled only just over £470 and were left entirely to a spinster of 36 who herself died ten years later leaving bequests to various sisters and nieces, one of the items being a Henry Moore seascape. Reading between the lines, the highly talented and attractive Lady Colin Campbell had been ruined by the divorce suit even though she was not found guilty; one feels she died a very lonely woman.

Of Captain Shaw, the magazine SOCIETY commented: *"He left the court without a shadow on his fair name and blameless, honourable and laborious life"*.

CHAPTER THIRTEEN
THEATRE FIRES

"There must be a limit somewhere to what an official can be expected to do, and . . . in the present case the limit has been passed"

About 1880 Richard D'Oyly Carte, the theatrical manager, decided to build a theatre especially suited to Gilbert and Sullivan comic opera. This was to be the Savoy and he chose, as architect, C. J. Phipps. D'Oyly Carte claimed that it would be a particularly safe theatre because it would be the first public building to be lit entirely be electricity; and Phipps was perhaps the best known theatre architect in the country. The claim about the lighting was reasonable; gas lighting had been a major cause of theatre fires because of the ease with which it could ignite costumes and curtains and because the burners generated so much heat. Phipps's professional judgement would, however, be found tragically deficient within six or seven years.

The Savoy Theatre opened on 10 October 1881 with PATIENCE. Ironically, within an hour of the start of the performance smoke was seen pouring through the proscenium opening into the auditorium, a spark from an electric battery having set light to some woodwork on the stage. But the fire was quickly dealt with and the show went on.

Thirteen months later, IOLANTHE had its first of nearly four hundred performances at the Savoy. Shaw was a regular theatre-goer and he was present that evening. During the second Act, the Fairy Queen singled out Private Willis as *"a man whose physical attributes are simply godlike"* and then continued, in song:

"On fire that glows with heat intense
I turn the hose of commonsense,
And out it goes at small expense!
We must maintain our fairy law
That is the main on which to draw —
In that we gain a Captain Shaw!

She continued with a verse that immortalised the Captain and which reminds us that he had become a very well-known public figure:

"Oh, Captain Shaw!
Type of true love kept under!
Could thy brigade with cold cascade
Quench my great love, I wonder?"

This was not as original as it may seem. Gilbert was a plagiarist and may well have got the idea from an earlier music hall chorus:

"My heart's on fire
Not all the Fire Brigade could
Subdue the flames
Though led by Mr. Braidwood"

Captain Shaw and the London theatre were not however linked solely by that Gilbertian chorus. Ways of preventing and controlling theatre fires had occupied much of his time and attention for several years.

In other countries, theatre fires had been innumerable and often horrifying: 800 casualties at St. Petersburg in 1836; 631 in Karlsruhe in 1847; and 1,670 in a Chinese theatre a couple of years earlier. But in London there was much official complacency. All London theatre fires since Shaw's appointment had been at night; since 1858, the only fatalities had been among firemen, not audiences. Most of the theatres were licensed by the Lord Chamberlain who was more concerned with possible indecency, lèse majésté or treason on the stage than with safety in the auditorium. But the matter was urgent, for the number of theatres in Greater London was to grow threefold during the second half of the century.

The near destruction in 1872 of the Oxford Music Hall, in Oxford Street, within two hours of the fire starting was an indication of what could happen to such a building; and to any people who might be inside it, particularly if fire broke out during a performance. But it was the 283 deaths caused by burning and trampling at a theatre fire in Brooklyn, five years later, that really brought the message home.

It was realised that the stage, the flies and back stage were areas of high risk and attempts had been made to divide off the stage from the audience by means of a fire-resistant wall and some kind of safety curtain. But the degree of protection was often illusory; and in many music halls, which were simply large rooms attached to public houses, there was no protection whatever.

In 1878 Shaw published his book, FIRES IN THEATRES. His comment that *"many of the monstrosities in the way of theatres which have disgraced our cities for years, should never have been allowed to exist"* endeared him neither to manager nor owners. His warnings, they argued, could have only one effect: to produce panic the moment there was any kind of emergency.

The publication of FIRES IN THEATRES, following hard on the heels of the Brooklyn fire, stirred the Government into extending the terms of reference of an already-existing Select Committee appointed to enquire into the constitution, efficiency, emoluments and finances of the Metropolitan Fire Brigade. It was now charged, also, with considering fire prevention arrangements in theatres and other places of entertainment. But, apart from recommending increased control over theatre construction in the Metropolis, it did little to tighten up legislation. There was an Amending Act the following year which gave the Board of Works certain powers to require alterations in existing theatres, but these applied only to theatres above a certain size and no more than *"moderate expenditure"* could be insisted upon. The circumspect manner in which the Board operated this modest legislation was still sufficient to generate a mass of complaints from theatre owners and managers. Then, a further terrible fire in 1880, at the Ring Theatre, Vienna, when about five hundred people lost their lives as they fought to reach unlighted exits, changed the climate of public and official opinion.

In response, the Home Secretary asked the Board of Works to report on all the London theatres, indicating what was needed to be done to make them safe, whether within or outside the limits of *"moderate expenditure"*.

So Shaw, by now 54 years of age, was at once launched into the most massive administrative task in the whole of his career. The resulting papers, although little known, make fascinating reading.

Typically, within a fortnight he had decided how he would organise the investigation. He would, he reported, need detailed drawings of each of the 41 theatres, full information about the number of people for whom each part of the theatre was licensed, distances of the direct escape routes into the street, a detailed description of the modes of exit, an explanation of the means currently used to protect the audience from the direct action of flame, heat and smoke, the arrangements for rescue, and a history of the theatre (including date of construction and of any alterations, and the name of the architect).

He warned the Board of Works that this task of great responsibility would place an enormous additional burden on those who did it and would involve *"a very considerable expenditure of time which, strictly speaking, we have not at our command"*. Simultaneously, he warned the theatre proprietors that it might be necessary to reduce the sitting or standing space considerably in some theatres to make escape easier, though he hoped *"at least in several cases"* to do this without ruining them.

He was immediately at work, inspecting the first seven theatres on his list. He made an initial visit himself, at a rate of two per day, and then a team from among his twenty-four most experienced officers and men made a detailed study of each building. Incredibly, they had completed their work at these seven theatres in five weeks.

It was quite out of character for Shaw ever to complain about his work load. But at the end of April 1882, three months after he had commenced this massive investigation and when he was working on the reports on the ninth and tenth theatres, he told his Committee:

"I consider this the heaviest duty which has ever been cast upon me . . . I presume the Committee will hardly need to be told that I am not in the habit of avoiding work, as every member must be aware of repeated instances of my undertaking heavy labour without a murmur, and especially of the enormous duty of taking over the Fire Escapes at a few hours' notice in 1867, when the order was issued only 48 hours before the work had to be commenced, and yet there was not a single mischance of any kind. In that case we accomplished what had to be done by working almost continuously for about 100 hours; but at the end of that time we were able to obtain some rest. In the present case however the labour and responsibility are so great, and have been so continuous, that I own to being almost overwhelmed by them."

He then described the two journeys made during the recess, and which have been referred to already in connection with the Colin Campbell Divorce Case. He continued:

"I mention these as instances . . . for the purpose of showing that I am not afraid of work, and that I carry out what I undertake even when, as at present, my strength is over-taxed. What I wish to point out is that there must be a limit somewhere to what an official can be

expected to do, and that in the present case the limit has been passed."

He went on, somewhat unspecifically, to request *"some immediate relief"*, and suggested that it was most unfair that the Home Office and the Lord Chamberlain's Office should call on another department (the Board of Works) and a *"very heavily worked"* official (himself) to undertake duties which they (the Home Office and the Lord Chamberlain) had in their charge, had professed for many years to be carrying out and for which they were being paid. He concluded:

"I came into the service of the Board as Head Fireman, and I most earnestly entreat that I may be allowed to carry on the duties of that position . . . and that I may be relieved from new work which was never contemplated when I was appointed."

Unreported discussions apparently went on behind the scenes and, a fortnight later, he came round to the view that since at the present rate the investigation would not be completed for another sixteen months it would be best to concentrate all the Brigade's resources on the exercise, leaving as much other work in abeyance as was possible. He was, he said, not prepared to sign any reports compiled by someone who was not a member of the Brigade.

So, the remaining thirty-three theatres were dealt with by late July, in a remarkable report running to 370 pages. It begins:

"It is impossible to convey any idea of the difficulties I have had to encounter . . . to reduce the subject to anything like method or system. It is not only that every house has been constructed on plans . . . wholly distinct from all other plans, but almost every part of every house is called by different names, according to the caprice of the owner or lessee . . . I have had to deal with no less than 34 . . . in some cases used differently in the same house at different periods of the year . . .

"In dealing with the exits from London theatres, it is necessary to call special attention to the perversity of ingenuity . . . for getting the visitors away . . . Every exertion seems to have been used to make the passages, corridors, landings and stairs as complex and tortuous as possible and . . . then to obstruct them by pay-boxes, cloakrooms, barriers, refreshment counters, single or double steps, and partial walls . . . The exits . . . in many cases . . . never become known to even the oldest frequenters of the houses. In some theatres the attendants seem to spend the biggest proportion of their time showing visitors the way . . . There should be some limits to . . . the distance from the spot in which the most remote visitor is seated to the point of absolute safety. I do not think this ought to exceed 200 or 250 feet, as every audience contains a proportion of stout, and old, and weak persons, who could not go quickly further than this distance without becoming exhausted, and in any case indirectly influence the speed of the whole audience in getting away."

He went on to make some general recommendations on: the maximum number of people to be brought together at one spot without crush barriers; the need for simple, separate exits; the compliance with building regulations before a licence could be granted; the manufacture and storing of scenery within the risk of an audience; the separate licensing of ancillary rooms, such as those for carpenters, scenery and refreshments; adequate emergency lighting; a strict inspection system; and the need to give on the licence a statement of the maximum number to be admitted to each part of the house. Theatres, contended Shaw, should not only be safe; they should be seen to be safe.

The report then detailed what had been found. It included: an absence of dividing walls so that a fire in one part would destroy the whole theatre; wooden ventilators over the stage that could be set alight by, say, a chimney fire; false ceilings of wood, of canvas, or of paper; the indiscriminate storage of inflammable props and rubbish; swinging, defective or unguarded gas fittings; a defective water supply; incompatible hydrants and branches; a below-ground theatre with fresh air supplied only by fans that could, equally, introduce smoke and fumes; an absence of gallery gangways, the patrons climbing over the seats to leave; a gallery staircase less that a metre wide; a junction of stairs and corridors bringing together five hundred people at one point; escape doors in bad repair, or habitually locked; a hose full of holes; inadequate roof support; workshops so positioned that a fire there would prevent any escape by the main exit; deficiency or absence of handrails on staircases; dilapidated staircases; and even a main wall in imminent danger of collapse whether there was a fire or not.

Shaw reported that at the Strand Theatre, which stood on the site of the present Aldwych Underground Station, it took nearly eleven and a half minutes on a busy night to clear the dress circle and stalls. Yet this theatre had false ceilings of wood, and defective gas and water supplies and fittings. Shaw concluded: *"The theatre, under its present conditions, would if once lighted burn as quickly as a match box or a prepared bonfire and is absolutely unsafe for the reception of an audience"*. It was immediately reconstructed, under the supervision of C. J. Phipps.

Also condemned was the Criterion Theatre, on land between Haymarket and Lower Regent Street. Shaw found it to be exceedingly well-managed and free from any of the worst faults he had noted elsewhere. But it was in a basement at three different levels, even the upper circle being reached by descending stairs. Because of the inadequacy of the ventilation the audience would suffocate if there were a fire, the number of people likely to escape being very small. As a result of the report the theatre was rebuilt with a portion of the adjoining restaurant removed so that part of it was open to the sky. *"The morning sunshine streams into the pit"*, said one visitor.

The ninety-year old Prince of Wales Theatre, earlier known as the Dust Hole, had a wall that was in danger of immediate collapse, although braced. It also had insufficient ventilation, unsafe lathe and plaster separation between stage and auditorium, dangerous wooden floors, a landing only three and a half metres by three metres on which up to 142 people might come together in an emergency, and defective water supply and fire fighting apparatus. Also, various dangerous trades were being carried out in different parts of the theatre. Shaw recommended it should be closed at once; as also should the Royalty Theatre because of its dilapidated condition. The former became a Salvation Army hostel until it was rebuilt as a theatre in 1903; the latter was reconstructed at once.

Only the two-year-old Princess Theatre, in Oxford Street, another C. J. Phipps creation, emerged with an unqualified good report. *"Those entrusted with the safety of the building"*, he wrote, *"have given great attention to the protection of the building from fire"*. Especially good were its means of escape. The new Savoy Theatre was also generally commended, though it should have been divided into more than one risk.

Shaw's report resulted in the immediate closure of several of the most dangerous theatres and in the remodelling of others. But, despite its details and the conscientious way it had been compiled, it only touched the fringe of the problem. There were in London, in 1882, over three hundred music halls and similar establishments that were outside the scope of the investigation, though not all of them were open every night. They ranged from vast purpose-built theatres, like the South London Palace of Varieties in Lambeth which flourished from 1860 to 1940 despite destruction by fire in 1869, and which housed about 4,000 to rooms above or behind public houses, like the Gun at Woolwich where a first-floor room of about 55 square metres, that is the size of a typical school classroom, was being used nightly to accommodate audiences of up to sixty people.

At least fifty-one of these three hundred-odd music halls were in two working-class districts, Bethnal Green and Stepney. The capacity of eighty-three of these London music halls is known and amounted to 40,000, an average of 475 people per building. Even if the capacity of each of the remainder was much less, say fifty each, that gives a further 11,000 or so places. So, over 50,000 places (seated or standing) were available in these premises, which were licensed but not subject to Shaw's inspection. They were not all open on the same night nor were they always filled to capacity, but theoretically at any one time 50,000 people were at risk in London, with no structural or other precautions to inhibit fire or assist escape, and in circumstances where panic could all too easily take place. The actual figure on certain nights may have been even greater, for some music halls and theatres doubtless escaped being licensed, even if for only a short while; and the calculations take no account of concert halls or private functions.

Less than six months after Shaw completed his reports one of London's largest theatres, the Alhambra, on the east side of Leicester Square, was burnt to the ground. Fortunately, the fire started two hours after the audience had gone home. It was a very tall building (32 metres from the basement to the apex of the roof) and very capacious. Shaw had reported that since it was not divided up by party walls any fire not extinguished within five or six minutes would be disastrous. In this he was correct. But, ironically, he had gone on to say: *"The external walls are of sound material and construction, and appear to be capable of resisting any fire or shock likely to occur within them"*.

Twenty-nine of the Brigade's available thirty-two steamers together with

131

over two hundred firemen (including the Prince of Wales) attended. The fire had quickly got a hold and, despite Shaw's optimism about the walls, one of them collapsed and so badly injured First Class Fireman Thomas Ashford that he died later in Charing Cross Hospital. Superintendent Hamlyn, who was accompanying the Prince, and three firemen were injured at the same time. In a separate incident, Fourth Class Fireman Henry Berg slipped on a ladder and fell head first to the ground. He, too, died of his injuries.

The Alhambra fire served, yet again, as a reminder of what might happen if a London theatre were occupied when fire broke out. It is a miracle that it never did, though certainly Shaw's reports must have diminished the chance of its happening. In the seventeen years before, there had been fourteen major theatre fires in London; in the next seventeen years there were only five.

Elsewhere, things were different. It has been calculated that in 1884 alone forty-one theatres were burnt down somewhere in the world, killing 1,200 people. Even in Great Britain, Shaw's work had had little impact outside London. When tragedy struck in the provinces, it came only four years after the publication of Shaw's report and in a brand new theatre designed by none other than the London-based architect, C. J. Phipps. The unfortunate city was Exeter. The Circus Theatre there had been burnt down twice and, in 1885, local businessmen commissioned Phipps to design a building that was modern and comfortable and safe.

Phipps was in his early fifties. He had been in practice for nearly thirty years and, after moving from Bath to London, had become a recognised authority on theatre design, contrary to the wishes of his parents who disapproved of such places, and contrary to his architectural training which had been Gothic and ecclesiastical. He had been responsible for the Gaiety (1868), the Variety, Hoxton (1869), the Vaudeville (1870); and, more significantly, the Princess (1880) and the Savoy (1881) (the only two London theatres soundly praised by Shaw in his report) and the Strand (1882) when it was rebuilt to take the place of the theatre condemned by Shaw.

No architect, therefore, was better placed than Phipps to be aware of Shaw's views on theatre design; and in a letter to Exeter Corporation he wrote: *"The theatre is designed in accordance with the Rules and Regulations of the Board of Works under the Act of 1878 and of the Lord Chamberlain, and having constructed over forty theatres I bring a somewhat large experience to bear on the subject"*. But the comment is highly significant: he was harking back to the 1878 Act rather than to Shaw's strictures of 1882; also the reference to the Lord Chamberlain was obviously meant to impress the provincial dignitaries yet had no technical significance at all. The suggestion, then, is that Phipps was prepared to trim what he must have known to be essential in safety terms to meet the wishes of his clients. Whether he was venal, incompetent or disinterested we have no way of knowing. Certainly, the theatre that he designed had almost every feature that Shaw had condemned: lack of partition between stage and audience, tortuous corridors, steep, obstructed and narrow stairs, low roofs and small exit doors. The local magistrates, doubtless ignorant of all the theatre's faults, inspected it on completion and granted it a licence.

It opened in the Autumn of 1886. On 5 September 1887, fire broke out on stage during a performance of ROMANY RYE. There had been several mishaps with the scenery during the first three Acts and in the middle of the fourth the drop-scene suddenly came down, narrowly missing one of the cast. More or less simultaneously, the curtain was lowered, smoke was seen, the curtain blew out towards the auditorium, someone shouted *"fire"* and there was panic. The twenty or so patrons in the dress circle and a more numerous crowd in the stalls easily escaped, and the crowded pit was evacuated with some injury. But in the upper circle and gallery it was a different story. The substantial audience there had been augmented at nine o'clock by half-timers, but those parts of the house had only one exit each, a second having been eliminated from the plans doubtless to save costs. The ILLUSTRATED LONDON NEWS commented: *"Shilling customers must not expect any care for their lives . . . The occupants of the boxes, who paid higher prices, had their safety well-provided for; and so it is at most of our theatres"*.

The fire quickly ran round the flies, down the wings, and caught the curtains alight, filling the house with smoke and flames. Within three minutes the fire, fanned by a draught through a large open door at the back of the theatre, was raging both on the stage and in the orchestra pit. Quickly, many in the gallery were suffocated, for another dictum of Shaw's that the architect had ignored was that the auditorium roof should be at least ten feet (three metres) above the highest seat. One hundred and twenty-three recognisable bodies were eventually recovered, human remains and a list of the missing accounted for a further sixty-five people, giving a total death roll of 188. This probably represented a quarter of all those in the building.

One might have expected Captain Shaw's involvement in the matter to have been only peripheral. But it so happened that on the day after the fire he was passing through Exeter on his way back from a short holiday in Spain and, not unnaturally, he halted his journey. He attended the second emergency meeting of the City Council that same day and was invited to speak. He accepted, but pointed out that he was not present in an official capacity and that it would be inadvisable for him to say much beyond the fact that there seemed to have been no want of exertion on the part of those responsible for the public services, the fire had obviously spread rapidly, and any outside help would have made little difference. The firemen appeared to have *"done well in their way"* but perhaps the tragedy had shown the need for a fire force controlled by the municipal authorities. He had in mind, no doubt, that according to some eye witnesses all the people huddled on the front balcony had been rescued with builders' ladders before the fire escape had arrived. When it did come, and some claimed it took twenty minutes or more, its use was confined to the removal of the dead bodies. In practice, a force of the kind envisaged by Shaw could have done little better; most of the casualties had died in their seats or in a mass of fallen bodies on the gallery stairs.

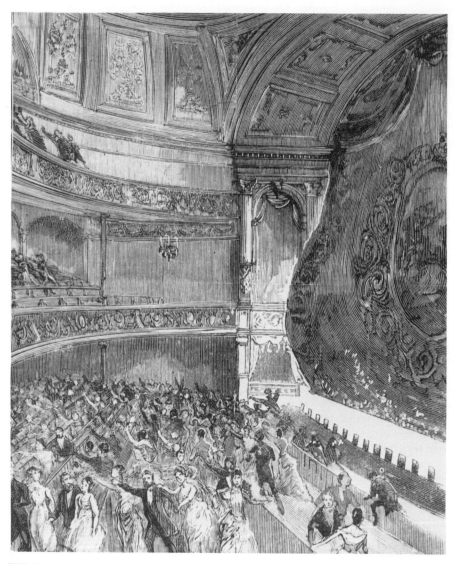

THE EXETER THEATRE FIRE (1887). During a performance the curtain was suddenly lowered, smoke was seen, the curtain blew out towards the auditorium, someone shouted "fire", and there was panic. (Photo: Devon Record Office).

THE EXETER THEATRE FIRE (1887). Some were brought down by means of builders' ladders. There is conflicting evidence about how long the Fire Escape took to arrive and whether it effected any rescues. (Photo: Devon Record Office).

THE EXETER THEATRE FIRE (1887). Many in the gallery were trapped and climbed out onto the roof. The watchers implored them not to jump but some did, a distance of forty feet. (Photo Devon Record Office).

The Coroner, Henry Hooper, soon found that he would be hampered by the refusal of the City magistrates, the men who had so recently inspected and licensed the theatre, to attend the inquest. In their view, the Coroner had no jurisdiction. Wisely, he sought Home Office support and, not surprisingly, the Secretary of State at once requested Shaw to assist in investigating fully the causes of the fire, its rapid spread and its fatal effects. He was also to investigate whether the disaster could be ascribed to defects of construction, to negligence or accident, or to any particular combination of causes. There followed a flurry of telegrams and letters, all of which survive: Shaw to the Chief Constable, advising him of the appointment; the Chief Constable to the Coroner, likewise; the Coroner to Shaw letting him know when the adjourned inquest would re-open; and Shaw to the Coroner saying that he would be arriving at the Rougemont Hotel at five o'clock on the Sunday (11 September). The Hotel's records, unfortunately, do not go back that far.

When Shaw reached the Rougemont he found a letter from the Coroner waiting for him. Hooper lived at Dawlish and as the last Sunday train left for that place at 6.45 he had not stayed to greet Shaw but would see him, it said, as soon as he arrived back on the first train in the morning, due in at 9.20. It is obvious from the letter that Hooper had never met Shaw, but was gratified and relieved to have his support.

This was understandable for feelings were running high in the City. A mass funeral at the new cemetery on the outskirts of the town had been attended by between 8,000 and 10,000 people; and on the day that the inquest re-opened, the DEVON AND EXETER GAZETTE carried this report:

"One of the London evening papers — the EVENING NEWS, a journal which chiefly owes its reputation to the fact that it reported verbatim the whole of the filthy details of the Colin Campbell case (in which, coincidentally, Captain Shaw had been involved) — sent a special representative to Exeter to 'work up' the fire. And most certainly the youth of five-and-twenty executed his commission. Reports of the most grotesque character have appeared in the EVENING NEWS . . . He attacked the Sheriff of Exeter and the surgeons of the City as persons guilty of irreverent conduct and he assailed the men who worked with unflagging heroism . . . The correspondent stated that drunkenness prevailed among the working men . . . laying out the bodies . . . a base and cowardly slander. He speaks of the funeral being attended by 'a jostling crowd of loose women, who carried lap dogs, bottles of gin, and luncheon baskets', and 'who raced as if they were following a hunt'.

"On Friday night the libels caused a feeling of intense indignation . . . The correspondent appears to have gone to the London Hotel. He was taxed with the authorship of the report, and . . . he was shown the door. He then went to the Rougemont (doubtless more up-market and so more secure) . . . The manager had difficulty in restraining the indignation of those . . . aware of his whereabouts. On Saturday morning it was suggested he should leave the City . . .

He proceeded to the Queen Street Station with a view to leaving by the up 12.40 train (but) . . . stayed . . . on the down platform until very nearly the last moment, apparently fearing recognition . . . (Then) Mr. N. O'Leary, an elderly man and lame having suffered severely with rheumatism . . . knocked him down. The correspondent . . . ran . . . to the Dispensary . . . His eye was blackened . . . He was afterwards escorted to the station by a policeman and left . . . by the 2.15 train . . . Those on the platform shouted, 'Three groans for the libeller. Go home . . .' The incident caused intense excitement throughout the City."

Shaw dominated the inquest because of his fame and because, not unnaturally, the local citizens were so stunned at what had happened. But he showed great courtesy and tact, saying of the magistrates only that if the gentlemen who were PRIMA FACIE responsible for the safety of life in the City had been present or represented by Counsel he would have gone a great deal further in his questioning than he had done. As to any evidence that might be given by Phipps he should, Shaw said, be examined *"for the sake of his own reputation and to assist the jury, and not for the purpose of shielding any authority not represented".*

In his summing up, the Coroner said that all the evidence pointed to the fire having started in the flies. The jury would need to decide whether its rapid spread was caused by the inflammable state of the building, the very dry summer or the absence of any proper means of fire extinction. They would also have to decide whether the gallery staircase, even if well-constructed and of proper dimensions, had been adequate for an area holding four hundred people. In that connection, they would want to consider Mr. Phipps' comment that the gallery audience had a second means of escape by jumping over into the upper circle, even though the people there would then need ten to fifteen minutes to disperse. The great majority of the bodies, he pointed out, had been found at the top of the gallery stairs where there was a check box and a post at an angle; the jury might consider that this post had contributed to the loss of life.

The theatre company, he suggested, could have done no more, and *"by employing an architect of Mr. Phipps's reputation they were consulting the safety of the public".* The management's position, in applying to the Justices for a licence, was different from what it would have been in London. There, the Metropolitan Board of Works had the power to make regulations for the protection of new theatres, and licences could be issued only if the Board were satisfied with the construction of the building. But, in the provinces, these laws did not apply. Therefore if, in the jury's opinion, the Justices had considered the theatre suitable and had come to the conclusion, rightly or wrongly, that the building was a safe one, that was the end of the matter though he did not accept their contention that their action could not be considered. If, on the other hand, they had failed to exercise discretion (however misguided) and had merely allowed matters to turn out as chance might let them, they were as amenable to the law as any other of the Queen's subjects.

After being out for nearly five hours the jury returned a verdict of accidental death. One rider censured the magistrates for not having inspected the theatre fully and for allowing themselves to be misled by the architect in the matter of exit from the gallery to the second circle; another rider regretted their declining to recognise the Coroner's court *"and their lack of courtesy to the Government Commissioner (Shaw) attending it"*. They also deeply deplored the fact that the architect had produced a building with so many structural defects, especially outside the pay office, and were surprised at his suggestion that climbing over the rail from the gallery to the second circle was a legitimate exit. Their ninth and final rider was, at the suggestion of the Coroner, withdrawn; it was that their being without any refreshments for many hours was *"a blot on the legal system of the country"*.

Captain Shaw was then formally thanked and he replied appropriately. He accepted an invitation from the Mayor to remain for a meeting of the Town Council at which he questioned the Surveyor on the size and pressure of the water mains and recommended hydrants one hundred feet (thirty metres) apart in the populous parts of the City and a hundred yards (ninety metres) apart in the outlying districts. He also suggested that as there seemed to be plenty of volunteers to work a manual pump it would be inadvisable to have a steam pump which would need a permanent staff. But, he suggested, the fire brigade needed to be improved greatly. Many of its members were physically unsuited and what was needed was a City brigade of smart, active young men. He would be very pleased to send down a skilled officer to help form and drill such a brigade. The offer was accepted.

In his official report, he commented that the original plans for the theatre had been altered or added to in almost every part of the building. The resulting faults were legion: complex exit routes; a failure to separate the dangerous workshop trades from the main building although land had been available for this purpose; a roof ventilator that had been reversed to keep out rain and draughts but which therefore prevented the escape of foul air and smoke; the absence of virtually any ventilation or smoke escape in the auditorium; unplanned openings in the proscenium wall; room and corridor partitions made of wood, lathe and plaster or match boarding, instead of fire-resistant materials; a fireplace in the lower flies; a fire hydrant marked on the plan as being in the flies (in error, said the architect), but not provided and the existence of which, according to several witnesses, would have made it possible to put the fire out at a very early stage; lumber stored under escape staircases; corridors floored with wood; corridors only three feet six inches (about a metre) wide; and backless gallery seats encouraging panic mass-escape, both within the gallery and into the second circle. There were, he wrote, other theatres as bad, but very few worse. Any one of these serious defects in design would have justified the issue of a licence being refused. The Company had engaged an architect and so had become responsible for the building works; the Company had then applied to the appropriate authority to be allowed to use that building as a theatre; and that authority had then granted a licence, *"thus informing the Company, the public, and all* concerned that the building was safe for the purposes of a theatre, and fit for the reception of an audience". Thus, he suggested, the licensing authority had become responsible on 12 October 1886 and were still responsible when fire broke out on 5 September 1887. He continued:

"At the first puff through the side of the curtains, the smoke made its way into the space over the gallery, at the second into the gallery itself, then into the upper circle, by which it passed by a so-called management door into the gallery stairs, and at the expiration of two minutes the lower edge of the cloud formed a diagonal line with one end at the footlights, and the other gradually lowering until in less than ten minutes it reached the pit, by which time the whole building except the vestibule and the dressing-rooms were one mass of flame. To sum up, the fire arose in the flies through accident or neglect . . . and the heavy loss of live was caused by the bad construction of the theatre."

He went on to point out that the jury, while severely censuring the licensing authority, had apportioned some of the blame to the architect. But, said Shaw, if the architect why not the contractor, the bricklayers and even the labourers who dug the ground for the foundations. In his view, and notwithstanding the verdict of the jury, the licensing authority had, on a certain date, assumed the whole and sole responsibility for the safety of the theatre and in doing so had relieved the Company and its agents and employees of any responsibility and *"the lessons and warnings of recent years had prepared all concerned for the terrible catastrophe precisely as it occurred"*.

This view that the architect had no professional responsibility to warn the magistrates of their errors of judgement may seem strange; it certainly did to the magistrates. In due course they responded with a two-and-a-half-page foolscap report in which they suggested that the general principle of their responsibility had been *"most unnecessarily and . . . unfairly strained"*. The Act under which the licence had been granted gave no indication that the structural condition of the building had to be taken into account; and even if it did they must be guided by expert advice and it was unreasonable to suppose them responsible for the expert's mistakes or errors of judgement. They had set aside the claims of local architects and had appointed a man who had designed more than forty-two theatres, eleven of them in the capital; and they were informed that in no instance had a licensing authority deemed it necessary to seek a second opinion on the structural safety of any building he had designed. Further, they had asked the Lord Chamberlain, in May 1886, whether there were any points in the new Bill for regulating new theatre building that they ought to know about and had been advised that it would be sufficient to study the then current regulations. They had relayed that information to Phipps and he had said that he knew them well and that they had *"in their essentials"* been complied with. It would have been a most unusual course had they doubted the competence and judgement of Phipps and, whilst deploring the awful loss of life, they could not be held responsible for the defective state of the law.

Another who felt that the jury had been unjust in their comments was Seth Bevan, a Plymouth contractor who had built the theatre. Two days after the fire, in a letter to the WESTERN DAILY MERCURY, he defended both the architect and the theatre Company; but the tragedy preyed on his mind and eight months later he shot himself.

Shaw's statement that the licensing authority must accept total responsibility for the safety of the theatre's patrons, whilst it had no force in law inevitably led local authorities for the first time to undertake their licensing function conscientiously. There soon followed the Public Health Amendment Act (1890) which enforced stricter fire regulations in any building where the public might gather and within a few years there were demands that all theatre planning should be subject to municipal or state control and that no theatre should even be erected if the plans suggested that it might not meet the requirements of the appropriate authority. In the meantime, there had been a substantial fall in the number of people prepared to risk their lives by going to the theatre at all. The Exeter theatre fire had horrified the nation.

On a lighter note, Shaw's stay in Exeter during the period of the inquest had been marked by an incident that shows that his enthusiasm and agility remained undiminished although he was within a few months of his sixtieth birthday. Between four and five o'clock on the Saturday morning after the disaster a fire broke out in two houses almost opposite the stage entrance to the gutted theatre. A neighbour thought it would be wise to summon Shaw from his bed at the Rougemont Hotel. This was done, and according to a newspaper account, *"a little before six o'clock, when the fire was still burning fiercely, the gallant Captain came upon the scene"*. He at once took an active part in directing operations and carried a hose up the fire escape and into one of the rooms and then called on a fireman to take over from him while he went to another part of the building. The newspaper continued:

"The activity shown by Captain Shaw was remarkable. He was here, there and everywhere, up ladders and down again in a moment. Nothing escaped his eye and the smartness with which he put the firemen through their duties was the subject of warm admiration on the part of the bystanders, the celerity with which he carried out the work being in marked contrast to the style in which fire extinguishing operations have been conducted at some recent fires."

CHAPTER FOURTEEN

SHAW ABROAD
"Vive le capitaine Shaw"

It will be recalled that the day after the Exeter theatre fire, Shaw was by chance passing through that city on his way back from Spain. He frequently went abroad for relaxation, but inevitably kept a weather eye open for local fire activities and sometimes, whether invited or not, gave professional advice. He always claimed that his absences from London enabled him to study foreign methods and so were of inestimable value.

In January 1883 he engaged in a somewhat undignified correspondence in THE CITIZEN with a Mr. Cowin, an insurance director, who had the final word.

It was, said Cowin, *"totally unnecessary for Captain Shaw to go out of Great Britain to pick up new ideas. There are firemen on this side of the water, men standing head and shoulders higher than he in his profession, who could teach him some ideas old and new, that he might with great advantage adopt. That gentleman has completely lost his temper in this controversy and I can only advise him to let his anger, like the recent Wood Street fire (a disastrous conflagration in the City), burn itself out".*

By contrast, THE TIMES, when he was about to retire in 1891 commented: *"The first of his valuable qualities was that of making use for home purposes, of the experience of other cities and other lands".*

At the start of his career in London, he had told the Hankey Committee, in 1862, that he had watched fire fighting in various places in America (where, it will be remembered, he claimed his own hotel had been burned down) and in France. His knowledge of the latter country enabled him to argue convincingly against the author and volunteer fireman, Charles Young, before the McLagan Committee of 1867. Young claimed that the Parisian SAPEURS-POMPIERS were *"a far superior formation"* whose officers were *"very scornful of the Metropolitan Fire Brigade arrangements".* Shaw replied that Young had never fought a fire nor been inside a fire station in his life. Seeing the fire from the outside of a mob, he suggested, was hardly a strong qualification. *"Those gentlemen in Paris,"* he declared, *"are intimate friends of mine and have assured me though Mr. Young had been in Paris and they had shown him what they could in less than an hour, his statement is utterly incorrect".* Further, said Shaw, the Paris Fire Brigade cost £100,000 a year to run, *"a sum quite beyond what this country would tolerate".*

Shortly, Shaw's enthusiasm for Paris ran away with him. When, during the Commune in May 1871, the French capital was besieged he wrote privately to the Foreign Secretary offering to organise, at a day's notice, a temporary fire-fighting force which would make everything safe within twenty-four hours of commencing work there. It was an extraordinary thing to do: he had not consulted the Board of Works, much less obtained their approval. Then, the Board received an official request for assistance from the French government (perhaps prompted by Shaw) and agreed to vote the necessary funds and to send as many engines and men as could be spared but, before the arrangements were completed, the need had passed. Meanwhile, Shaw had gone to Paris in a private capacity and was so widely acclaimed that, according to one account, he was accompanied to the railway station on his return to England by a body of firemen shouting: *"Vive le capitaine Shaw"*.

His employers of less than six years viewed the matter differently and censured him, whereupon he pointed out that to have awaited their instructions would have meant delay, and when a fire needed attention no delay could be tolerated. However, after a sharp exchange of words the matter was dropped. VANITY FAIR, commenting on the incident, said: *"He is, besides being the first fireman, one of the most popular men in London, and he well deserves his popularity"*. It is doubtful whether the Board of Works agreed.

It is probably not coincidence that one of the strongest supporters of the French was Bertie, Prince of Wales and that among those in Paris during the siege was the Duke of Sutherland. The views of these two men may well have saved Shaw from the worst of the Board's wrath. Coincidentally, another person in Paris at the time was Lieutenant Butler who, later, would be involved with Shaw in the Colin Campbell divorce case.

Shaw returned from Paris with one idea firmly in his mind. As he later wrote in FIRES AND FIRE BRIGADES:

"The most perfectly constructed buildings in the world are perhaps those of France, especially in and about Paris, where gypsum and other materials useful for resisting fire are to be found on the spot, and therefore cost nothing beyond the cost of lifting; and this . . . became especially apparent during the terrible time of the Commune in 1871, when there was not as much as a single instance to be discovered of fire having passed from one house into another."

Shaw also attempted to make his mark in Egypt. He reported to his Committee, in January 1871, that the Foreign Office had invited him to give advice *"on the protection of Cairo from fire"*. He understood that this somewhat wide-ranging request had emanated from the viceroy, but here again the idea may have come from the Duke of Sutherland who had supported, and attended the opening of, the Suez Canal in 1869. When Shaw eventually went, he not only drilled a force for the Khedive but also reported on fire protection in Alexandria, Ismailia and Port Said as well as Cairo. These exertions were not very fruitful for, as THE FIREMAN pointed out sixteen years later, very little advice had been acted upon.

Then, in 1882, Shaw returned to the United States. At the very last meeting of his Committee before the Summer recess he said that he might probably wish to be absent from London for about a fortnight after the Board resumed. He expected, he said, to be back before the end of September but as he proposed to take rather a long journey he thought it well to warn them. The Committee was aware, he said, that the previous year he had not been away at all. In the event, he did not return until some time in the first half of October.

142   The idea for the visit had probably come from the Prince of Wales who

had been there the previous year, when he had attended a massive parade of volunteer firemen. Shaw sailed in the BALTIC and stayed at the Victoria Hotel, New York. In Cincinatti, he attended a national convention of fire engineers during which he was made a Life Member of the National Association of Fire Engineers of America. He established some personal friendships; but many were sceptical of his reputation and had an aversion to anyone with an English accent, especially someone who was so obviously a *'gent'*. Unfortunately, too, he was less tactful than he might have been as, for instance, in New York when the Fire Commissioners wanted to impress him with the speed of turn-out. He purposely pulled the wrong alarm with the result that the men galloped off to the location that had been chosen by the fire chief without noticing that the telegraph indicated a different one. Later, at a display in City Square, both he and President Gorman were drenched by inexperienced and over-enthusiastic firemen.

Probably he did not understand the exuberance or brashness of a nation that was taking half a million newcomers annually from Europe; and he certainly had a bad press. The FIREMAN'S JOURNAL OF AMERICA, for instance, said that he was critical both of American firemen and of their methods. This he denied. His mission, he said, was to learn and, having visited the principal cities of Europe and America, he considered that New York had as fine a body of firemen as any place in the world.

The British magazine, THE FIREMAN, suggested that the Americans might have taken to Shaw more if he had been a man *"more nearly approaching the standard of their own refinement, who would cut coarse jokes and chew tobacco and generally adapt himself to their company"*. But that was not Shaw's life style and he left behind a poor public image even if he made friends with many individual firemen, some of whom he visited again in later years or entertained at Southwark. He chronicled his professional reactions in FIRES AND FIRE BRIGADES, where he wrote:

"The Americans long ago took the lead in steam fire engines; but they stopped where they had begun and at this moment nearly all their splendid machines are far too heavy and unwieldy for the work, and the same may be said of almost everything they have in use.

"So heavy have their hose and other appliances become that they cannot be carried on the engines, and consequently every station has extra horses and coachmen at, of course, a considerable cost . . . Moreover . . . the men are wrapped up in heavy oilskins and sou-westers which retard their action and prevent them from getting down to their work."

In the year 1884, he went to Berlin though for a shorter period, missing neither the last Committee meeting before the recess (on 6 August), nor the first one after it (on 30 September). Then, in 1887, after his two further stays in the States he went to Paris where he inspected the ruins of the Opèra Comique. He told reporters that he made a point of visiting the scene of every great fire, and doubtless with his massive theatre report of the previous year in mind, he referred especially to the Ring Theatre in Vienna and others in Rouen and Nice. This visit to Paris must have taken place on his way to Spain from which he returned coincidentally with the Exeter theatre fire.

It is not clear where he went in 1888 but he had not returned by the time the Committee re-assembled in October for what was in fact (though unrecorded) its 500th meeting. The Second Officer simply stated that as Shaw had not returned to London he, Simonds, had written the reports and was attending on Shaw's behalf. He does seem, by this time, to have been pleasing himself about his absences from London during (and after) the Summer recess. Indeed, he had moved from a position when, in 1882, he had warned in good time that he might be back a fortnight late, through that of warning his employers after he had gone that he would be missing on their return, to a situation only six years later (1888) where he simply did not turn up at the time he was due back. His later employers, the London County Council, would be less complaisant.

Whether he was ever accompanied on these trips by his family seems unlikely for, in 1889, when he went to the Swiss Alps THE FIREMAN noted that his wife and two daughters *"as is their annual wont went to Homberg where they remained for about three weeks, making a short stay at Fokestone on their way home"*.

On this occasion, whilst Shaw was in the Alps, it was the Chairman of the new London County Council Fire Brigade Committee, Colonel Howard Vincent M.P. who was taking a working holiday in Paris and reporting back afterwards on what he had seen. He explained that the Paris Brigade was organised on a military system. The Colonel of the Brigade (in effect Paris's Captain Shaw) was *"an officer of much distinction (who) . . . until recently held a high post at the military college of St. Cyr. The officers,"* he reported, *"are all carefully selected and the men, young and athletic, are far superior in physique to the ordinary French infantry soldier"*. He found London better provided for than Paris in engines, fire escapes and the river service; the French horses were inferior and, because of the defective granite pavements, were slower to respond to a call. The constant change of sappers was a great handicap to efficiency; and, *"if a proportion of London firemen are older, they have the advantage of steadiness and experience. There can be no doubt,"* he concluded, *"that the Navy . . . is a better school for fire work than the Army"*.

It is an illustration of how the creation of the London County Council had diminished the autocracy of Shaw, that it was his Chairman, not he, who made the Paris visit. And when, in 1891, some fifty representatives of French fire brigades came to London, it was the Chairman (on behalf of the Council) who played host and who, after a demonstration, conducted the party through the workshops, stables and stores. For Captain Shaw, the sands of time were running out.

CHAPTER FIFTEEN
SHAW UNDER NEW MANAGEMENT
"We do not want a military man nor do we want a society drawing room darling . . . We want an administrator — one who would be the servant of the committee"

For much of his working life, Shaw's employer was the Metropolitan Board of Works. Its members were elected by the Common Council of the City and by London's Vestries and District Boards. One third of the members retired each year but their re-election, if they wished it, was almost automatic. The system of indirect election was unpopular with all democratic reformers; and there was much apathy, even in the direct elections to the Vestries.

The Board was hindered by not having the name *'London'* in its title. London might be the seat of government, the home of the sovereign, the centre of the legal system and learned professions, the hub of the literary and scientific world and the heart of the Empire; yet it could not speak in its own name except through the City of London. The Act that had created the Board referred only to a *'metropolis'*, not to a particular place called London. The rest of its title, too, was somewhat mundane and suggested that it was no more than a glorified works contractor. In 1855 THE TIMES had hailed the new scheme for London's government with great enthusiasm; only four years later it was describing the Board as a failure and as being incompetent and irresponsible, corrupt and inefficient. These accusations were subsequently fanned by the many associations that advocated the reform of London's government.

It was the 1888 Local Government Act that created the London County Council (LCC) and ensured that, from the following year, the Metropolitan Fire Brigade would pass into its hands though, for legal reasons, the name remained unchanged until 1904. The creation of the London County Council was the fulfilment of a campaign for a unified government of London that had been started by the Liberals in 1876. Accordingly, its elections were fought on political lines from the very beginning. Candidates selected by the Liberal Associations, and ranging from Liberal Unionists to Fabian Socialists, called themselves *'Progressives'*; the Conservative Associations, trusting that independence in local elections would work in their favour, gave no overt help to a *'Moderate'* party, which was clearly Conservative in inspiration. From the first, the elected Councillors had leaders, whips and party meetings, although there is no evidence of a disciplined party group.

The first elections for the new Council were held in January 1889 and the result was an overwhelming victory for the Progressives, who won 73 of the 118 seats. The most prestigious of the successful Progressive candidates was Lord Rosebery, a former Foreign Secretary, who became one of the representatives for the City. He was elected to the chair by 104 votes to 17, and one of his first duties was to preside over the election of Aldermen, a particularly acrimonious affair as negotiations between the parties to share the seats broke down and, on a vote, all but one of the seats went to a

Progressive.

The Metropolitan Board of Works went out of office in a most ignominious fashion. It was due for dissolution and for replacement by the LCC on 31 March 1889. Its last days were occupied in committing the new (as yet impotent) Council to heavy capital expenditure and to raising the salaries and pensions of its officers. THE TIMES commented, on 20 March:

> "London will feel that it is well rid of a body so blind to its own dignity, so unmindful of the plainest precepts of duty, so indifferent indeed to ordinary restraints of decency, as the Metropolitan Board of Works has shown itself to be in the last few weeks. The gravest suspicions of corruption and malversation will attach to its memory."

It was due, at its last meeting on 22 March, to receive massive tenders for engineering works, but the (Conservative) Government feared the worst and so brought forward its dissolution by eleven days to prevent the tenders being dealth with. Not for nothing had it come to be widely known as the Board of Perks.

When the Council's provisional Fire Brigade Committee met for the first time, on 1 March 1889, Shaw was invited to prepare a report on the state of the Brigade and to make recommendations for improved fire cover. This he did with great gusto and little tact, circulating it to the London newspapers at the same time as he put it up to his Committee. He said that if all parts of the LCC area, which was greater than that covered by the former Board of Works, were to be equally and adequately protected there was need for thirty-two new fire stations, twenty-five more steamers and twenty-five additional manual engines. The number of fire escapes needed to increase from 127 to 472. All in all, the cost to the Brigade of these improvements would be £275,000 annually and every Londoner would have to pay 1s 2d (6p) a year for fire protection. New Yorkers, he pointed out, were paying nearly five times that amount. Some of his recommendations were quickly met at least in part, 113 additional men being recruited, and some new fire stations being built chiefly on the outskirts of London. The number of escape stations, hose carts, fire alarms and fire hydrants was also substantially increased.

The additional expenditure was proposed, inevitably, by Progressives, but opposition came not only from the Moderates but also from other Progressives, especially James Ambrose, a Limehouse provision merchant, who only served on the Fire Brigade Committee for seven months; and from Joseph Thornton, a brush manufacturer from the New Kent Road, who represented Bermondsey.

The deployment of more resources and attempts to produce greater cost-effectiveness were accompanied by increased interference in the Brigade's work by the elected Members. Finding, for instance, that in the past Shaw had been given (or had taken) delegated authority in the matter of all but exceptional stores expenditure, it set up a sub-committee which would in future consider all items, both as to quantity and price. Later a very angry Shaw drew his Committee's attention to an article in THE STAR

CAPTAIN SHAW SHORTLY BEFORE RETIREMENT (circa 1891). This is perhaps the best surviving photograph. It illustrates, particularly well, his employers' comment: "He is an absolute-minded man and does not like any interference". (Photo: London Fire Brigade Library).

(24 February 1891) which alleged that, before the LCC had taken over, members of the Brigade had been guilty of gross dishonesty and misconduct, both in connection with the stores accounts and in association with contractors who had charged, and been paid, for work they had not done. His suppressed fury was hardly assuaged when Nathan Moss, a Notting Hill cabinet factor who represented Hoxton as a Progressive and who had recently been Chairman of the Fire Brigade Committee for a year, admitted that he had spoken to a STAR reporter on this subject, though he denied that he was responsible for the views expressed in the article.

The general attitude of many of Shaw's new masters was best set out perhaps by John Burns when, later, there was a discussion in Council about the kind of Chief Officer that was wanted to succeed Shaw on his retirement.

"We are told we want a man to command," he said. *"Well, we do not; we do not want a military man nor do we want a society* **147**

drawing-room darling. (Laughter). We want an executive officer, we want an administrator — one who would be the servant of the Committee, and not a man to command, which invariably means a man who would devote a great deal of his time to circumventing the desires and instructions of the Committee and conducting himself in the way that a man with a large salary generally does, to the exclusion of those administrative duties which he would perform if his salary were a little smaller."

An incident that happened about two years after Shaw had finally gone also shows the kind of men he was having to deal with, THE TIMES of 4 December 1893 noting:

"An extraordinary case, which has to accentuate in a remarkable degree the strong feeling of indignation which prevails throughout the ranks of the Metropolitan Fire Brigade in regard to the manner in which they are treated by the members of the Fire Brigade Committee . . . occurred on Saturday at the station of the Brigade in Farringdon Street. A stranger entered the station, and seizing hold of the 'Occurrence Book' proceeded to read it. The fireman on duty asked him his business and he declined to tell it. Thinking the man was a lunatic, the fireman called in a police constable and ejected him. He then produced a card which showed that he was a member of the Fire Brigade Committee, and, re-entering the station he again opened the 'Occurrence Book' and inserted a memorandum to the effect that the fireman on duty had insulted him . . . The men state that the arbitrary manner in which the Fire Brigade Committee is dealing with all ranks is becoming perfectly unbearable. The members of the Committee, it is said, not infrequently telephone to headquarters for vans to carry them about . . . On the recent occasion of the presentation of medals to the men in Hyde Park the members of the Committee crowded into Captain Simonds's van (he was, for a short while, Shaw's successor) without asking his permission or intimating what their intentions were, and drove off to the National Liberal Club, leaving the Chief Officer of the Brigade to wait until his van returned."

Yet the striving after greater efficiency and the detailed interference by members of the Council did nothing to prevent the first public display by the Brigade, after it was taken over by the LCC, deteriorating into a shambles, something that would surely never have happened if Shaw had been left to organise it himself. To make matters worse, it was held on Horse Guards Parade and the principal guests were the Prince and Princess of Wales. Its aim was the public distribution of medals; the date, Saturday 25 May 1889, only a few weeks after the LCC had resumed responsibility. Arrangements were in the hands of Colonel Howard Vincent MP, who had been elected Chairman of the Fire Brigade Committee although a Moderate. He had pointed out that as Commanding Officer of the Queen's Westminster Rifle Volunteers he could arrange for that body of men *"to keep the ground"*. There would, he promised, be an enclosure near the saluting point for Council members and their friends and *"distinctive non-*

transferable tickets" would be issued to facilitate their admission.

Shaw was left to organise the march past which, naturally, he did with great care and panache. Five vans, five manual pumps, twenty-two steamers and 118 firemen would enter from Birdcage Walk and take up pre-arranged positions; the Prince and Princess would then arrive and drive past; then they would go to the saluting point, past which the engines would walk, then trot and then gallop; then all hands, except the coachmen, would dismount and form a hollow square in front of the Royal party; eight men would receive medals from the Princess; the Prince would address the firemen; the Chairman of the Fire Brigade Committee would thank Their Royal Highnesses; and the firemen would mount, gallop past once more and leave by Birdcage Walk.

So much for the theory. Five days after the event, the Fire Brigade Committee met and the Chairman seems simply to have outlined what had been planned. Then, brush manufacturer Joseph Thornton proposed a motion regretting that the Police authorities had not made *"more efficient arrangements"*, but the motion found no seconder, and there the matter rested. It is, indeed, to the newspapers that one has to turn to find out that what actually took place were *"some of the most remarkable scenes ever witnessed on a State occasion"*.

No enclosure had been marked out for the visitors; when the hundred men of the Queen's Westminster Rifles arrived they found that the crowd was milling about all over the parade ground; Lord Rosebery, the LCC Chairman, together with his children, was trapped somewhere in the mob; the Royal Party, numbering eleven and including all the Prince's grown-up children, had great difficulty in forcing a way through, Miss Shaw (the reports do not say which one) had equal difficulty in reaching the Princesses to present them with a bouquet; when she got there the Princesses had to let her take refuge in their carriage until some brawny firemen managed to transfer her to a steamer; the march past had to be abandoned; the medal winners had to fight their way to the point of presentation; Captain Shaw could not make himself heard; and the other speeches were dispensed with. Shaw was livid; so were the firemen; so, too, no doubt was the Prince. Questions were asked in the House; there had been, it was said, some misunderstanding between the LCC and the Police.

Disaffection was growing on all sides. The men were discontented; the officers were discontented; Shaw was discontented; and so, too, were the members of the Council.

In March 1891, seven hundred members of the Brigade petitioned for more money; in the previous year, for the first time in the history of the force, they threatened to go on strike, over boots. They should, they claimed, have had new boots at Christmas, but they had not. The threat was effective. This was all part of the broader picture of increased working-class militancy, illustrated for example in a letter, in May 1891, from the Wandsworth branch of the Amalgamated Society of House Decorators and Painters. This enquired whether it was true that painting at the Brigade stations was done by the firemen and, if it was not true, whether the Society might have details of the work that had been entrusted to **149**

MR. ROBERT LYON, PECKHAM. A marine salvage surveyor and a Progressive on the new LCC, he behaved with considerable insensitivity when Shaw resigned, at which time he was Chairman of the Fire Brigade Committee. (Photo: ILLUSTRATED LONDON NEWS).

MR. NATHAN MOSS, HOXTON. A Notting Hill cabinet factor, he was a Progressive on the new LCC and was one of Shaw's bitterest critics. He was, for a year, Chairman of the Fire Brigade Committee. (Photo: ILLUSTRATED LONDON NEWS).

contractors. A month later, the Council's architect dealt with a complaint from the Asphalte Employees Protection Society that Claridges' Patent Asphalte Company had paid sub-standard wage rates for work done at various fire stations; he also reported that carpenters at work on a new fire station at Wandsworth had gone on strike.

This militancy by working men, whether firemen or artisans, was anathema to Shaw and to his senior officers, six of whom had by the beginning of 1891 handed in their resignations in the twenty-one months of the LCC's existence. The world they had known was rapidly changing; and they were disinclined to change with it. Even some ideas that were laudable and indeed idealistic they viewed with scepticism, as when Thornton the brush maker suggested that meetings to be held in the parish of St. George the Martyr, Southwark, to sound out ratepayers' views on the question of free libraries might by matched by meetings of staff to discuss the same matter at Fire Brigade Headquarters.

Shaw himself was the subject of increasing harassment. One petty example of this occurred in January 1890. The Chairman of the Fire Brigade Committee, currently Nathan Moss, the cabinet factor, drew attention to a paragraph in the DAILY TELEGRAPH which stated that on the occasion of Lord Napier's funeral a detachment of the Fire Brigade, under Captain Shaw, had been drawn up in the churchyard. On whose authority, he wanted to know. Shaw, rather lamely, said that as some of his family had expressed a wish to see the funeral he had applied to the City Commissioner of Police for places. That gentleman had suggested that Shaw might like to have some men in uniform with him; Shaw had accompanied them in one of the police vans. Thornton moved and Robert

Lyon, another Progressive and a Peckham marine salvage surveyor who was to become next Chairman of the Fire Brigade Committee, seconded a motion on the subject. It was that *"the explanation tendered by the Chief Officer of his conduct on this occasion is not satisfactory"*. Neither was it; and he should have known better. He expressed regret, but relationships had hardly been improved by conduct that was at least politically insensitive and perhaps also both bloody-minded and arrogant. Shaw was becoming his own worst enemy and increasingly Members strove to take him down a peg or two.

Four months after that incident, he submitted to his Committee the programme for a performance by a detachment of the Brigade at the annual exhibition of the National Physical Recreation Society at the Royal Agricultural Hall. They noticed a statement that the men would appear *"by the kind permission of Captain Shaw CB"* and they at once resolved to advise the Society that they *"strongly objected"* to the words used and wished them to be expunged.

The very next month there was ill-feeling over Brigade drill. This had become an elaborately-staged Wednesday afternoon spectacle and was such a social occasion that admission to good vantage points was by ticket. The ever-troublesome brush maker, Thornton, complained to the Committee that his information was that Wednesday drill was of a special character and that ordinary ratepayers who had asked to be present were being roughly turned away by firemen. Shaw disarmingly told the Committee that, although his wife was at home on Wednesday afternoons to receive visitors, the drill on that day of the week was the same as that on any other and he had never received any complaints of the kind alluded to. It is again easy to see faults on both sides. One may conclude that each wanted to be rid of the other.

CHAPTER SIXTEEN
RESIGNATION
"A magnificent way of resigning"

One sign of the changing climate nationally was the creation, in 1887, of the National Fire Brigades Union, originated by provincial volunteers who described themselves, significantly, as *"workers, not idlers, or ornamental gentlemen"*. When, in 1880, Shaw had been invited to become connected officially with the volunteer firemen he had declined; now, in 1887, he accepted the Presidency of the new Union.

In June 1891, he led its first parade at the Crystal Palace, in front of the Emperor of Germany and the Prince of Wales. London was not represented and, since the fifty-six brigades present marched past in alphabetical order, Shaw rode on the engine of the Aberystwyth Fire Brigade. This was somewhat ironical, for it was an ancient machine that had been bought second-hand from Glasgow for £72; even more so because it was to be one of Shaw's last public appearances. A few days earlier, he had tendered his resignation.

That resignation was to achieve more column inches in the national newspapers than would be conceivable now for any world figure. It was not because of the deed itself — Shaw was over sixty-three — but because it was recognised as a significant political matter in which all the newspapers took sides, according to whether they were against the new LCC (i.e.,

THE CRYSTAL PALACE GALLOP PAST (1891). Shaw had for many years been unsupportive of volunteer firemen but in 1891 he led its first parade at the Crystal Palace, before the Emperor of Germany and the Prince of Wales. (Photo: British Library).

sympathisers of the Conservatives and Moderates) or for the LCC (i.e., backers of the Liberals and Progressives). By picking up any newspaper of the time and reading one paragraph about Shaw's resignation, one can tell immediately where that paper stood on the political issues of the day and, especially, what it thought of London's new governing body.

Shaw had taken a few days' leave over Whitsun and, as soon as he returned, he reported that he wished to be away from London between 9 and 12 July, a period when he was normally never out of Town. But the dates had been chosen with great care, and indeed cunning.

With equally careful timing, he wrote his letter of resignation on 26 June, the day after his Committee met. On the same date (or even previously) he wrote to the Prince of Wales to tell him what he was doing, and the Prince's Secretary replied that *"for the sake both of the Fire Brigade and of London"* the Prince sincerely regretted to hear of Shaw's intention. The resignation was reported to the Committee, almost as a footnote, at their meeting on 2 July (as Shaw had obviously intended), so that its full impact and any Committee discussion would necessarily take place at its next meeting on 9 July — the first day of Shaw's absence on leave.

The letter was starkly simple and was addressed merely to *"The London County Council"*. It read:

"Gentlemen

Having completed 30 years' service in the Brigade I desire to obtain my pension in accordance with the regulations.

I shall however be glad to remain in charge for any reasonable time to be agreed on, if your honourable Council considers that such a course will be of advantage to the Department, pending the appointment of my successor.

I have the honour to be, Gentlemen,

Your obedient servant,

Eyre M. Shaw

Chief Officer, Metropolitan Fire Brigade."

When the Council heard of the resignation, a Member asked the Chairman of the Fire Brigade Committee whether any reason had been given for it. He replied that all he knew was what was said in the letter. THE GLOBE commented that, happily, whatever the reason it had nothing to do with Shaw's health and strength or with any need for repose. But the journal LAND AND WATER went a lot farther. It described the LCC as *"that extremely self-sufficient body of amateur everythings"*, and said they would never find another Captain Shaw. The amount of work he did would have to be divided among many and the firemen under him had been *"like a happy family under the direction of an affectionate father"*. For his courage, his powers of organisation, his even temper and his great endurance he had become a household name throughout the land. He had been driven from his post by *"senseless and ignorant heckling"*. It was, it concluded, *"the patient British Public that will have to pay the cost of this, the latest and gravest blunder of that ridiculous mushroom body, the London County Council"*.

THE TIMES, in more measured terms, described his admirable relations with his men who were devoted to him, and his constant search for new methods of prevention, detection and extinction of fire. The Metropolitan Fire Brigade was better organised, better equipped and more able to perform its duties than the brigade of any other European capital or of any American city. THE REFEREE, however, took a more unusual line, suggesting that it would eventually be realised that fire could be extinguished by what it called vibratory physics, the *"setting up of some counter-vibration of the ether"*. The office of chief fireman, it said, *"will some day be as obsolete as that of the medicine man of the Red Indians"*.

By 4 July, two days after the Fire Brigade Committee had noted the receipt of Shaw's letter of resignation, speculation was beginning to grow as to what had prompted it, the HAMPSHIRE INDEPENDENT hoping that whatever difficulties had arisen might be removed; and THE OBSERVER of 5 July suggesting that certain *"fussy members"* of the Committee had made his life unbearable by their interference.

The middle fortnight of the month produced evidence of conflict within both the Fire Brigade Committee and the Council over the absence of any expression of regret by Members at the resignation. Edmund Boulnois for instance, the proprietor of the Baker Street Bazaar, Conservative MP for East Marylebone and later to be leader of the Moderates in the LCC, expressed surprise that there was none; on the other side, John Williams Benn, Liberal MP, publisher, grandfather of Tony Wedgwood Benn and later to be leader of the Progressives and Chairman of the LCC said, rather obscurely, that he could quite understand his colleague's desire *"to advertise his friend Captain Shaw at the expense of those who had done their duty properly"*. He was quite sure that the final report would be *"interlarded with sufficient expressions of regret"*.

The irascible Joseph Thornton, the Progressive New Kent Road brush maker, said he saw no reason why the Committee should pay a compliment *"where one had not been earned"*, or why the Committee should be courteous *"where ordinary courtesy was not shown to them"*. Some members of the Committee at least, knew why the resignation had been offered.

The Chairman, Sir John Lubbock, trying to pour oil on troubled waters, said that he hoped the public would not draw any inference as to the Council's opinion on the matter by what had been said. He thought everyone recognised the valuable service rendered by Captain Shaw and, for his part, he hoped the resignation would not be final. THE GLOBE complained that the letter of resignation had been placed before the Committee just as if it had been *"an indent for soap"*, and suggested that if Captain Shaw had no difference of opinion with a Committee which included such men he *"must have the temper of an angel"*.

But whatever the reasons for Shaw's resignation, it was only a part of a broader picture. On 20 July, a month or so after Shaw had written his letter, THE TIMES reported the resignation also of Superintendent William Port. There were, it said, seven officers at the head of the Brigade (Shaw, the Second Officer and five superintendents) and, of those seven, five had resigned since the LCC had taken over the Brigade a little more than two years previously; another superintendent, William Hutchings, was to die on active service the following month. THE TIMES omitted to say that all five who had resigned were of retirement age. Shaw was sixty-three and had served thirty years; Superintendent Hamlyn had been one of the oldest men in the Brigade when he left after thirty-seven years; Superintendent Palmer had been almost sixty and had nearly thirty-six years' service behind him; Superintendent Campbell was fifty-five, with thirty years' service; and Superintendent Port, although a mere fifty-three years of age, had served nearly thirty-three years and was the last active fireman in London to have worked under Braidwood and at the Tooley Street fire. It was misleading of THE TIMES to refer to *"constant changings and shiftings which cannot but be the reverse of beneficial"*; the LCC had inherited a team of senior officers who were highly experienced but also aged; their retirement shortly would have been inevitable under any regime. It took a paper from north of the Border, the SCOTTISH LEADER, to point out that the resignations had all come close together because those concerned had deferred their retirement until a new pension scheme came into force.

By the time Shaw's resignation was next considered by the LCC, the Fire Brigade Committee had got round to expressing regret. It had discussed the matter in some detail on 9 July when, it will be remembered, Shaw had arranged to be on leave. Colonel Howard Vincent, a Moderate and the Committee's first Chairman, complained at the way the letter had been reported to Committee on 2 July and passed to the Council without any recommendation. The current Chairman, Robert Lyon, apologised, but said that as the contents of the letter had already been made public (by Shaw) he had thought it best to pass it on to the Council informally in advance of any discussion on it. An attempt to amend the proposal that the minutes of 2 July should be confirmed, which amendment would have had the effect of excluding references to the letter as it had been irregularly placed before the Committee, was defeated by four votes to three. No one had come out of this well: Shaw should not have made the contents of his letter public; the Committee should have foreseen the effect of passing on the letter to the Council without comment; the Chairman of the Committee should have advised the Chairman of the Council in confidence; and the Council should have refrained from discussing the letter publicly until the Fire Brigade Committee had considered it. A week of nationwide wrangling and speculation would then have been avoided.

At their 9 July meeting the Fire Brigade Committee was surprisingly unanimous in recording its regret at receiving Shaw's resignation from the post which he had held *"for the long period of thirty years with conspicuous success and with great advantage to the safety of life and property in the Metropolis"*. More predictable was the motion by Joseph Thornton (supported, on this occasion, by Nathaniel Hubbard, a Herne Hill coal merchant) that Shaw should receive a pension smaller than that to which he was entitled. That uncharitable motion was lost by two votes to nine.

155

SUPERINTENDENT WILLIAM PORT. The last active fireman in London to have worked under Braidwood and at the Tooley Street fire. He retired immediately after Shaw resigned. He was then 53, with nearly 33 years' service. (Photo: London Fire Brigade Museum).

SUPERINTENDENT CHARLES CAMPBELL. Campbell began his fire career as a parish engineer in 1855, was absorbed into the Brigade and was promoted to Superintendent in 1880. He retired shortly before Shaw; He was then the oldest Metropolitan fireman. (Photo: London Fire Brigade Museum).

SUPERINTENDENT WILLIAM
HUTCHINGS. Captain Shaw had great
confidence in Hutchings. He had joined the
Fire Brigade Establishment in 1862 and was
promoted to Superintendent in 1885, over the
heads of more senior men. He died of blood-
poisoning in 1891. (Photo: London Fire
Brigade Museum).

CAPTAIN SHAW: A CARTOONIST'S
IMPRESSION. Shaw was very tall and slim - hence
his nickname, "the long 'un". When he "weighed
in", as a guest at Sandringham in 1878, he turned
the scales at 13 stone 3 lbs, in uniform. (Photo:
London Fire Brigade Library).

The Committee, on the same day, received two petitions that had been set out with almost indecent haste. One was from Mappin Brothers asking if they might submit designs and estimates *"in the event of the Council desiring to present Captain Shaw with a testimonial"*, and pointing out that they had designed and were making *"the beautiful Gold Casket and Badges for presentation to the German Emperor on the occasion of his visit to the Guildhall"*, the following day. The other petition was from the Second Officer, J. Sexton Simonds, applying for the (as yet unadvertised) Chief Officer's post. He felt confident, he said, that he would carry with him *"the loyal support of most, if not all, the officers and men of the Brigade"*; a curious piece of self-depreciation.

When the full Council next met, on 21 July, they had before them the Fire Brigade Committee's expression of regret at Shaw's resignation. This was tabled as a formal motion and then George Fardell, a Moderate representing Paddington, moved an amendment that Shaw should be asked to reconsider his decision. John Hutton, a Progressive best known as the proprietor and publisher of the ABC Railway Guide, seconded. The amendment was carried and the substantive motion was then passed by forty-three votes to thirty-six, which is hardly the *"substantial majority"* described by the MORNING POST. It indicates that Shaw had a lot of supporters among the Progressives; but reports of the meeting show that these did not include either John Williams Benn, who protested that the Council was going cap-in-hand to Captain Shaw and thereby setting a precedent, or Joseph Thornton whose attempts to say why he thought Shaw had resigned were constantly interrupted. It was obviously the Radical wing of the Progressive group that opposed Shaw; and Nathan Moss, the Notting Hill cabinet factor and previous Chairman of the Fire Brigade Committee, indicated the reason. The Council would, he said, lose all control of its officers if the resignation were not accepted. Under the Board of Works *"the Fire Brigade Committee had practically been Captain Shaw"* (he presumably meant the reverse), but the Committee was now determined to think for itself. THE TIMES, however, observed: *"The sagacious, temperate and capable members (among the Progressives) are unable to put any effective check upon the escapades of their colleagues"*. In fairness to Benn, though, he did later point out in a letter to THE TIMES that he had never spoken to Shaw in his life and was simply urging, *"purely for administrative reasons, that the Council, much abused as it is, was not called upon to grovel in the way suggested by Mr. Fardell"*. He was, he said, second to none in recognising Shaw's splendid work for London.

The BIRMINGHAM MAIL suggested at this point that, if it came to a choice between abolishing the London County Council or Captain Shaw, the majority of Londoners would probably prefer to dispense with the Council as the lesser of the two evils. On the other hand the *'popular'* Radical paper, the PALL MALL GAZETTE, suggested that if despite all Captain Shaw's efforts the force would *"tumble to pieces"* as soon as he retired, there was something seriously wrong. THE DWARF took up the same theme, and concluded: *"Bismarck is Chancellor no more; yet*

Germany thrives".
Shaw was, meantime, quick to respond to the invitation to reconsider his decision to retire. The letter though was obscure in its implications; and was no doubt intended to be so.

"I am much obliged for this compliment," he wrote, *"and I do not hesitate to say that I would gladly do anything in my power which would enable me to remain where I am; but I am compelled to look at all circumstances from a point of view which may not have presented itself to your notice, and I regret to have to express my conviction that, under the existing conditions and terms, I could not continue to hold my position with advantage either to your honourable Council or to myself."*

The new Radical mass-circulation evening paper, THE STAR (which, with the DAILY CHRONICLE was the Progressives' most constant friend) pondered Shaw's phrase, *"existing conditions and terms".* There must be *'conditions and terms'* in any municipality, it suggested. *"The public who elect the Council",* it continued, *"expect that it will safeguard the public interests, supervise public expenditure, and not shift its duties onto the shoulders of an irresponsible official".* The Metropolitan Board of Works had had a wonderful capacity for shirking its duties and, under it, Captain Shaw had exercised his functions *"untrammelled by close supervision".* The present Fire Brigade Committee, on the other hand, had shown a zealous regard for the public interest. The Chairman of the Committee had actually taken the trouble to attend fires (an act described by THE SPORTSMAN, a couple of days later, as *"an altogether needless piece of zeal").*

"All this was new to Captain Shaw," continued THE STAR. *"He tried to thwart the Committee, but it insisted . . . in exercising the control which the public had entrusted to them . . . The 'conditions and terms' it has imposed have been purely in the public interest. It would be intolerable if a public officer, whoever he is, and however capable he may be, enjoyed unlimited power coupled with absolute irresponsibility. In a well-governed municipality there is no place for autocrats."*

The PALL MALL GAZETTE, in similar vein, suggested that the resignation was being treated *"with all the gravity and anxiety due to a national crisis";* though, it might have added, without the unanimity among the press that such a crisis would probably have created.

THE TIMES suggested that interference with Shaw had been prompted by *"the meddlesome vanity of Jacks-in-office luxuriating in the brief day of their power".* But JUSTICE, the paper of the Socialist Democratic Federation which was, at that moment, the largest Socialist party in London, took an opposite and much more succinct view: *"Captain Shaw has resigned, and a good thing too. London has read about enough of the bumptiousness of this overrated 'pal' of the Prince of Wales and the Duke of Sutherland."*

Increasingly, the provinces were showing an interest and taking sides. The West Yorkshire Fire Brigade Friendly Society, based at Cleckheaton, sent a resolution to the LCC Fire Brigade Committee urging that the Council should unanimously refuse to accept Shaw's resignation; and the BRISTOL TIMES AND MIRROR and the NOTTS GUARDIAN, in exactly the same (presumably therefore syndicated) words condemned the LCC. On the other hand, the BOLTON EVENING NEWS, the SHEFFIELD INDEPENDENT, the LIVERPOOL POST and the LEICESTER MERCURY (all with identical text) supported the Council. So, too, did the BRADFORD OBSERVER, which suggested that no official of a provincial municipality would ever dream of adopting an attitude similar to Shaw's. The SUSSEX DAILY NEWS ventured to suggest that the attitude of THE TIMES to the whole matter was ludicrous, and considered that there was probably *"some lack of tact on both sides"*. Few impartial observers, then or now, would probably dissent from that.

Even the American papers joined in. The NEW YORK HERALD criticised the LCC and concluded: *"It is exceedingly liberal in spending other people's money, but beyond that it can offer no claim to distinction. We should not predict for it a lengthened career, and its epitaph does not seem likely to be flattering to its brief existence"*. By contrast (in style as well as view), the BALTIMORE UNDERWRITER claimed:

> *"No American underwriter or fireman outside of (SIC) the snobocracy has ever had any use for that superlative snob, Eyre M. Shaw . . . His weak side and his blind side, his defects and deficiencies have always been better understood on this side of the Atlantic than in his own bailiwick."*

By the last day of July, demands were growing for some kind of inquiry or official investigation into the whole matter. A certain Heathcote Harding, of Ravenscroft Park, managed to get a letter on the subject published in THE STANDARD, the MORNING POST and THE ECHO all on the same day, and for three or four days newspapers both in London and in the Provinces pursued the same theme; but the idea then ceased to attract attention.

In its place, the matter began to be seen in relation to the next LCC elections. LAND AND WATER, for instance, on 1 August commented:

> *"As soon as it becomes known that a really good man cannot . . . serve the Council with advantage to them or himself . . . no first-rate men will care to become candidates for County Council offices. Consequently, the work will be done in an inferior way by inferior officers."*

The paper expressed the hope that Londoners would secure the return of a Council *"wholly different from the present (one) . . . The ratepayers . . . have little more than six months to get ready . . . Politics cannot be left out"*. The WESTERN MORNING NEWS, too, felt that Shaw's resignation was likely to be held against the Progressives in the forthcoming election, *"and for that reason will be kept for some time longer before the public"*.

Another element that was creeping into the papers by early August was speculation about Shaw's future. The WEEKLY DISPATCH, a paper addressed particularly to London tradespeople and their assistants, referred to his *"magnificent pension"*; but others sought to employ his undoubted talents. Wotton Isaacson, the Conservative MP for Tower Hamlets and a fellow member of the Carlton Club, asked the First Lord of the Treasury whether the Government would consider attaching Shaw to a department of State so that *"his valuable services might be retained for the benefit of the country"*. The Chancellor of the Exchequer, in reply, said that whilst it was well-known that Captain Shaw was an officer of distinguished ability, he knew of no vacant office where his services could be used. The MANCHESTER COURIER and the WHITEHALL REVIEW suggested with some strong force of logic that he should become the first Inspector-General of Theatres.

By this time, most of what could be said had been, and with the onset of the Summer recess all went quiet. All, that is, except a *'silly season'* rumour attributed to the London correspondent of the MANCHESTER GUARDIAN, and published in THE STAR and, next day, in the EDINBURGH EVENING NEWS and the BELFAST NEWSLETTER, that Shaw had withdrawn his resignation. Shortly, both THE ECHO and THE STAR were publishing emphatic denials from Shaw.

In late September, the papers again carried speculation about his future. The BELFAST MORNING NEWS confidently told its readers that Shaw intended to stand for the LCC, he was certain to be elected and he would then *"of course be found a place on the Fire Brigade Committee"*. That would have created an interesting situation. Meanwhile, the BIRMINGHAM DAILY GAZETTE and the SHEFFIELD DAILY TELEGRAPH reported that four Parliamentary constituencies were anxious to have him as their Member, and the DUNDEE ADVERTISER, THE STAR and the ST. STEPHEN'S REVIEW all named the West Division of Southwark as one of them, whilst the LEEDS MERCURY — perhaps with a less clear telephone line — had it as one of the Divisions of Suffolk. FIGARO was infinitely more vague *"He is going to winter in Rome, and when he comes home he will have other fish to fry"*.

Although Shaw's response to the invitation to reconsider his decision to resign had been dated 24 July, the Fire Brigade Committee made no effort to consider the matter again until their second meeting after the recess, on 24 September (Shaw had been away on the day of the previous week's meeting). The Committee deliberated the letter in private for some time and Shaw was then called in *"and was asked to explain in writing what were the terms and conditions to which he referred in his letter"*. A Special Meeting would be held in eight days' time (later changed to eleven) to consider the matter further. It was five days before the Clerk confirmed in writing to Shaw what was wanted of him.

Shaw refused to be drawn. He did not send his reply until the day of the meeting, and it was both dignified and disingenuous:

"I hold a very strong belief that the existing arrangements are not such as to conduce to the success of the Brigade in carrying out its arduous duties, and, being unwilling to make any complaint, or ask any favour, I have claimed the pension to which I am entitled.

161

At the meeting of the 24 ultimo, I was under the impression that the wish of the Committee was that I should give my views with regard to the mode with which the Brigade could be safely and properly worked, and I endeavoured to make it understood that I was willing to do this; but the wording of the communication to which this is a reply is so clear and definite, as referring to the past and not to the future, that it seems to be impossible for me to go beyond my present statement, which is a simple repetition of that which I made on the 24 ultimo.

I am sure that the Committee would not wish to place me in the false position of seeming to make complaints when I have successfully avoided making any; but, if the desire is that I should make suggestions as to the future working of the Brigade, I shall be quite prepared to bring forward proposals which I think will be useful to all who are interested in the success of this department of the Council's business."

After the Committee had considered this letter, they instructed the Clerk to reply which he did, as follows:

"The Committee have received your letter . . . which they regret to find does not contain the information they understood you to promise to endeavour to give them at their meeting on the 24 ultimo. They have instructed me to ask you again to give a definite reply . . . and also to explain the grounds of the statement . . . of today of your 'very strong belief that the existing arrangements are not such as to conduce to the success of the Brigade in carrying out its arduous duties'. The Committee feel that it is due to them that you should inform them what are the existing arrangements to which you refer.

I may point out to you that any statement you may make to the Committee respecting the past would be likely to be of assistance to them in regard to the future . . ."

But Shaw was too astute to fall for that, as his reply written two days later shows. It ran:

"In reply to your letter of the 5 instant, I have to inform you that I have nothing to add to what I have already said.

The Fire Brigade Committee and the members of the Fire Brigade Committee are quite aware of their own proceedings without explanation from me or anyone, and I think it will probably be acknowledged that I have faithfully done my part in carrying out all instructions which I have received.

With regard to the past I do not see how I can made any statement which might not be interpreted as a complaint, and the Committee is already acquainted with my views on this point.

If I had wished to make a complaint I should have made one, but I considered such a course inconsistent with my position, and I continue to hold the same view."

At long last, the Committee realised that it would never obtain from Shaw a statement that would enable it to vindicate its actions. It resolved that the correspondence should be submitted to the Council and intimated that it was considering the conditions of service for a new Chief of the Brigade.

Naturally, the newspapers once more took up their by now customary positions. THE STAR attacked Shaw's refusal to be drawn and suggested that the correspondence did him little credit. *"In attempting to throw mud at the Council,"* it said, *"Captain Shaw has got bespattered himself"*. THE TIMES thought it was *"a magnificent way of resigning"*, but it certainly did not prove he was right and the County Council hopelessly wrong. THE ECHO, however, suggested that the richest city in the world could not afford to have tried, trusty and responsible officers subjected to irritating interference by those *"who are neither experts nor the result of natural selection"*.

At this point Shaw's opponents opened up a barrage of criticism about his pension. THE STAR suggested he would receive nearly £1,000 per annum in retirement and that whereas he received a pension equal to two-thirds of his salary a subway inspector received only one-third of his former earnings. The position, said the newspaper, should be reversed.

Inevitably Joseph Thornton, sarcastically described at this point by the SOUTH LONDON MAIL as *"the highly intellectual and gentlemanly representative of Bermondsey"*, opposed the proposals for Shaw's pension. As Shaw had received more than £40,000 during his thirty years' service he ought to have made provision himself for his retirement. It was not Shaw, suggested Thornton, who had brought the Brigade to its present condition of efficiency, but the superintendents, the engineers and the men. The BRITISH ARCHITECT, too, suggested that the proposed pension would be *"a handsome salary for doing nothing"*. The SUSSEX DAILY NEWS, however, said that Shaw had been underpaid in his post, it was no one's business but his own whether he had saved any money and, anyway, he had probably been *"paying pretty heavily for the insurance of his life"*. In the same debate, and in similar spirit to that of Thornton, John Burns welcomed Shaw's retirement and said he was convinced that the new Chief Officer would be able to reorganise the Brigade. *"The engineering department,"* he claimed, *"would not do credit to a second-hand ironmonger's in a back street"*.

Two days later, on 22 October, Shaw attended a meeting of the Fire Brigade Committee for the last time. There was considerable discussion of the appointment of a new Chief Officer. But absolutely no reference is recorded as having been made to the fact that it was his last time in attendance and no vote of thanks was proferred for his thirty years' service.

The previous day he had been 'at home' to a representative of the journal PICCADILLY, who wrote that Shaw did not like newspapers and was never slow to say so, but on this occasion he had been in *"a fairly loquacious mood"*. He had told the reporter: *"I was born on 17 January 1828"*; previously, he had generally allowed himself to be quoted as being two years younger than he really was. He refused to be drawn on the reasons for his resignation and as to whether he would contest Southwark in the next Election. To a reporter of the SOUTH LONDON NEWS, who obviously had not been invited to interview Shaw at home, he was much

163

more brusque. Having agreed that he had been asked to contest West Southwark *"our representative was proceeding to further interrogate the gentleman when the latter said sharply, 'I have nothing further to say. Good morning"* '. Upon which, wrote the reporter, *"the Captain placed his hat upon his head and departed".*

The day after Shaw's last Committee meeting, the Liberal DAILY NEWS described the *"general gloom"* prevailing among the officers and men at Headquarters. Perhaps they agreed, though unable to express the thoughts themselves in such flowing terms, with THE WORLD which, a few days later, described the LCC as:

> *"the grand organic embodiment of the combined Bumbledom and Jacobinism of the Metropolis . . . It has managed to unite in itself the worst attributes of an English vestry with the worst attributes of a French revolutionary club . . . No English vestry could well display grosser ignorance or denser stupidity than it does . . . No French revolutionary club was . . . more dangerous in its designs or more oppressive in its practice . . . The miscellaneous collection of notoriety-hunting busybodies, faddists, crotchetters and charlatans who form the active section of its members, utterly refuse to be cribbed, cabined or confined by the statutory provisions which define its legitimate powers and capacities."*

So, after a torrent of words that can rarely have accompanied the resignation even of a government, 31 October 1891 dawned. The morning papers carried the news that Shaw had been awarded the KCB: he had been appointed a Companion thirteen years earlier. TRUTH, a powerful enemy of cant and hypocracy, commented that anyone who was surprised that Shaw had had a KCB conferred on him rather than a baronetcy had overlooked the fact that a KCB was *"infinitely more esteemed"*. It could only be secured *"by brilliant service, whilst the other is generally acquired in turn for contributions towards the funds of the party in power"*. It continued: *"A successful officer receives the KCB; any successful tradesman can, if so minded, procure a baronetcy".*

But the prize for malevolence of a kind that so frequently characterised the Victorian press must go to REYNOLD NEWS which obviously disregarded on this occasion the fact that one of its regular readers was Bertie, Prince of Wales.

> *"Flunkey Shaw,"* it said, *"has not only got his savings and his pension, but also a KCB and is now presumably happy, since he is just the kind of small-minded man likely to set a high value on an empty title as well as on a solid pension. This mark of recognition is probably intended by our Tory class Government as a snub to the Democratic County Council of London."*

During his final day in the Brigade Shaw, dressed in plain clothes and accompanied by Lady Shaw and their children Anna and Clarina, took leave of his colleagues. Three hundred men, about half the total force, assembled for the event. These included the four Superintendents, all of whom were fairly new in post, and also three retired Superintendents (Campbell, Hamlyn and Port) who had served under him for most or all of his thirty years.

Curiously, there is much conflict in the newspapers of the time about what was presented at the ceremony. Second Officer Simonds made the presentation of two pieces of plate (or a candelabrum or a pair of silver candelabra) purchased by subscription among the men. Also, an address was read setting out the Brigade's appreciation for Shaw's *"incessant zeal, unflagging energy and constant devotion to duty"* which, it said ambiguously, in spite of many and great difficulties, had brought the Brigade to its present state of efficiency.

Turning to Anna Maria, Captain Simonds said that in Lady Shaw the Chief Officer had had a helpmate for many years; and in his daughter Anna (curiously, referred to in several places in the report in THE TIMES as "Hannah") the men and their wives had a devoted friend on their beds of sickness, and when they were injured or dying Miss Shaw had set a noble example to the women and children. *"As the name of her father"*, he continued, *"would be emblazoned on the scroll of time so Miss Shaw's name would be engraved on the hearts of all connected with the Metropolitan Fire Brigade"*.

Shaw who, according to the MORNING ADVERTISER *"nearly broke down altogether"*, replied:

"I thank you from the bottom of my heart and I will always retain a lively recollection of our work together. I would add a few words about your duty. Your duty is to preserve over five million people from fire who have elected a certain body to represent them, and to them you owe your duty. I know from past experience that you will amply carry this out. My last words to you are, be loyal to those whom you serve."

Despite Shaw's words and the nature of the occasion THE STAR could not avoid the comment: *"The moral of which we take to be is that precept is better than example"*.

Simonds then presented to Mrs. Shaw a gold bracelet studded with diamonds and rubies (or a sapphire ring, or a diamond and ruby ring) and to Miss Shaw a diamond and amethyst gold brooch (or a gold bangle bracelet in diamonds and amethysts). As the company left, Shaw shook hands with everyone at the door, the rest of his family standing by his side and doing the same.

Later Shaw received, also, an inscribed silver salver, a tea and coffee service and a cabinet of silver plate from the insurance companies constituting the Fire Offices Committee; and from the medical department of the Brigade, a George III silver goblet, richly embossed and bearing a commemorative inscription. Subsequently, too, the officers and men of the Brigade presented Clarina with a silver inkstand in recognition of the good feeling which had for so many years existed between them and his family.

The DAILY NEWS, in reporting the event, drew attention to the coincidence that it was because of the great Tooley Street fire that Shaw had succeeded Braidwood when he did, and the last fire attended by Shaw in uniform was at Mark Brown's wharf in the same road.

Shaw's last report to his Committee was dated the same day as his retirement, 31 October 1891. It read:

"*. . . The number of fire stations, which in 1861 was 13 is now 59; the number of firemen, which was 113 is now 706; the quantity of hose, which was under 4 miles in length, is now over 33 miles . . .*

The system of telephones and of call-points which formerly did not exist, now extends over the whole of London.

The attendances during my time have been as follows:

FALSE ALARMS	CHIMNEY CALLS	FIRES
32,335	86,645	55,004

Total calls: 173,984

In addition to a large number of coachmen and pilots, there have passed through my hands 2,796 men of whom some have died or been killed, some have been pensioned, many have got appointments at home or in the colonies, and there remain 706 thoroughly trained and disciplined officers and firemen in splendid order, and capable of carrying on their duties with spirit and determination under all circumstances likely to arise.

The force is now fully recruited to the last man of the authorised number, and every member of it has been as fully trained and instructed as the time of his service has made possible . . .

I have completed every reference made to me from Committee and answered every letter which I have received, and there are no arrears of work in my department . . ."

With staggering malevolence the Committee, when it received the report five days later, agreed only on the Chairman's casting vote to print it in full for submission to the Council; and, although Shaw's resignation was formally announced as having taken place, there was again no resolution of thanks, appreciation or good wishes.

Meanwhile, at five minutes to midnight on Shaw's last day as Chief Officer of the Metropolitan Fire Brigade, he sent from Southwark to every fire station in London the message:

"Captain Shaw on leaving wishes to say goodbye and good luck to all members of the Brigade".

A few days later, he and Lady Shaw left for Paris. They later went on to Italy although he was back in London early in December to receive the Freedom of the Worshipful Company of Coach Makers and Coach Harness Makers, the Master of the Company being Edmund Boulnois, the later leader of the Moderates on the LCC.

In the meantime, the LCC sought a successor. There were forty-one applicants for the post and nine were interviewed. The Fire Brigade Committee nominated, as first choice, the Second Officer, J. Sexton Simonds. The General Purposes Committee rejected him in favour of the Fire Brigade Committee's second choice, W. R. Campbell, an army Captain. Council, however, reversed the decision by a decisive majority (49-11) — perhaps because Campbell was said to be a protégé of Shaw. Simonds was appointed but five years later left in disgrace over financial malpractices. The next time round, the wrong decision was again made. Sidney Gamble, a well-educated and experienced fire officer of undoubted ability and integrity, who had become Simond's Second Officer was passed over and a naval officer, Commander Wells, was appointed from among eighty-three applicants. After only seven years he left to become Chief Agent of the Conservative Party and was succeeded by another naval officer, Captain Hamilton. His term of office lasted only five years and, when he left to become a Director of the Army and Navy stores, THE FIREMAN commented: *"He knew nothing about fire fighting when he took over the command . . . and that knowledge . . . had not greatly increased when he left"*.

All three of these men, Simonds, Wells and Hamilton commanded the Brigade while Shaw was still alive. He must have watched their arrival, their contribution and their departure in awe and despondency.

CHAPTER SEVENTEEN

RETIREMENT AND DEATH
"The public confidence which has been so unreservedly placed in him has been fully deserved"

Perhaps Shaw's career was best summed up by THE FIREMAN immediately after his retirement. It said:

"Captain Shaw's chief gift was in organisation . . . His work was to foster the gradual growth of the institution, and to adapt it to the wants of . . . an already overgrown but still growing city . . . The staff . . . was kept well in hand. The discipline was . . . exceedingly rigorous; but we don't think that men of average ability and good conduct found it insupportable.

No doubt there were some complaints, and much which has been written as to the intense affection existing between the chief officer and the staff is, to those who know the facts, mere gush . . .

That there were some weak spots in the Captain's administration was, to a certain extent, inevitable. No man can be most excellent in every department. Captain Shaw was not an engineer, and his decisions on such mechanical points as came before him for decision sometimes brought a smile to the professional man . . .

Whether he ever attained the supreme excellence (as a fireman) . . . which his predecessor (Braidwood) exhibited, whose firemanship was the wonder of competent critics, is a matter of opinion which we should hardly care to decide. But, on the whole, when everything that can be said against the Captain's administration is allowed to the full, it cannot be denied that the public confidence which has been so unreservedly placed in him has been fully deserved."

Shaw must have read these comments with some satisfaction. At least equally, he must have enjoyed the rather plaintive report of the Fire Brigade Committee made in the January following his October retirement. He had, so it was claimed, removed the furniture from his office at Headquarters without prior notice, claiming that it was his own property since it had been presented to him 27 years earlier. So that the new Chief Officer should have somewhere to sit and work, expenditure not exceeding £100 was recommended to the Council.

On his retirement Shaw had to vacate Winchester House and he moved to 48 Rutland Gate. All the children, except Anna, had by this time left home. Massey, aged 35, was still a bachelor and would remain so until he was 74; Bernard, 34, had married and had presented Captain Shaw with a first grandchild six months before his retirement; Anna, 32, would nurse her father to the end; Clarina, 30, would die a bachelor at 77; Cecil, 29, was abroad and also would die unmarried; and Zarita, 27, had married in May 1890 Henry Le Bas, a stockbroker. Two further grandchildren were born after his retirement: a third Eyre Massey, whose father was Bernard and who was killed in World War I; and Geraldine Le Bas who died, as Lady McNee, in 1975. The eldest grandchild, another Bernard, was knighted and is now in his nineties. There were no great-grandchildren.

The early 1890's may well have been a golden period for Shaw. He was retired, he was famous, he was highly regarded, he was living in comfort with his wife, and he was still enjoying good health. He became a Deputy Lieutenant for Middlesex and was given the Freedom of the City of London. He became Chairman of the Metropolitan Electrical Company; this was absorbed by the Southern Electricity Board at the time of the nationalisation of the industry and unfortunately its pre-1930 records have been lost. Then, too, in 1895 he accepted a seat on the board of the Palatine Insurance Company which had been founded nine years previously.

But two years later, in 1897, Lady Shaw died, of heart failure after being ill for a week with influenza. The journal TRUTH wrote of her:

"Lady Shaw, by her unfailing amiability, her kindness to both rich and poor, and on account of her genuine character, had won the affection and respect of all whose privilege it was to have come into contact with her ... Lady Shaw and her family made the headquarters of the Fire Brigade a centre for the distribution of generous and intelligently-directed assistance to the poor and suffering of the district."

She was buried in a new family grave at Highgate Cemetery, very close to Fireman's Corner.

At the end of 1898, Shaw's own health began to deteriorate. He was taken ill at home and rushed to a nursing home with paralysis of the legs due to thrombosis. His right leg had to be amputated. Later, his left leg had to be removed as well and this limb, according to the family, was later displayed in the Hunterian Museum, though whether because of some clinical peculiarity or because it was the leg of a famous person is not known. The amputation was carried out by Sir Thomas Smith, Surgeon-extraordinary to the Queen and later to be in attendance at the operation on Edward VII on the day planned for that monarch's Coronation. Smith had been a surgeon at St. Bartholomew's for many years and was described as *"a dexterous operator, a sure guide in all difficult questions of diagnosis"*, and popular with students who appreciated his wit and humour. There is a family story that, after the operation on Shaw, Smith was seen walking the hospital corridor with the leg dangling over his shoulder; perhaps that was the nature of his *"wit and humour"*. Smith was a trustee of the Hunterian Collection, which lends credibility to the story of the leg being displayed there; Professor R. J. Scothorne, Professor of Anatomy at the University of Glasgow, has made extensive enquiries on this point but can find no record of the case nor of any such exhibit. The Collection was, in any event, bombed during World War II.

A curious story about Shaw when he had already lost one of his legs appeared in the LONDON FIREMAN, in 1975. Its author claimed that the story was based on original research. If it were true, it would make Shaw even more remarkable than he was anyway. It arose from *"a fact uncovered by an Austrian researcher"*. He was named as Erich Kemper (that should have read 'Kamper') who was, said the writer, *"perhaps the foremost Olympic historian in the world"*. The article related how Shaw

CAPTAIN SHAW IN RETIREMENT. Shaw lived in retirement for 17 years. At first he enjoyed good health but later had a thrombosis which led to the amputation of both legs. (Photo: Sir Bernard Shaw).

had taken part in the 1900 Olympic Games, when he was 72 (the author in fact said seventy because he had, like so many other writers, got Shaw's year of birth wrong).

According to the article Shaw, one-legged and in his seventies, had helped crew the yacht OLLE to victory and so was probably the oldest-ever winner of an Olympic Gold Medal. The writer conceded that the medal could not be found and that Shaw's sole surviving descendant had been unaware of the achievement. *"But"*, continued the article, *"that Shaw won the medal is beyond dispute even if one had the temerity to question the painstaking thoroughness of Erich Kemper's (SIC) research (for) . . . the British Olympic Association in their archives lists one E. Shaw as a member of the crew"*.

However it seemed suspicious that the family knew nothing of the medal or of the achievement, and that Shaw should have entered himself as *"E. Shaw"*, whereas he always signed *"Eyre M. Shaw"* and was known in Fire Brigade circles as *"Massey Shaw"*. Also, even allowing for Shaw's vitality and stamina it seemed remarkable that a one-legged man of seventy should crew the winning boat.

Unmoved by the suggestion that one should not have the temerity to question Erich Kamper's research, and equally by a repetition of the story in the DAILY TELEGRAPH of 29 July 1976, enquiry was made first of the British Olympic Association. Far from their having an E. Shaw listed in their archives as a member of the winning 1900 crew they pointed out that they did not come into being until five years later and therefore had no first-hand information on the 1900 Games. Next, the matter was raised with Erich Kamper, in Graz (Austria). His reply, translated, reads as follows:

"It is mentioned in . . . my 1972 edition of the Encyclopedia of Olympic Summer Sports, that there was a report in the French journals for the year 1900, that the winner of this particular yachting class was noted as 'Exshaw' (without Christian name or initials) and of French nationality. Since a name of this nature is hardly known in French and it was established after further research that it seemed to be that of an Englishman, my English colleague Dave Terry was consulted . . . He suggested that it could be that there had been a typing error, and instead of an 'x' there should have been a full-stop, so that 'Exshaw' should have read 'E. Shaw'. But since then we have been able to establish that this was a mistaken supposition. My Olympic colleague in Hong Kong, Ian Buchanan, who has for many years concerned himself with details about all British Olympic medal winners, was able to establish without doubt that the winner in that particular class in 1900 was in fact called Exshaw, a very well-known yachtsman who happened to have a second domicile in France, in the Arcachon area. An exchange of letters with the Mayor there enabled him to confirm . . . that there was a gentleman called Exshaw, with the Christian name of William, who was born in 1866, and who died in 1927 on board his yacht . . .

Therefore, it is established that Captain Sir Eyre Massey Shaw had   **171** *nothing to do with the 1900 Olympic yacht event but that the winner was in fact William Exshaw. His name was therefore correctly mentioned in the French sources with only the slight error that he was described as a Frenchman . . . "*

At the time when William Exshaw was winning his Olympic Gold Medal, Captain Shaw was reminiscing for a journal, MAP:

"When I retired and claimed the pension to which I was entitled . . . there was a general idea that I was a martyr; but I never by word or act gave countenance to any impression of the kind. It is true that I was quite aware that a small but compact phalanx of the governing body had 'banded themselves together under a curse, saying that they would neither eat nor drink till they had slain Paul', but I had faith in the overwhelming majority . . . and never for a moment doubted either their strength or willingness to support me so long as I was not in obvious fault.

But there is another side to such a question, and that is the feeling that life under these circumstances is not altogether agreeable. Frequent attacks from a section of a constituted authority may elicit only a small amount of ridicule or contempt from the great majority of the same body, but are often a serious obstruction, and always a grievous annoyance to a busy official . . .

Sometimes after an exceptionally hard week during which I may have attended one Fire Brigade Committee and one Board meeting, given evidence before two sittings of a Select Committee of the House of Lords or Commons, and extinguished some forty fires, involving an average of three or four hours' heavy labour and responsibility at each, besides conducting all the business, instruction, discipline and finance of the Brigade, it was a little trying to find myself denounced in unmeasured terms at a public meeting of the Board for gross neglect and mismanagement because one of the numerous fire engines under my control had failed to earn the approval of someone who saw it at work, and happened to be a friend of the accusing Member.

If only members of a governing body who make these accusations on imperfect information, could hear the remarks of their own very subordinate officials on such occasions, I am sure they would be deeply interested, and would certainly more fully understand the position in which they place their responsible officers . . .

It is said that a certain schoolmaster, being informed that his school was about to be visited by a king, asked that he might be permitted to keep his hat on during the royal visit . . . The king afterwards enquired the reason for this strange request, and the schoolmaster frankly replied: 'Your Majesty, if I were seen to take off my hat to anyone, my influence with the scholars would be gone for ever'.

This story . . . might, with advantage, be studied by those individuals occasionally found among elected public bodies, whose principal idea of governing is always to 'pitch into' their officials . . .

THE FUNERAL CORTÈGE LEAVING HIS HOME. On the morning of Shaw's funeral, a Station Officer and eight firemen attended at his house in Belgravia, bore the coffin to the hearse and marched alongside it to the church. (Photo: London Fire Brigade Museum).

THE FUNERAL: AT THE GRAVESIDE. At Highgate Cemetery, a huge crowd was present to see the arrival of the coffin. The path from the gate to the grave was lined with firemen. (Photo: London Fire Brigade Museum).

ANNA
WIFE OF
SIR EYRE MASSEY SHAW
DIED DEC. 15, 1891

SIR EYRE MASSEY SHAW K.C.B
LATE CHIEF OF THE LONDON FIRE BRIGADE
DIED AUGUST 25TH 1908

ANNA SHAW.
DIED APRIL 18TH 1921

CAPTAIN SHAW'S GRAVE. A modest one by Highgate Cemetery standards. Appropriately Shaw, his wife and
his elder daughter — all of whom served the Brigade for so long in their different ways — lie adjacent to Fireman's
Corner. (Photo: London Fire Brigade Libary.

CAPTAIN SHAW'S HELMET, AXE AND UNIFORM BELT. The firemen wore brass helmets; Shaw's was of silver. It and his axe and belt were later presented to the Fire Brigade by his family. (Photo: London Fire Brigade Museum).

But I must certainly add that on the whole . . . I have received great consideration and on many occasions great forebearance."

By 1905 Shaw was increasingly frail, and his grandson remembers him socialising at Stanhope Gate, Hyde Park. He was confined to a wheelchair, but still looked very dignified. His daughter Anna was invariably with him. The Rutland Gate house had been given up for a smaller one at 114 Belgrave Road, but when death came of heart failure, on 25 August 1908, he was staying at the Grand Hotel, Folkestone. He was eighty.

Ten years earlier, two months after Lady Shaw's death, he had made his last will. He left everything to his faithful daughter, Anna. His other children, except perhaps Massey, were already provided for. Both witnesses to the will were of the St. James's branch of the Palatine Insurance Company. Later, the family presented the London Fire Brigade Museum with his silver helmet, his axe and his uniform belt with its silver buckle.

The funeral is still remembered more than seventy-five years later by Shaw's grandson, probably the last-surviving participant. It took place on Saturday 29 August. A station officer and eight firemen attended at 114 Belgrave Road, at 10.15 in the morning. They bore the coffin to the hearse and then marched on either side of it to St. Saviour's Church, St. George's Square. After the service, the coffin was borne on the hearse to Highgate Cemetery where it was met by a large detachment of the London Fire Brigade and by deputations from the National Fire Brigades Union, the

176

London Salvage Corps, the Metropolitan and the City Police, the Metropolitan Water Board, and other fire brigades. The King, who as Prince of Wales had so enjoyed Shaw's company, sent Sir Archibald Edmonstone as his representative.

The firemen in attendance were volunteers for the task, preference being given to those who had served under Shaw. They wore full dress uniform including fire boots and medals; each had a neckerchief tied round the left arm. They formed up in two ranks from the grave towards the lower gate, to receive the hearse. Shaw received what he would most have desired — a fireman's funeral. According to one correspondent, the coffin bore the simple inscription: *"Sir Eyre Massey Shaw, died 25 August 1908, aged 78 years"*. If it did, it was wrong. He was eighty.

The memorial is a modest one by the standards of Highgate Cemetery. The inscription reads: *"Sir Eyre Massey Shaw KCB, Late Chief of the London Fire Brigade, died 25 August 1908"*. The grave also bears the names of: Anna, his wife; Anna, his daughter; who died of a cerebral haemorrhage in April 1921; Cecil, who died in 1912; Clarina, who died in 1938 of angina pectoris; Eyre Massey, Captain Shaw's eldest son, who died of syncope in 1939; and the same Eyre Massey's wife who died of a coronary thrombosis in 1954. But only Captain and Lady Shaw and their daughter Anna are buried in the grave; Cecil was interred in Suez and the others were cremated.

So, Captain Shaw and his wife and daughter, all of whom served the Fire Brigade for so long in their different ways, lie immediately alongside the memorial to London firemen killed in the course of duty. This is fitting, for Captain Shaw was the greatest fireman London — and perhaps the world — has ever seen.

NOTES ON SOURCES

For further details of the people and institutions named, please see under ACKNOWLEDGEMENTS.

CHAPTER ONE
A START IN LIFE

Cork County Library; the Hon. Secretary of Monkstown Golf Club; the Rector of Cobh; and, above all, Trinity College Library, Dublin. Quotations from M A P, 27 October 1900. *PACE* the DICTIONARY OF NATIONAL BIOGRAPHY.

CHAPTER TWO
SAILOR, SOLDIER, FIREMAN

Sir Bernard and Lady Shaw; R. A. Burchell, Lecturer in American History and Institutions, Manchester University; Malcolm Pillar, researching Victorian Torquay; New York, Torquay and Sheerness Libraries; the Hon. Librarian of the British Historical Society of Portugal; the Librarian of the British Association at Oporto. The TORQUAY DIRECTORY AND SOUTH DEVON JOURNAL and the SOUTH EASTERN GAZETTE. Reference to (but no reliance placed upon) Major J. Douglas Mercer's RECORD OF THE NORTH CORK REGIMENT OF MILITIA. Quotations, again, from M A P.

CHAPTER THREE
THE FIRST YEAR IN LONDON

The Committee minute books of the London Fire Engine Establishment and the Establishment's General Record of Fires in 1861, both at the Guildhall Library; the REPORT OF THE SELECT COMMITTEE ON FIRES IN THE METROPOLIS . . ., 1862. G. V. Blackstone's A HISTORY OF THE BRITISH FIRE SERVICE, 1957; Charles Roetter's FIRE IS THEIR ENEMY, 1962; Sally Holloway's LONDON'S NOBLE FIRE BRIGADES, 1833-1904, 1973.

CHAPTER FOUR
SHAW IN SOCIETY

The Earl of Caithness, Lord Clanmorris and, especially, Elspeth Huxley and her mother, the Hon. Mrs. Grant. The Staffordshire Record Office and the Library at Windsor Castle. The Acting Secretary of the St. James's Club and the Secretary of the Carlton Club. The minutes and associated papers of the Main Drainage Committee (1865-66) and of the Fire Brigade Committee (1866-89) of the Metropolitan Board of Works at the London Record Office. The minutes alone comprise 22 volumes and about 10,000 foolscap pages of manuscript.

CHAPTER FIVE
DECISION AND CONFLICT
The minutes and associated papers of the Main Drainage and Fire Brigade Committees of the Metropolitan Board of Works. Sally Holloway and G. V. Blackstone (see under CHAPTER THREE). Charles F. T. Young's FIRES, FIRE ENGINES AND FIRE BRIGADES . . ., 1866.

CHAPTER SIX
SHAW AND THE VOLUNTEERS
The minutes and associated papers of the Fire Brigade Committees of the Metropolitan Board of Works and of the London County Council, the latter also at the London Record Office. The monthly journal, THE FIREMAN, commencing in May 1880. G. V. Blackstone (see under CHAPTER THREE).

CHAPTER SEVEN
CHARITY AND FALSE PRETENCES
The minutes and associated papers of the Fire Brigade Committees of the Metropolitan Board of Works and of the London County Council, the latter also at the London Record Office. The monthly journal, THE FIREMAN, commencing in May 1880. G. V. Blackstone (see under CHAPTER THREE).

CHAPTER EIGHT
SHAW AND HIS MEN
The minutes and associated papers of the Fire Brigade Committee of the Metropolitan Board of Works. W. Eric Jackson's LONDON'S FIRE BRIGADES, 1966. H. E. Lockhart-Mummery, a Harley Street specialist, advised on the prescription and need for diarrhoea mixture.

CHAPTER NINE
LEADER AND HERO
The minutes and associated papers of the Fire Brigade Committee of the Metropolitan Board of Works. THE FIREMAN.

CHAPTER TEN
INVENTORS' CORNER
The minutes and, especially, the associated papers of the Fire Brigade Committees of the Metropolitan Board of Works and of the London County Council. The minutes of the Governors and of the Governors' House Committee of Royal Holloway College. Edward A. Sibbick, of Osborne House. John Durham's TELEGRAPHS IN VICTORIAN LONDON, 1959.

CHAPTER ELEVEN
AT HOME WITH THE SHAWS
The minutes and associated papers of the Fire Brigade Committee of the Metropolitan Board of Works. The 1871 census returns at the Public Record Office. The London Fire Brigade Museum. The Greater London Council Plans Repository.

CHAPTER TWELVE
THE COLIN CAMPBELL DIVORCE CASE
THE TIMES, 16 November to 22 December 1886. Anita Leslie's EDWARDIANS IN LOVE, 1972. Lord Mowbray, Segrave and Stourton.

CHAPTER THIRTEEN
THEATRE FIRES
The associated papers of the Fire Brigade Committee of the Metropolitan Board of Works. The East Devon Area Record Office, Exeter; the West Country Studies Library, Exeter. Sally Holloway (see under CHAPTER THREE). Diana Howard's LONDON'S THEATRES AND MUSIC HALLS, 1850-1950, 1970.

CHAPTER FOURTEEN
SHAW ABROAD
The minutes and associated papers of the Fire Brigade Committee of the Metropolitan Board of Works. THE FIREMAN.

CHAPTER FIFTEEN
SHAW UNDER NEW MANAGEMENT
The minutes and associated papers of the Fire Brigade Committee of the London County Council. K. G. Young's unpublished London University PhD thesis: *'The London Municipal Society, 1894-1963: a Study of Conservatism and Local Government'*, 1973.

CHAPTER SIXTEEN
RESIGNATION
The minutes and associated papers of the Fire Brigade Committee of the London County Council. Two albums of newspaper cuttings, collated by Zarita Le Bas (Captain Shaw's younger daughter) and held by the family.

CHAPTER SEVENTEEN
RETIREMENT AND DEATH
Sir Bernard and Lady Shaw; Erich Kamper, Sportredakteur. London County Council Fire Brigade papers at the London Record office.

PEOPLE, PLACES AND ORGANISATIONS

References to Captain Shaw, and to the London Fire Engine Establishment, the Metropolitan Board of Works and the London County Council and to their Fire Brigade Committees are omitted since they appear PASSIM. Also omitted are general references to "London" and to countries. For places in London see, initially, under that name.

*Accounts often fail to indicate which daughter is referred to. In such cases both have been indexed.